ADVANCED OPTIONS TRADING

APPROACHES, TOOLS, AND TECHNIQUES FOR PROFESSIONAL TRADERS

KEVIN M. KRAUS

New York   Chicago   San Francisco   Lisbon   London
Madrid   Mexico City   Milan   New Delhi   San Juan
Seoul   Singapore   Sydney   Toronto

For Gayle Marie and my wonderful children

Thank you for all the support and encouragement.

RISK DISCLOSURE

There is risk in trading or investing in commodity, financial and equity futures, equities, options on futures, and equity options. The information in this publication has been carefully compiled from sources believed to be reliable, but its accuracy is not guaranteed. Use it at your own risk. Trade recommendations or strategies presented in this publication are not recommended based on the risk suitability of the reader, rather general recommendations and strategies based on typical market trading. Consider your risk suitability before trading or investing in any risk investment. Read the risk disclosure information provided with your trading account carefully.

HYPOTHETICAL PERFORMANCE RESULTS HAVE MANY INHERENT LIMITATIONS, SOME OF WHICH ARE DESCRIBED BELOW. NO REPRESENTATION IS BEING MADE THAT ANY ACCOUNT WILL OR IS LIKELY TO ACHIEVE PROFITS OR LOSSES SIMILAR TO THOSE SHOWN. IN FACT, THERE ARE FREQUENTLY SHARP DIFFERENCES BETWEEN HYPOTHETICAL PERFORMANCE RESULTS AND THE ACTUAL RESULTS SUBSEQUENTLY ACHIEVED BY ANY PARTICULAR TRADING PROGRAM.

ONE OF THE LIMITATIONS OF HYPOTHETICAL PERFORMANCE RESULTS IS THAT THEY ARE GENERALLY PREPARED WITH THE BENEFIT OF HINDSIGHT. IN ADDITION, HYPOTHETICAL TRADING DOES NOT INVOLVE FINANCIAL RISK, AND NO HYPOTHETICAL TRADING RECORD CAN COMPLETELY ACCOUNT FOR THE IMPACT OF FINANCIAL RISK IN ACTUAL TRADING. FOR EXAMPLE, THE ABILITY TO WITHSTAND LOSSES OR TO ADHERE TO A PARTICULAR TRADING PROGRAM IN SPITE OF TRADING LOSSES ARE MATERIAL POINTS WHICH CAN ALSO ADVERSELY AFFECT ACTUAL TRADING RESULTS. THERE ARE NUMEROUS OTHER FACTORS RELATED TO THE MARKETS IN GENERAL OR TO THE IMPLEMENTATION OF ANY SPECIFIC TRADING PROGRAM WHICH CANNOT BE FULLY ACCOUNTED FOR IN THE PREPARATION OF HYPOTHETICAL PERFORMANCE RESULTS AND ALL OF WHICH CAN ADVERSELY AFFECT ACTUAL TRADING RESULTS.

CONTENTS

INTRODUCTION

"Whenever you find yourself on the side of the majority, it is time to pause and reflect."

—Mark Twain

Mark Twain's simple words ring true in many aspects of life, but in investing, this statement is a solid piece of advice. So often investors follow the masses and the mass media into a trending market direction only to have a reversal of fortune create a sudden change in the capital flow in the market.

In creating *Advanced Option Trading in Volatile Markets*, I wanted to bring you advanced trading and option techniques to allow you to follow the trending masses while learning to offset the risk of significant changes in market direction.

In this book we cover a great deal about volatility and the effects of volatility on market trading. Volatility ebbs and flows; it is not a fixed or necessarily predictable aspect of the market. Your job as an investor, trader, or financial professional is to learn to manage volatility using advanced strategy and trading discipline.

To be a successful investor or financial professional today, you must have a full understanding of the advanced strategies available for your portfolio as well as an understanding of how these strategies are utilized by other investors.

I wanted to bring advanced strategy to a level that was quickly and easily understandable and to avoid a bunch of flowery language and complicated mathematics that often discourage busy people from learning advanced portfolio management.

I hope you enjoy *Advanced Option Trading in Volatile Markets* and feel free to visit my Web site at www.kkraus.com.

Chapter 1

THE NEW MARKET

Trading in the New Market

Trading in today's markets is more challenging than any time in history. Wide price swings in equity, debt, currency, and commodity instruments and their representative indices have created a significant increase in market risk and capital requirements. In order to begin understanding how to use option trading strategies to manage portfolio risk and improve profitability, we have to understand the landscape of the markets of today and the outlook for markets in the future. Identifying and understanding the nature of market participants and their influence on the market is critical to successful trading. We need to also understand how the expansion of technology and the growth in knowledge of individual traders have changed the landscape of investing over the past several years.

Significant increases in participation and publicity of hedge and index funds have increased awareness of the influence these groups have. Television and industry experts often cite "the funds" as the culprits of market volatility, and in many ways they are. But "the funds" are just as subject to the increased risk as anyone else, only in much larger dollar figures. The question is who and what are "the funds" and how do you effectively manage your personal investments or your client's portfolio risk in the volatile climate created by fund traders and global investing. Fund managers themselves must learn to improve risk management in order to maintain positive returns in volatile markets or the assets may travel to the fund next door. Let's look at the major groups of market participants and how they are constructed and what their individual trading goals are.

Hedge Funds

The first and arguably the most powerful fund group is the hedge fund. *Hedge funds* are commonly limited-membership, private investment groups which are comprised of funds from professional and wealthy investors. These funds are limited by Securities and Exchange Commission (SEC) regulation to sophisticated investors and small numbers of investors at any one time. This is not however, a representation of their market strength in that these funds can have assets in the hundreds of millions or billions in assets under management. Hedge funds have extensive freedom in their investments and may spread their wealth across broad ranges of investments, equities, commodities, debt, or currencies because they are not specifically registered investment companies with the SEC. This investment freedom also enables hedge funds to direct large amounts of capital at particular market sectors, individual companies, broad indices, or even individual commodities at any given time.

Hedge funds are frequent "short sellers" in equity and derivative markets, meaning that the funds sell shares that they have often borrowed or may short futures contracts in order to buy them back at a lower price. Short selling is inherently risky; however, funds with deep pockets can sell large quantities of stock or futures positions in a short period causing a cascade in market price. The skilled hedge fund manager will use this opportunity to profit for the fund as other funds or smaller investors are liquidated on program sells and preset risk protection sell orders commonly called sell stops, or other risk management tools. This massive short selling capability may be regulated further in the future because of risk to individual investors and business interests, however, even with regulation, the power and wealth of these funds will be a formidable force for the foreseeable future.

Hedge funds can also be long market players, long-term players, or even day traders. Their scope and flexibility is what makes them a source for volatility and unpredictability. The nature of the market is that there is always a bigger fish, so even extremely wealthy hedge funds must constantly be managing risk and will be well served in the future to employ option strategies in their risk management as well.

Index Funds

Index funds are another influential group of funds. Index funds differ from hedge funds in that they are created under SEC regulation as investment companies using pools of capital from investors of all types. This group includes many funds that follow preset trading guidelines and formulas for trading. As an example, The ABC1 fund follows the S&P 500 index. Therefore, the fund will be obligated to be invested in a percentage of each of the stocks in the S&P 500 or a modified formula of those stocks or their representative futures contracts. Since it is obligated by its prospectus to invest in each of the S&P 500 stocks in a percentage of its total asset value, the fund will change its holdings based on assets under management more so than because of changes in market climate. This means that the ABC1 fund will have a less significant impact on the market or at least be slower to react to changes in market than will a hedge fund with the freedom to make wholesale asset changes. The ABC1 fund may be affected significantly when large numbers of investors begin to liquidate positions in recessionary or defensive economic periods.

Mutual funds are often classified as a type of index fund because their goals often fall in line with a particular trading objective. This objective is often classified as growth, income or index, meaning that the fund will specifically tailor its investments to the objective. Mutual funds pool large amounts of investor capital from retail and business investors and use the buying power to create large-scale positions. Mutual funds offer individual and corporate investors a simulated diversified portfolio in a single investment vehicle. They also offer sector opportunities for investors with an investment goal of capitalizing on industry-specific fundamentals or trends. They present a vehicle without the risk of direct investment in a single company or futures contract. For regulated investment companies, the funds investment objectives are spelled out by a prospectus that includes how the funds invest and divest to reach the specified performance goals. Mutual funds have a significant downside for many short-term investors in that the funds cannot be liquidated on an intraday basis and are often too diversified to have large short-term gains. A mutual funds share value or net asset value commonly referred to as NAV, is calculated based on the settlement prices for the day of the underlying instruments. Mutual funds are popular medium-term, long-term, and retirement planning vehicles, but are not necessarily for active short-term traders.

Exchange-Traded Funds

Exchange-traded funds (ETFs) are relatively young index fund investment vehicles and are growing in popularity for a number of reasons. They typically have lower management fees than their mutual fund counterparts, and, unlike mutual funds, ETF instruments can be traded intraday. This allows for active short-term trading in ETF securities and the ability for smaller investors to take advantage of diversified short-term positions. ETFs are a group or basket of securities represented by a net asset share value that is traded in open market. ETFs can be constructed of narrow sector-based securities or composed of securities from a broad index. ETFs also can be constructed of groups of commodity, equity, or financial futures contracts or even cash commodity products.

One of the interesting developments in the ETF market is the growing ETF options market on the underlying ETF securities. ETF options are becoming popular tools for position hedging as well as for direct investment. We discuss more about using ETF options later.

Pension Funds

Pension funds are similar to hedge funds in that they do not necessarily have a prospectus that must be followed for the placement of investment funds. However, a pension fund must have an investment statement filed with regulators, and it must follow government regulations regarding the protection of employee retirement funds. The funds are directed based on the objectives of the fund and can be in almost any sector. These funds often have a portion invested in the related company's stock or other related industries and are frequently heavy participants in low-yield, high-security instruments like Treasury bonds, high rated corporate bonds and municipal bonds. Pension fund assets under management can be massive in scope, such as the largest U.S. pension fund, the California Public Employees Retirement System, which in recent history topped $260 billion in assets under management.

Retail Investors and Traders

The retail investment market has changed more than any other category of market in the past decade. The evolution and expansion of online trading and 24-hour financial market coverage has brought the individual trader closer to the market then ever before. Investors are able to make snap intraday market decisions from their desk at work or home computer at any time.

Many of today's broker-dealers operate exclusively online or have large online trading operations which account for a growing portion of total market activity. Individual traders can now be a factor in increasing market volatility as information disseminates through the Net or modern media and individual traders can adjust their positions to react to market news quickly and less expensively than ever before. The online trading community can affect index fund positions quickly and without significant warning as investors may choose to add or subtract mutual fund or ETF positions frequently based on market movement and news.

This online community includes a surprisingly large number of individual online day traders who are buying and selling all day long. Day traders are not new, but the convenience of Internet trading has attracted a much more diverse and reactive group of individual traders. Many firms allow traders to operate on smaller account balances which may reduce the risk tolerance of the investor. These smaller more reactive traders may lack trading discipline, or they may be trading on monetary risk rather than basing their decisions on technical objectives. It is common for small investors to be unable to see a position through because of the lack of understanding of risk, lack of risk management skills and a lack of capital. This lack of discipline and capital to sustain a long-term market risk causes market reactions that increase overall market volatility. Individual traders may not be able to move the market on their own, but as a combined group who may react similarly to major market events, they can have significant influence.

In addition to changes in market participation in recent years, changes in the infrastructure of the market and the means by which trades are executed have had a dramatic impact on increases in volatility and the speed at which market participants react to changes.

Modernization of the Market

The effect of the modernized retail investment market is increased access to markets and, as mentioned above, possibly a less disciplined market investor making decisions on small capital. In decades past, professional trading advisors and registered representatives might have assisted small investors with market stamina and maintaining long-term investment goals. The lack of investors obtaining professional advice in a growing portion of the market can also account for an increase in short-term or even intraday market volatility.

Another major effect of the modernized retail market is the reduced cost of trading. Online retail brokerage firms have substantially reduced trading fees because of the lack of hard capital overhead and costs of a traditional brokerage. Maintaining hundreds or thousands of offices nationwide with tens of thousands of employees is very expensive in comparison to a warehouse full of servers and information technology professionals. Lower trading costs in equity and derivative markets have increased small investor tolerance to active trading.

There are also many positive aspects to the modernization of the market. Small investors are more in touch with the market, thereby making the overall market a more active part of everyday life. People feel more in touch with the effect of markets on their personal finances when their investment statement arrives daily as e-mail rather than once a month from the post office. More importantly, there has been a huge closure in the gap between the large and small investor in many markets. The Chicago Mercantile Exchange and The Chicago Board of Trade are perfect examples of the closing of the gap. In the past, large traders had special privileges and dedicated personnel on the floor of the futures exchanges and often were able to manipulate the market effectively with large orders. Today, with more computers than people on the trading floor, the balance has shifted. Order management systems handle the order matching for electronic contracts in place of the human bid-offer process of years past. The large investor in electronic or e-mini contracts has no more advantage in the bid-offer process than the small investor with a single contract. Many derivative markets still have a large investor operation requiring a certain number of contracts in order for the service to be utilized; however, it is likely that in the coming years these operations will be replaced by their electronic counterparts. The loss of the human open outcry auction system also has reduced the number of independent floor traders or locals active in the market. These traders did provide liquidity to the market, especially on an intraday basis, but the decrease in spread differential, especially in thinly traded markets, has at least made up some of the monetary difference to the small investor. Most of these traders have simply moved off the floor to carry out the same type of operation via electronic trading.

Government Intervention

The future of government regulation and intervention in the marketplace is difficult to predict. Recent government intervention using public funds for capital investment in many sectors has the potential to change the big picture of financial regulation and institutional ownership in the long term. New regulation in the market has the potential to affect market participation by wealthy investors and funds by further defining the range and scope of their investments. One of the negative aspects of new market regulation is increased compliance costs for regulated funds, brokerage firms, banks, and assorted investment companies. Large private investors may seek investment opportunities in nonregulated or foreign markets rather than in regulated markets.

Foreign Participation

The modernization of the market is occurring all over the world, and there is greater participation on behalf of foreign investors and governments then ever before. Competing exchanges and marketplaces are growing in the Middle East, Asia, and Europe. The more global the economy becomes, the more global factors will affect trade in domestic markets.

Agricultural commodities are a prime example, with modernized farming booming around the world, and competition is growing in all global markets for agricultural products. Agricultural traders must be monitoring fundamentals in Asia, South America, Europe, and North America as each market can significantly affect the global supply-and-demand picture more than ever before. Alternative fuels and developing nations consume increasingly more grain products annually, applying additional stress on a tight supply chain. Rain in central South America means more to this supply chain than it did five or ten years ago.

The energy crisis precipitated a massive transfer of wealth from the U.S. economy to energy-rich nations. These funds will fuel markets around the world for many years to come and will further the economic globalization we've seen in recent years. Many of these participants will return the funds to U.S. markets, but it is likely that some developing markets will also benefit from this wealth and diversify the global economy. Diversification means that money will be moving from market to market in larger amounts, reacting to global events and further increasing volatility.

Market Psychology

Psychology is not a new factor to the markets; in reality it is the markets. Markets are driven more by emotion today than ever before. Later in this book we look at statistical and technical aspects of trading options and their underlying products. However, before we can begin to understand making money with options or managing risk with options, we must understand and accept the unknown in market behavior. In your analysis you should understand that the unquantifiable factor in the markets is the mind of the investor. You cannot predict the reaction of individual investors or portfolio managers large and small to any event with any significant degree of certainty. You also cannot predict how one fund manager will react to the movements of another on any given day.

As an example, in the late 1990s you might have been inclined to be short the silver market based on the technical picture or an option strategy. You short silver in one fashion or another with a solid rationale on a technical high in the exact month that a wealthy individual decides that silver is the metal of the future and invests billions of dollars over a short period of time. No mathematical, fundamental, technical, or other abstract analysis could predict this type of event.

The market effect of the September 11 attacks on the World Trade Center had at first the expected effect of liquidation of capital from the market. The quick recovery in the market may not have been expected and caught many people by surprise. The psychological aspect of the market is the main reason we have a need for risk control.

Advanced option trading, along with technical option skill and knowledge, is about an advanced mindset in the market. You must build your understanding of how market psychology affects your trading objectives and how to make wholesale emotional market shifts work for your benefit or at the least not be a disaster.

The first place to start understanding the unpredictable nature of the market is to begin to understand it in you. Twenty years of trading have taught me that I am my own worst enemy when logical market motion begins to fail. When everything that should happen doesn't or what shouldn't happen does, it is difficult to control that defensive mechanism that causes reactionary market decisions. I often see traders, managers, and investors make impulsive position changes only to see their original position succeed. Some time later in response to one bad decision, they hold another ridiculous loser for no reason, and the cycle perpetuates itself.

Market discipline is one of the hardest skills to manage and is the reason why there are thousands of "systems" to which a trader can turn for the decision-making process.

One my first goals with new traders, experienced or not, is to help them understand the nature of risk and trading and then devise a risk control strategy to reduce the risk of emotional trading decisions. As a trader, investor, or portfolio manager, having a known and defined risk on a position creates sensible decision making and often provides the emotional leverage that enables you to move on and take advantage of other opportunities.

Utilizing options in your portfolio is a method of controlling the emotional risk of the market. Options can be utilized not only as independent investment vehicles but also to define risk, build cash against future market risk, and diversify portfolio risk across markets. The wonderful thing about options is that they provide a mechanism for defining time, price, and risk while also opening up opportunity.

Throughout this book we will be discussing the risk of trading options with both limited and unlimited risk. You should be aware that options trading also has inherent psychological risk that is separate from the underlying position as well. Options are also often victims of psychological rather than statistical pricing and sometimes can be worse than their underlying security. Options typically trade somewhat less frequently than their underlying security or derivative so they tend to have a wider range between bid and offer prices. Changes in the supply and demand of available options can also be a risk to option trading causing the option to not perform as expected versus the underlying asset. Options can also become market indicators of their own. Options with particularly high open interest or volume at a particular strike price may become a price target to traders near expiration. There is a constant watch on the strike prices creating demand and adjustments to strategy in the underlying to defend or target those strike prices.

Summary

As a financial professional or individual investor, the current dynamics of the market are critical to your decision-making process, investment objectives, and risk control. As markets advance further in the future, volatility is not likely to be significantly reduced so improving your strategy, market mindset, and use of options may help smooth the road and help you avoid the pitfalls of trading in high volatility.

Chapter 2

UNDERSTANDING OPTIONS

Our focus in this book is advanced option trading strategy and how to utilize it effectively in high volatility. It is important to make certain that you have the proper background on options in order to understand more advanced material later in the book. With that in mind, let's do a quick review of the basics of what options are and how they function in the market.

Options Basics

An *option* is the right, but not the obligation, to the underlying instrument at a particular price and particular time. The *underlying instrument* can be a stock, futures contract, Exchange Traded Fund, index security, interest rate, or other market-traded instrument with options available. There are two types of options traded on the market, call options and put options:

- A *call option* is the right, but not the obligation, to buy the underlying instrument at a particular price and particular point in time.

- A *put option* is the right to sell, or be short, the underlying instrument at a particular price and particular point in time.

Let's look further at our definition of an option:

- An option is the right, but not the obligation—an option gives the option buyer the right to buy or sell (call or put) the underlying instrument.
- At a particular price—this price is determined by the option purchased and is referred to as the strike price. As an example, if ABC Company is trading at around $15.00 and there is an option strike price at $16.00, then the $16.00 call option would give the call buyer the right, but not the obligation, to be long or buy ABC Company's stock at $16.00. A buyer of the $16.00 put option would have the right, but not the obligation, to sell or be short ABC Company's stock at $16.00.
- At a particular point in time—options are limited term instruments, meaning they have a set date at which they will expire. This term can be as short as a few days or a year or more into the future.

Each option is represented by the month of expiration, the strike price, and the type of option, for example the ABC Company, August, $16.00 call option.

Option Premium

Options have a cost commonly referred to as the option's premium. Just like a car insurance policy has a premium for you to buy a certain amount of coverage for your car, an option has a similar theory. You are paying a premium for the right, but not the obligation, to the market. This premium is determined by supply and demand in the market. Like other securities, options are bid, offered, and traded actively on the market. They are traded separately from their underlying instruments and often on different trading exchanges.

Writing Options

Similar to the way an insurance policy has an underwriter or someone who is willing to take the risk that you will not wreck your car, an option has a writer as well. Option writers are investors who are willing to take the risk for a price or premium that the option will have no value at expiration or that the premium will be reduced and that they can purchase back the option at a lower price.

This risk process is not exactly the same as shorting a futures contract or selling short in equities because options writers are not necessarily betting that the underlying market price will go in a particular direction. They are just counting on the market to remain above or below a certain point. We discuss writing options later in the book, but for now it is most important that you understand that the premium is the risk value of the option. An option seller or writer is taking the risk and demanding premium for that risk. As in most every investment, the more assumed risk the investor takes on, the more reward the risk taker wants in return.

ATM, ITM, and OTM

There are three expressions commonly used for referring to the distance an option is from the current underlying instrument price:

- *At the money (ATM):* This means that the strike price of the option is in very close proximity to the current underlying instrument pricing. If ABC Company is trading at 15.00, then the 15.00 call would be considered at the money.
- *In the money (ITM):* This refers to options for which the underlying instrument price has surpassed the option's strike price in the direction of the option. If ABC company is trading at 15.00, then the 14.00 call option would be considered in the money.
- *Out of the money (OTM):* This refers to options for which the underlying instrument price has not yet reached the strike price of the option. Again this would be in the direction of the option, call versus put. If ABC Company is trading at 15.00, then the 14.00 put option would be out of the money.

You will see these expressions used in commentary, analysis, and information relating to trading options, including many of the strategies you'll be learning later. Most often you will find traders using at the money or out of the money options in their trading strategies.

Intrinsic and Extrinsic Value

An option premium is composed of two values: intrinsic value and extrinsic value.

Intrinsic value is present in options that are in the money. This value is related to the option's strike price and the current price of the underlying instrument. A call option has intrinsic value when the underlying price is higher than the strike price of the option. A put option has intrinsic value when the underlying price is lower than the strike price of the option.

Here is how intrinsic value on a call option is calculated:

$$\text{Underlying price} - \text{strike price} = \text{intrinsic value}$$

This is how intrinsic value on a put option is calculated:

$$\text{Strike price} - \text{underlying price} = \text{intrinsic value}$$

Extrinsic value can be described as the risk value of the option. The risk value is made up of several components. One of these is time value, which is the length of time that the option writer or seller will assume risk for the sale. A 5-year life insurance policy premium is much cheaper than a 15-year policy premium because the insurance company is exposed to risk for an additional 10 years on the 15-year policy. Options are no different; time has risk, and therefore time has a premium cost to the buyer. Time value can be present in options that are in the money, at the money, or out of the money. Time value is the portion of premium in the options price that is above and beyond the intrinsic value. If an option is at the money or out of the money, then the option would have no intrinsic value and would have time value only. Time value can also be considered the risk value of an option. When you purchase an option, you are compensating the writer for the risk and time of selling the option. Included in the time value of the option is the risk assumed from the volatility of the market. If the market price fluctuates wildly, the writer naturally assumes that there is more risk than if a price is very stable, so the time value of the option would be further increased on the more volatile options. The longer the time remaining until the option expires, the more the perceived risk of the option and therefore the higher the premium. More time, more risk, more premium.

Time Decay

Time decay is the expression of the decreasing risk value of the option resulting from the decrease in time before expiration. A good example of time decay or risk value decay is U.S. Treasury bonds. These have active options in each month with the same underlying contract for as many as three months. Figure 2.1 shows three U.S. 30-year Treasury bond options in three different months. Each has the same pricing on the underlying Treasury bond contract because they all follow the same underlying June futures.

In this example, we have the April, May, and June U.S. T-Bond 126 call options. The near option (April) has a last price of 215. The May option shows a price of 336, and the June option is priced at 428. The option has more risk of significant price changes between now and June than it has in April, so the option has more value in June.

In addition to risk premium, there are other factors contributing to option time value. The funds required to place the option

Symbol	High	Low	Bid	Offer	Last
TR-J09,C126	162	200	162	215	219
TR-K09,C126				336	342
TR-M09,C126				428	435

Figure 2.1 U.S. Treasury bond serial options—Powered by CSMXpress

position, either in cash or margin, have an interest cost over time that is also part of the time value. As time becomes shorter, the interest collectible on those funds over the period before expiration is lower. If the option represents a futures contract on a physical commodity, it is also likely that there will be storage costs and interest on the physical item that can also make up a portion of the time value.

Expiration and Exercise of Options

As we've discussed, options are a limited term instrument. Options have a set date at which they expire. You should clearly understand what happens when your option reaches the expiration date and what is going to be required of you as the investor or your client. U.S. equity options in general expire on the third Friday of the expiration month unless the third Friday is a holiday; then they expire one day early. Options on futures do not have a standard for all markets. Expiration of futures options is based on the terms listed for the individual contract or type of commodity. For example, CBOT (Chicago Board of Trade) grain options expire around the twenty-fifth of the month before the expiration month. So a March corn option will expire around February 25, while Feeder cattle options usually expire on or near the last day of their expiration month.

You should have a financial calendar handy to show you the expirations of stock and commodity options or at least bookmark a calendar online so that you can refer to it as needed.

If an option expires, it means that the option has been held to the expiration date and the option is out of the money, or at least close enough to the money so that the trading costs of exercising the option cannot be justified. When the option expires, the position is removed from the account and the entire premium paid by the option buyer is lost which in turn means the option writer has retained the entire premium paid by the buyer.

When an option is exercised, it means that the option is converted into the underlying instrument. If it is a typical U.S. stock option, then it represents 100 shares of the underlying stock. If the option is exercised, the investor is now responsible for the financial aspect of the 100 shares of stock. Options on U.S. futures contracts typically represent one futures contract. If the option is exercised, then the financial ramifications of the underlying futures position are realized, good or bad.

In-the-money or at-the-money options are typically automatically exercised by the exchange, although it is standard practice with U.S. equity options to make certain that an at-the-money option is at least ½ point in the money, (¼ point for institutional investors) to allow for covering the costs of trading. Futures markets do not have a standard for covering trading expenses. If your option is at the money, the option will most likely be exercised even if the costs of trading cause you to lose on the position.

There are two different styles of options used in the market with respect to expiration. In a European style option, the option cannot be exercised prior to the expiration date. This style of option does not carry the risk to the writer of the buyer exercising the option ahead of expiration. American style options can be exercised at any time during the life of the option. This typically happens only on options that are "deep in the money" meaning that they are so far in the money that there is little or no time value remaining, but it is possible that an option may be exercised at any time and at the buyer's discretion . If an option is exercised prior to expiration, the exerciser loses any premium value above the intrinsic value of the option.

Options Symbols

Options quotes seem like cryptic code with no rationale, but once you learn the system, you will be able to quickly work through the options quotes. Let's take a look at equities first because they are a bit more complex then their futures counterparts. An equity option symbol is made up of three parts: first the root symbol, then a month code, and finally a strike price code.

Equity option symbol = Root option symbol + month code
+ strike price code

In Figure 2.2 you can see a sample of a stock option ticker symbol. In the tables shown in Figure 2.3 and Figure 2.4 you can see the month and strike price codes. The root symbol is the symbol for options on the underlying stock or instrument. The root symbol is not necessarily the same as the underlying stock ticker symbol, so make sure that you look up the option symbol for the stock in question.

In Figure 2.3 we show the expiration month codes for stock options. Call options are from A–L, and put options are M–X.

In Figure 2.4 you can see the strike price codes for equity options. You will be looking for the strike prices nearest to the current price

Option Symbol	Stock Symbol	Expiration Code	Strike Price
BAHK	BA (Boeing)	H	K

Figure 2.2   Stock ticker example

	JAN	FEB	MAR	APR	MAY	JUN	JUL	AUG	SEP	OCT	NOV	DEC
Calls	A	B	C	D	E	F	G	H	I	J	K	L
Puts	M	N	O	P	Q	R	S	T	U	V	W	X

Figure 2.3 Equity option month code table

Month	Code	Month	Code
January	F	July	N
February	G	August	Q
March	H	September	U
April	J	October	V
May	K	November	X
June	M	December	Z

Figure 2.4 Equity option strike price table

of the underlying stock. Correlate that row of prices to the code letter. This will be the last letter of your ticker symbol.

Using Figures 2.3 and 2.4, practice putting together option ticker symbols if you are not familiar with the codes. Try putting together an April 40.00 call for Wal-Mart (root symbol WMT). From Figure 2.3 you can find the April column and the call option row and you will see the symbol is D. From Figure 2.4 you can find the 40 strike price and the letter associated with it at the beginning of the row will be H. You should come up with the symbol WMTDH.

The symbols will vary a bit between different quote systems and electronic trading platforms, but the code will remain this same. Some quote systems will have a dot in front of the code to denote that it is an option quote; some may have a .X or .O after the code. There are variations among providers, but just being familiar with the code system should make it possible for you to work with any of the systems.

Futures and options on futures have a completely different coding system, but it is a bit easier. The futures symbol is made up of the commodity symbol, month code, year, strike price, and option type. In Figure 2.5 you can see the month codes for futures and options on futures.

For example, the S&P 500 index futures contract has the symbol SP. If we wanted to watch the ticker symbol for a July 2009 S&P 500 800 call option, the combination would be SPH09800C. Again, different quote systems and trading platforms have variations of this base symbol, but you will have the essence of using your

Code	Strike Prices						Code	Strike Prices					
A	5	105	205	305	405	505	N	70	170	270	370	470	570
B	10	110	210	310	410	510	O	75	175	275	375	475	575
C	15	115	215	315	415	515	P	80	180	280	380	480	580
D	20	120	220	320	420	520	Q	85	185	285	385	485	585
E	25	125	225	325	425	525	R	90	190	290	390	490	590
F	30	130	230	330	430	530	S	95	195	295	395	495	595
G	35	135	235	335	435	535	T	100	200	300	400	500	600
H	40	140	240	-340	440	540	U	7.5	37.5	67.5	9.5	127.5	157.5
I	45	145	245	345	445	545	V	12.5	42.5	72.5	102.5	132.5	162.5
J	50	150	250	350	450	550	W	17.5	47.5	77.5	107.5	137.5	167.5
K	55	155	255	355	455	555	X	22.5	52.5	82.5	112.5	142.5	172.5
L	60	160	260	360	460	560	Y	27.5	57.5	87.5	117.5	147.5	177.5
M	65	165	265	365									

Figure 2.5 Futures option code table

quote and order entry systems. Always check with your quote or trading platform provider for its symbol system.

Options on futures do not necessarily have an expiration in each month so it is important to reference your financial calendar to determine which month codes will apply to the individual option contract.

Option Chains

Now that we have a basic understanding of the options symbol system, let's take a look at some real option quotes on the option chain in Figure 2.6. In the option chain you will find the current pricing for each strike price. In addition to the most recent trade in the last category, you will find the daily high, low, bid, and offer/ask prices as well as current volume and open interest.

This particular chain is in a straddle format and shows call options on one side and put options on the other with the strike price down the middle which is handy for working spreads. Figure 2.6 shows a

Symbol	Last	Change	Call Bid	Ask	Volume	Open Int	Strike Price	Symbol	Last	Change	Puts Bid	Ask	Volume	Open Int
WMTFC	N/A	0.00	33.85	34.00	0	0	15.00	WMTRC	0.04	0.00	0.01	0.04	25	189
WMTFB	N/A	0.00	31.25	31.50	0	0	17.50	WMTRB	0.06	0.00	0.01	0.05	2	371
WMTFD	N/A	0.00	28.75	29.00	0	0	20.00	WMTRD	0.05	0.00	0.05	0.08	20	4,670
WMTFS	N/A	0.00	26.35	26.50	0	0	22.50	WMTRS	0.14	0.00	0.06	0.09	2	474
WMTFE	24.50	0.00	23.80	24.05	2	0	25.00	WMTRE	0.17	0.00	0.09	0.12	36	654
WMTFT	21.20	0.00	21.35	21.60	22	22	27.50	WMTRT	0.24	0.00	0.14	0.17	50	917
WMTFF	17.80	0.00	18.90	19.15	64	85	30.00	WMTRF	0.27	0.00	0.21	0.24	48	1,951
WMTFZ	15.40	0.00	16.60	16.70	2	273	32.50	WMTRZ	0.41	0.00	0.31	0.34	25	663
WMTFG	14.28	1.11	14.26	14.35	70	219	35.00	WMTRG	0.60	0.00	0.46	0.49	31	1,761
WMTFU	11.55	0.50	11.95	12.05	10	217	37.50	WMTRU	0.68	0.19	0.68	0.71	20	3,737
WMTFH	9.25	0.35	9.75	9.85	20	575	40.00	WMTRH	1.00	0.30	1.01	1.03	117	4,463
WMTFV	7.85	1.15	7.70	7.80	170	799	42.50	WMTRV	1.47	0.45	1.47	1.51	161	6,785
WMTFI	5.75	0.80	5.85	5.95	8	1,894	45.00	WMTRI	2.25	0.55	2.13	2.16	64	9,475
MTFW	4.35	0.65	4.26	4.30	52	2,739	47.50	WMTRW	3.05	0.60	3.00	3.10	36	8,647
WMTFJ	3.00	0.45	2.90	2.94	1,499	30.935	50.00	WMTRJ	4.10	0.95	4.15	4.25	70	11,547
WMTFX	1.86	0.26	1.87	1.89	1,440	12,455	52.50	WMTRX	5.75	1.05	5.65	5.70	82	5,512
WMTFK	1.14	0.22	1.10	1.14	1,142	15,461	55.00	WMTRK	7.60	0.91	7.35	7.45	40	6,536
WMTFY	0.64	0.14	0.61	0.64	286	5,960	57.50	WMTRY	9.45	1.15	9.35	9.45	20	2,272
WMTFL	0.33	0.07	0.31	0.34	84	9,476	60.00	WMTRY	11.96	0.86	11.55	11.65	7	1,402
WMTFA	0.17	0.02	0.15	0.17	10	5,246	62.50	WMTRA	15.35	0.00	13.90	14.00	10	210
WMTFM	0.10	0.00	0.08	0.10	10	3,525	65.00	WMTRM	17.50	0.00	16.30	16.40	6	879

Figure 2.6 Basic option chain—Wal-Mart, Inc.

basic option chain, and you will find this type of option quote provided by most online brokerage houses as well as most of the financial media sites. For more advanced trading, the basic option chain is missing vital information needed for effectively making option trading decisions.

If you are not currently using option analysis software for your trading, you might consider checking into the various offerings from software companies and Internet resources. The Internet is an excellent resource for finding option pricing modeling applications. You can find offerings from many different sources including free software downloads, JavaScript applications, predesigned spreadsheets for Excel, and services offering fee-based software applications. Many of these programs are relatively low or no cost, while others can be several hundred dollars a month with real-time data feeds.

The most important part of any software or online application is that you, as the trader or analyst, be able to perform an analysis and develop information over the basic option chain. Throughout this book we demonstrate fee-based software-generated option chains, and models. Figure 2.7 shows the expanded capability of software in presenting the relevant information.

You can see in Figure 2.7—Wal-Mart, Inc., option chain—that we are able to expand our view by analyzing theoretical option value, implied volatility, and the Greeks. (See below.) By using a software analysis program you can more effectively lay out your potential strategy and gather more information regarding the risk and reward potential of the position.

You should also be aware of the limitations of these programs. Remember that options models, including the ones we demonstrate throughout this book, are theoretical and based on assumed

Actuals	WMT Common					
	WMT		49.19	+0.25		
Options	JUN <98>					
57.5 calls	T.Prem	MktPr	MIV	Delta	Gamma	Theta
55.0 calls	1.10	1.10	30.6%	28.7	4.91	-1.28
52.5 calls	1.92	1.92	32.5%	40.8	5.24	-1.60
50.0 calls>	3.00	3.00	34.3%	53.4	4.99	-1.78
47.5 calls	2.64	4.33	35.8%	65.0	4.29	-1.81
45.0 calls	1.86	6.05	38.8%	75.0	3.37	-1.77
55.0 puts	1.29	7.10	29.9%	-71.3	4.91	-1.20
52.5 puts	2.19	5.50	32.8%	-59.2	5.24	-1.59
50.0 puts>	3.19	4.00	33.8%	-46.7	4.99	-1.73
47.5 puts	2.85	2.85	35.4%	-35.0	4.29	-1.76
45.0 puts	1.97	1.97	37.2%	-25.0	3.37	-1.66
42.5 puts	1.45	1.45	40.9%	-17.3	2.33	-1.56

Figure 2.7   WMT option chain–Powered by Option Vue 6

and/or fixed values which may or may not be accurate with respect to the stock or derivative option you are analyzing. These models also do not always account for factors such as changes in volatility, commissions, dividends, and splits which can radically affect the pricing model.

The Greeks

The term "the *Greeks*" refers to a set of mathematical equations used for deciphering the potential for movement in an options value versus the underlying stock or derivative position. Letters from the Greek alphabet are assigned to these equations, hence the name. Understanding how to use the Greeks effectively is critical to your ability to price options effectively and predict the risk and reward of an option. There are multiple levels of Greeks in option modeling

Actuals		IBM Common			Legend			
	IBM	91.95	-0.96	Symbol	Trade	Last	Chg	

Options			APR <30>					JUL <121>				
110 calls	MktPr	MIV	Delta	Gamma	Vega	Theta	MktPr	MIV	Delta	Gamma	Vega	Theta
105 calls	0.31	32.3%	13.6	2.07	5.76	-2.15	2.90	35.0%	31.5	1.69	18.7	-2.58
100 calls	0.96	33.3%	25.0	3.02	8.39	-4.15	4.70	37.7%	39.4	1.83	20.3	-3.15
95 calls	2.50	35.8%	41.1	3.69	10.3	-6.12	7.10	40.9%	48.1	1.89	21.0	-3.58
90 calls>	5.20	39.9%	59.7	3.67	10.2	-6.87	9.10	40.0%	57.5	1.86	20.6	-3.45
85 calls	8.40	39.5%	77.2	2.87	7.97	-5.27	11.42	38.3%	66.9	1.72	19.1	-3.05
80 calls	13.10		89.9	1.68	4.68	-3.14	15.00	40.6%	75.8	1.48	16.5	-2.81
100 puts	10.40		-75.0	3.02	8.39	-5.57	12.50	34.4%	-60.6	1.83	20.3	-2.77
95 puts	5.63	36.8%	-58.9	3.69	10.3	-6.26	11.00	42.9%	-51.9	1.89	21.0	-3.69
90 puts>	3.50	42.5%	-40.3	3.67	10.2	-7.28	7.80	41.1%	-42.5	1.86	20.6	-3.48
85 puts	1.85	44.5%	-22.8	2.87	7.97	-6.20	5.60	41.9%	-33.1	1.72	19.1	-3.30
80 puts	1.05	49.6%	-10.2	1.68	4.68	-4.99	4.05	44.0%	-24.2	1.48	16.5	-3.06
75 puts	0.52	52.9%	-3.32	0.70	1.96	-3.35	2.95	46.7%	-16.4	1.17	13.0	-2.75

Figure 2.8 IBM option chain—Powered by Option Vue 6

formulas; however, most options traders use the following four in the first order of Greeks: delta, vega (academically referred to as kappa) theta, and rho. One Greek is used in the second order— gamma. There are actually 10 second order Greeks and 20 third order; however, for our discussion we use only these the five given above. Each of these terms relates to one factor in the estimation of the theoretical value of an option given the time remaining, volatility, and interest rate. Let's go through each of them individually using an option chain or matrix. Figure 2.8 shows a full option chain on IBM common stock, and it shows two different terms of expiration.

You can see in the figure that IBM is trading at 91.95, which makes 90.00 the strike price for at-the-money options. The 90 call is actually slightly in the money, and the 90 put slightly out of the money, but they are the closest option to the current price.

Delta

Delta measures the sensitivity of the option's value to a change in the price of the underlying, in the example above, the underlying is IBM. For call options delta is denoted by a number between 0 and 1.00, with 0 representing no movement of the option as the underlying changes price; 1.00 means that the option is matched with the movement of the underlying, dollar for dollar. For puts, delta is represented by a number between 0 and −1. Delta in this case is shown normalized for dollars, so the figure represented is number of dollars you would gain or lose in option value should the underlying move by $1. Again, refer to Figure 2.8 if IBM were to go to 92.95 tomorrow, then the 90 call option would gain $59.70, and the 90 put would lose $40.30. The opposite would happen if IBM were to drop that same dollar amount. Remember, these are theoretical probable values resulting from a mathematical formula. They are not set in stone.

Delta is related to the distance from the current market price either in the money or out of the money. The farther in the money an option becomes, the stronger the delta. Eventually a deep in-the-money option will have a delta of 1.00. At-the-money options will always have a delta of around .50 because the delta of the at-the-money call and the at-the-money put when added together should equal 0. The farther away the underlying price moves from the option strike price, the lower the delta. A deep out-of-the-money option will have a very small delta. For example, the 75.00 put option has a delta of only 3.32, meaning that if IBM drops to 91.95 tomorrow, the option would gain only $3.32.

If this were an option on a futures contract, the delta would more often be expressed as a percentage of change. So if CBOT corn were to move 20 cents per bushel and the option had a delta of .40, then you would expect the option to change by 8 cents. The same concept, but the number of different pricing variables on futures contracts, makes a standard dollar amount difficult to establish.

Delta is one of the most critical components for constructing your trades properly and with the appropriate risk control. When we analyze the individual option strategies, we discuss more about delta management and delta-neutral trading. Delta neutral means that we are trying to achieve a delta of the overall position to zero or close to it in order to reduce the effect of change in the underlying.

Gamma

Gamma is a second order of delta, meaning that the values for gamma come from the result of delta. Gamma measures the change in the delta with the movement of the underlying. Like delta, it is based on $1 or one point of movement in the underlying.

A larger gamma indicates that the delta is sensitive to the price movement on the underlying. You can see in Figure 2.8 that the gamma is the highest in the strike prices immediately surrounding the current underlying price. It is not always true that the at-the-money calls are the highest; however, it is very common. What gamma helps us do is assess how much the rate of price change will increase or decrease as the underlying changes. This information is valuable when you are attempting to accomplish delta-neutral positioning or delta hedging.

Commodities hedgers often use delta hedging in order to accomplish the correct protection from price movement in the underlying. For example, a livestock operation may use delta hedging and options to protect a late August or September cash cattle sale that will still have time value remaining when the cattle are sold. Using options spreads also creates a need for delta hedging because the offsetting option positions can reduce the overall delta to where additional positions may be needed. By using gamma, we can discover how much the delta will adjust, and we will then be able to more accurately predict where the option pricing will be if the market moves a certain distance.

Theta

Theta is the calculation of how the passage of time affects the price or premium of the option. If the Greeks are normalized in dollars as we have them in Figure 2.8, you can see the dollar amount that the options value will drop for each day that time passes. In Figure 2.8 the April 90 call has a theta of −6.87 meaning that the option will drop by $6.87 per day in time value. Note that the longer-term July 90 call option has a theta of −3.45, just over half the April option. The longer the term until expiration, the slower the time value decay.

It is also important to notice that as you move farther away from the money, the theta tends to weaken as well. This is not a significant factor because the time decay is present on all the options. However, as a function of the overall value, the decay rate will be slightly slower.

Vega

Vega is the measurement of the sensitivity of the options price or premium to change in volatility in the underlying. If volatility increases, the options value will increase; if volatility decreases, then the value of the option will decrease. Vega tends to be strongest in the at-the-money options rather than in-the-money or out-of-the-money options. Vega is shown as a factor of a 1-point change in volatility in the underlying asset. So if we look again at the July 90 call from Figure 2.8 which is at 9.10 and we can see the Vega is .20.6. If the underlying volatility rises by 2 percent with no change in the underlying price, we would expect this option to be theoretically priced at $9.50.

Rho

Rho is the measure of the sensitivity of the option to changes in interest rates. When interest rates are low, rho is not nearly as necessary to track as it is when interest rates are higher or when they are in a position to be moving higher. Interest is an issue with options because the value of the money not yet committed to the underlying asset during the life of the option.

Rho is most important to long-term options or LEAPS (Long-Term Equity Anticipation Securities) because the value of the unspent capital is more significant over time.

Chapter 3

VOLATILITY AND OPTIONS

Market Volatility

We've outlined some of the major changes in market participation in recent years with the growth of new markets, changes in market participants, and the basics of options. The last decade brought new meaning to the term "volatility" in markets around the world with new standards of price movement and volume. This new volatility has affected nearly all sectors from agriculture and energy to equity and financial markets. To manage market volatility in your portfolio, it is important to understand the basic cause of market volatility and its effects. In this chapter we discuss volatility and what it means to successful trading and managing risk now and in the future.

What Is Volatility?

Volatility is defined as the measure of instability in the price of a security instrument. Simply said, volatility is the measure of price movement risk on a particular stock, future, or other security. The higher the volatility of the instrument, the greater the assumed risk of significant changes in price over a period of time. This often correlates to direct risk, in that if the price change is dramatic, the risk of the price being contrary to your position increases. What makes studying volatility important in your portfolio is the understanding of the risk you are undertaking with a particular position or group of positions both now and in the future. We can break volatility in to three common indicators—current, historical, and implied.

Current Volatility

Current volatility is the measure of the active volatility of a position. Current volatility can be calculated with the standard deviation, most often a 20-day period. Figure 3.1 shows the 20-day standard deviation volatility chart for Home Depot Corporation.

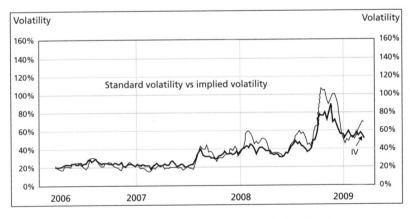

Figure 3.1 Volatility of Home Depot—Powered by Option Vue 6

You can see in the figure that Home Depot experienced a spike in volatility in October 2008 which reached up to over 90%. Remember, volatility is an indication of the range of movement in the stock price and the average risk of the price based on the period selected. In this case we used the standard deviation at 20 days. If you look at the chart in Figure 3.2 you can see that the volatility is not necessarily an indication of market direction as Home Depot stock fell sharply during the rise in volatility.

Historical Volatility

Historical volatility is the pattern of current volatility over a span of time. As referenced above, current volatility is actually a short-term historical average; however, historical volatility gives an accounting of the price movement and risk of a particular instrument over a longer period and makes it possible to better project the future risk of the instrument. This historical volatility is in no way a guarantee of future risk or volatility to a market, but it is a baseline that makes it possible to see unusual patterns in the future. The instrument could have significantly higher or lower levels of volatility which may be outside the investment objectives. By looking at historical volatility, we get a sense of suitability in relating the instrument to the objective.

In Figure 3.2 we can see the result of the volatility in Home Depot stock over a period of time. We can see that Home Depot's stock in the center area of the chart began experiencing wide daily and weekly price swings as well as a significant change in trend. If you have access to historical volatility charts through your brokerage house or data service, you may find them a helpful trading tool along with your analysis of price charts. Remember the wider the

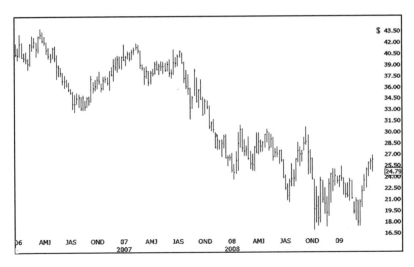

Figure 3.2   Home Depot daily chart
Image Courtesy of FreeStockCharts.com

average price range swings on a daily basis, the higher the volatility will be over a period of time.

Implied Volatility

Implied volatility is the forward looking volatility indicator. Implied volatility is related mostly to options, but can be on other securities as well. Implied volatility is the measure of sentiment regarding a particular option and its underlying security or a group of options and securities in the case of index options. You can think of implied volatility as a measure of investor fear and anticipation regarding the future price of an option.

Implied volatility is derived from the option premium versus the underlying price and the time remaining. In today's world implied volatility is calculated most often with software applications rather than with pencil and paper. Implied volatility is one of the most important factors in option trading. We focus a great deal on using high implied volatility in many of our strategies.

Volatility on Parade

To effectively demonstrate the new market volatility we are discussing, let's look at a few exceptional examples of recent volatility and massive price movement. Figure 3.3 shows the CBOT soybean futures over four years or so with the most striking part of the chart beginning in September 2006. Soybeans began a rally based on fundamental crop issues and massive index and hedge fund buying that culminated in gains of over $11.00 per soybean contract. The margin on the CBOT soybean futures contract changes as market volatility increases risk, but futures margin requirements exploded during this period. At-the-money call options during this period were a full $1.00 per bushel or more (5,000 bushel contract or $5,000 per

Figure 3.3 CBOT soybeans weekly
Image Courtesy of CSM Futures Group

dollar per bushel). Some of the weeks displayed in this chart had 5, 10, or even 15 thousand dollars' worth of trading range.

In Figure 3.4 we show what many consider to be the best market indicator for investor sentiment regarding the market. This is not an indicator of market direction, just market sentiment. The VIX index, or The Chicago Board Options Exchange(CBOE) volatility index, shows the average volatility of S&P 500 stocks. By calculating the volatility of the options, the index represents the sentiment of options traders with respect to the next two option expirations.

In Figure 3.4 we have highlighted the section representing the fourth quarter of 2008. This very clearly shows the increased volatility across the full market if the fairly diverse group of stocks represented in the S&P 500 are experiencing this level of daily volatility. Option volatility during the last half of 2008 was extreme in almost every market. As we look beyond 2008 and to the first quarter of

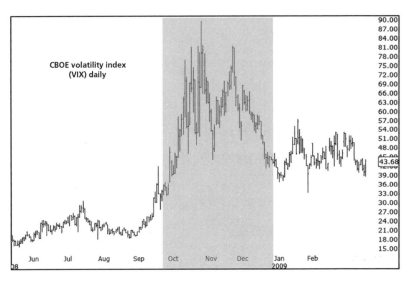

Figure 3.4   CBOE VIX index
Image Courtesy of FreeStockCharts.com

2009, we can see some resumption of range to the volatility, but if you imagine a midline in the volatility for the first quarter, you are looking at something like 45 percent in comparison to the third quarter of 2008 at around 20 percent average volatility.

We must be prepared to adjust to this increased level of volatility on a more permanent basis and make a new level be a part of trade construction, portfolio management, and risk control. If at some point in the future volatility returns to normal, we can use the lessons learned from high volatility to be even more effective in periods of low volatility.

Another interesting demonstration of volatility shows the reaction to volatility demonstrated by the VIX index in Figure 3.5. Figure 3.5 is a chart from the iShares 20-year bond fund in the same period as the VIX chart in Figure 3.4. During the last quarter of 2008 there was a large exodus of cash from the equity market into safety areas,

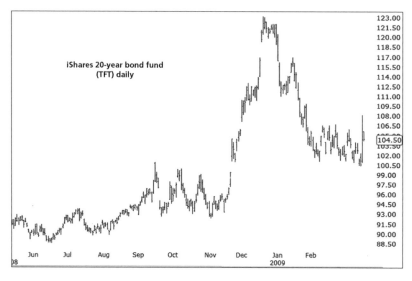

Figure 3.5 iShares Daily Chart
Image Courtesy of FreeStockCharts.com

which is the cause of the large price spike in the Treasury fund. We can correlate almost exactly the peak in the S&P 500 option volatility from the VIX chart to the beginning of a period of increased volatility and massive influx of cash into the debt market. As volatility reached exceptional levels, the risk tolerance and confidence of investors caused the movement of funds from equity to debt. It is clear that as investors began to feel the exceptional volatility in equities, the liquidation of equity assets began, and the money had to move to safer areas. It is important to study volatility not only in the market you are attempting to trade in but also in related and opposing markets as well.

Volatility Cause and Effect

Volatility can occur as a result of a number of things, everything from quarterly earnings reports to crop conditions in Brazil. In the case of the last quarter of 2008, volatility developed as a result of a mass exodus of cash from many markets as the credit crisis reached critical mass and investors began to flock to cash and safety. In contrast to the equity volatility, commodities markets were experiencing increased volatility for several quarters prior to the fourth quarter for a multitude of reasons. Increased energy demand and reduced supply created an environment in which energy product pricing created a ripple effect through every aspect of commodity production. Producers, transportation suppliers, end users, and retailers all were affected. The soybean chart in Figure 3.3 is a perfect example of how increased pricing and volatility cross into a storm of market fluctuation.

Commodity options during this period saw a dramatic increase in premium because of the increased implied volatility. Call option premiums in agriculture and energy were especially affected through most of this period. The major consideration to the inflated premium is the elevated risk to option traders. As we discuss option strategies, it is important to understand that the increased volatility can work in favor of the option trader, but also represent a significant element of risk.

Also, volatility does not necessarily result in higher pricing; it is the indicator of dramatic swings in price. Increased market volatility is often caused by increased interest on the part of speculators and large institutional traders regardless of the current direction of market prices. If a market is demonstrating volatility, then high-risk traders are more attracted to short-term trading opportunities. This perpetuates the cycle and further increases short-term volatility. More money moving means more volatile price swings.

In this way volatility becomes a self-fulfilling prophecy as one form of volatility attracts another. As markets experience decreasing assets from negative market information, volatility can increase as traders and investors see downward trends develop and begin running for the door. Volatility is also not a directional indicator in that as markets peak or bottom, volatility can decrease until a new direction is established. Volatility also builds into news events, earnings reports, and other known but unpredictable market events. After the event, volatility tends to reduce somewhat quickly, reverting back to preevent levels.

There is a tendency to see increases in volatility as markets rise and decrease as markets fall. This is an aftereffect and not necessarily a leading indication. The explanation for increasing volatility in uptrending markets may be more psychological than anything else, in that many traders do not understand short-trading the market, so money flows more freely into uptrends creating increasing volatility then as the trend reverses traders pull capital from the market causing decreasing volatility. This pattern of long-side volatility isn't likely to improve until investors in general develop a better understanding of short market positions.

Short-side volatility is often a contest between larger market players with knowledge and expertise in trading short positions and those participants trying to exit existing market positions. This contest often takes place between hedge funds and index funds. Individual investors are typically averse to the risk of short market trading and are mostly contributors to downward market volatility, primarily from a liquidating standpoint rather than any short market position.

Volatility and Trading Objectives

The correlation between volatility and the underlying risk to the portfolio is not an issue that can be fixed to a point or statistical guideline. Common market thinking suggests that as volatility increases on one or more positions in the portfolio, the entire portfolio is at additional risk. This is not necessarily true in all cases. The risk is dependant on the investment objectives of the portfolio and the current contents of the portfolio. Some investments do well in up trending volatility, while others will increase in risk significantly. If the portfolio has a significant percentage of assets like options that have exposure to volatility, then the assets may have to be adjusted or compensated for so that the increased volatility can be neutralized.

It is important to understand the current trading objectives and risk tolerance of the portfolio in order to create strategies to adjust for volatility. If the portfolio is set up for a time-based objective, say a retirement portfolio for a middle-aged person, then short-term volatility changes are less significant in trade planning. Long-term investors want to avoid high volatility option acquisitions that may decrease in value due to decreasing volatility; in general, volatility will have less effect on the buy and hold investor. Daily, weekly, or even annual volatility changes may not necessarily cause a need for adjustment in strategy.

A retirement portfolio for an investor nearing retirement with an income or growth objective will have significantly higher risk from increasing volatility. Large swings in price may affect the ability of this type of investor to draw consistently on a portfolio. In this situation volatility should be monitored carefully and consideration should be given to moving assets to areas less affected by volatility such as cash equivalent markets.

With any investment, your first and foremost duty in risk management is to determine your objectives and risk suitability Let's look at some common investment objectives and how options can fit into the portfolio mix.

A small investor who has an investment objective of retiring at age 65. The goal of the portfolio is time-based and total value based. The objective is to have a certain amount of money at a certain point in life so you set up a portfolio for growth for several more years. Volatility is going to play less of a role in your risk management decision making than will proper diversification and quality products. You want to make sure that the stocks, bonds, and funds that you are invested in will first and foremost survive until your goals are reached. You want the investments to grow until they are of value to provide acceptable income

The current volatility in the market is likely to be a major consideration only upon entry, exit, or shifting positions unless the objective is short term. Time-based or retirement-based investors often have a very conservative approach to investing, so this must be taken in to account when they decide what options strategies to apply to a portfolio.

When using options with this investment objective, you must keep in mind that options by nature are limited because they cannot be held indefinitely. Options must have an expiration date; therefore, as a risk management strategy they are somewhat short term in nature. By short term we mean, even long-term expiration options are three years or less. This does not mean that options cannot be used in a portfolio with the above objective. Quite the opposite is true. Options can help build significant value by capturing premium through writing options, limiting risk during periods of instability to preserve portfolio value, and defining risk on higher risk and aggressive positions. Long-term investment objectives are an ideal situations for adding option trading to the portfolio. If the portfolio has more of a fixed long-term structure and goals, many option strategies are open for the long-term benefit of the portfolio. Investors with this objective are often viewed as averse to risk and often reject options based on the common view that options are risky, however, with the right strategy option trading can improve risk management.

A lifestyle type of investor often has a much different objective. The investor is likely to be more willing to speculate with the objective to make my life better today and tomorrow or to simply increase my wealth. A lifestyle type of investor is going to expect a more significant return on investment in a much shorter period of time. This type is not necessarily a sophisticated or qualified investor, so you must be clear on the risk suitability for investing with options.

Volatility is going to be much more of a significant factor because frequently smaller, less sophisticated investors have monetary risk tolerance rather than technical market risk tolerance. Option strategies can help this investor improve risk management by limiting risk, increasing premium income, and offsetting changes in volatility. This investor will sometimes have more in-depth market knowledge, but the risks of option trading should be well understood before undertaking any strategy. Options can be utilized by this investor on a long-term, short-term, or even intraday basis. Options strategies can help smaller and average net-worth investors prevent short-term market fluctuations from significantly affecting their ability to maintain a position. Options can also be used by this investor to increase leverage on limited resources using purchased options and reduce cost basis with option writing.

For sophisticated and accredited investors, options are an obvious choice because of the ability to capitalize on the massive leverage options offer in equity, debt, and futures markets. We cover more about leverage when we talk about each option strategy, but as the high volatility of today becomes the average volatility of tomorrow, understanding volatility management will be more important to these investors than ever before.

Options on Futures

We will discuss a great deal about volatility in relation to equity markets, but we will also utilize examples of futures contracts and options on futures in our discussions.

Derivatives, or futures, are contract instruments between two parties for the exchange of a commodity. It could be a physical commodity, cash instrument, or financial instrument. Futures contracts do not specify the price. The price of the contract is determined in open market trading on a futures exchange. Futures contracts do specify the commodity, the quantity of the commodity, quality of the commodity, and the terms of delivery with respect to time and place.

There are two types of futures contracts: those that provide for physical delivery of a particular commodity and those that call for an eventual cash settlement rather than delivery. Most futures contracts these days are cash settlement, but you should be aware when trading options on futures that you could end up exercised into the underlying futures contract and be subject to delivery of the commodity any time after the first notice day. Futures contracts are leveraged instruments, meaning they represent a certain quantity of whatever is represented by the contract. The amount of funds required to trade the contract is significantly less than the cash value represented by the contract. If you wish to trade options on futures and you are not experienced with them, we recommend seeking a professional broker to help you with your futures market option education before trading.

Options on futures contracts carry substantial leverage in relation to the dollars needed for margin, but again you should be aware of the risks involved in options trading. Because of the leverage nature of the futures market, investment objectives must be defined a little differently than an equity or debt investment objective. Futures and options on futures are often designated in one of two manners, either speculative or hedge. A speculator is the investor who is trading in futures strictly to make a profit. Most equity investors are speculators as well. A hedger is a person or business that is using the options on futures or the underlying futures contracts to offset risk in their business inputs and outputs. For example, a hedger might be a corn ethanol plant that is buying corn on the futures market to offset the risk of rising input costs. That same business might also short ethanol futures or options to offset the risk of falling fuel prices. The volatile nature of the futures market and the limited term of the individual contracts make futures trading a shorter-term investment. It is not possible to hold indefinitely an individual futures contract or option on a futures contract. This short-term flow of capital tends to create a higher average historical volatility than their equity counterparts.

Each of these two types of futures investors can take advantage of the leverage and capital advantage of trading options by being able to define risk with purchased options or capture premium from written options.

Summary

We now have an introduction to what volatility is and how it is important to good trade decision making. We also have a better understanding of the causes and effects of volatility and the market reaction to it. It is important to research current and historical volatility for markets that are part of a trading objective and to make certain in the new market that the trading objectives are being followed.

Chapter 4

BUYING OPTIONS

Buying options is the most commonly used option strategy among investors and traders in the marketplace. Professional and nonprofessional investors alike use purchased options to access and leverage the market with limited risk. It is their limited risk nature that makes them so attractive. Buying options allows the investor the right to the underlying market at a particular strike price without the necessity of committing the full capital amount and without putting the underlying asset at risk.

The strategy of buying options outright can be complex when it comes to managing volatility. Many professional and nonprofessional investors underestimate the effect of volatility on purchased options and are left with a bad taste in their mouth if volatility suddenly drops. Experience working with professional investment and fund managers has shown that even though the depth of knowledge about options has increased 10-fold over the last several years, the basics of buying options is a mystery to many of those who manage portfolio risk for themselves and others.

We start out with covering the basic strategy of purchasing calls and puts and then look at how to avoid the pitfalls of volatility and time value decay when you're using purchase options in your portfolio or for your clients. In our models we use small quantities of options to demonstrate costs and breakeven more clearly. Our initial examples demonstrate commission rates based on standards of a single commission for fewer than 1,000 shares and a single futures contract for most firms. The calculations remain the same for underlying and option breakevens with larger quantities. Just remember that the calculation of commissions and fees is based on the rate for the quantity. Depending on the size of the portfolio you are managing, you may be trading 10 options or 10,000.

Buying Call Options

The goal of buying a call option is to gain the right to a long position in the underlying asset at a particular price with limited risk. This can be either an independent investment or an enhancement of risk control to another position. The advantage is that the call option is obtaining a long position with only the premium paid for the option at risk. Let's look at an example of a call purchase using an at-the-money call on Home Depot common stock and the breakeven scenario for the purchase.

In Figure 4.1 we show the purchase of one May $20.00 call option for Home Depot, Inc. In the "trade" column, +1 represents the purchase quantity. This gives the buyer the right to purchase 100 shares of Home Depot common stock at $20.00 per share. The "last" column shows the purchase price of $2.33 per share. In the "Acutals" row at the top of the figure, you can see that the price of the underlying market at the time of this purchase was $20.71. With the call strike price at $20.00 and the underlying Home Depot stock at $20.71, the call option has an intrinsic value of $0.71.

Actuals	HD Common					
	HD		20.71	+0.38		
Options	**MAY <62>**					
30.0 calls	Trade	Last	MIV	Delta	Gamma	Theta
27.5 calls		0.08		5.14	3.08	-0.29
25.0 calls		0.36	45.8%	17.6	6.80	-0.84
22.5 calls		1.04	50.6%	38.1	9.01	-1.34
20.0 calls>	+1	2.33	58.4%	60.6	8.23	-1.56
17.5 calls		3.00		78.9	5.62	-1.21
25.0 puts		4.90		-82.4	6.80	-0.78
22.5 puts		2.72	47.5%	-61.9	9.01	-1.23
20.0 puts>		1.40	51.9%	-39.4	8.23	-1.37
17.5 puts		0.69	60.1%	-21.1	5.62	-1.19
15.0 puts		0.28	66.4%	-9.41	2.96	-0.76

Summary	Net Reqmts	Gross Reqmts	Cash Flow	-$248
Init	$248	$0	Cur. Value	$0
Maint	$248	$0	Gain/Loss	$0
Cash/Init	-1.00		Commis	$14.95

Figure 4.1 Buying a Home Depot $20.00 call option—Powered by Option Vue 6

Call option: Underlying – strike price = intrinsic value

The remaining $1.62 in premium is the time value on this option.

Total premium – intrinsic value = time value

Let's look at the breakeven for this option and at what point it starts becoming profitable. A single $20.00 call option gives us the right to Home Depot at $20.00 per share on 100 shares. We have spent $2.33 per share in premium which we need to add to our strike price; we also need to add our costs of trading.

$20.00 strike price + $2.33 premium = $22.33 + costs of trading
= breakeven

Some summary cost figures are given at the bottom of Figure 4.1. These show a total cost of the option of $248 or $2.48 per share, which is the $233 in premium plus commissions set at $14.95 by default. This commission level may be a high or low figure for your trading costs. On larger quantities the effect of commission is spread across the total purchase premium, but remember to add the commissions and fees to the bottom line. If you are buying 10 options, then the cost will be .1495 per share. We now know that our breakeven is at $22.48 per share, meaning that Home Depot stock must rise to $22.48 by expiration in order for us to break even. Any price above $22.48 would be profit on the position.

Prior to expiration, the option will gain value if the market rallies thereby creating an opportunity to sell the option for a profit. Note that the option we've purchased in Figure 4.1 has a delta of 60.6 meaning that for each $1 of stock price movement, this option should gain 60.6 cents of that $1, with the delta increasing as the option goes further into the money. Let's look at how this option position gains value as the market moves. We have now purchased the at-the-money call option, and the delta on this option is strong at 60.6, so, assuming volatility remains constant, if Home Depot stock rises $1 tomorrow, we have a projected gain of $60.6 and a projected delta increase or gamma of 8.23 on the same increase in price. We will lose the time value for the day (theta) of $1.56 and come out with a net gain of approximately $59 on the $1 underlying price move.

In Figure 4.2 you can see the projected profit or loss on the option as the underlying price increases.

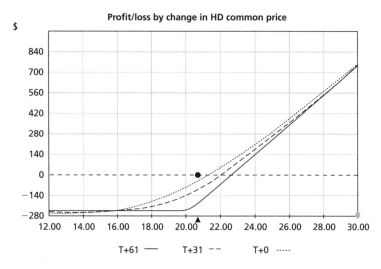

Figure 4.2 Home Depot $20.00 call model—Powered by Option Vue 6

The horizontal axis shows the price of Home Depot stock with the small arrow at $20.71 indicating the current underlying market. The vertical axis shows the profit/loss on the purchase of the $20.00 call in dollars. The dotted line that sweeps upward represents the profit and loss on the $20.00 call option if the price was adjusted with 0 time value decay, that is, if the underlying changed value today. The dashed line represents the profit and loss with only 30 days remaining until expiration, and the solid line represents the expiration day of the option. The dotted horizontal line represents breakeven on the position. Where the lines cross is the breakeven point for each period. Notice that the more time passes, the higher the underlying price must be to reach breakeven.

The objective of buying the $20.00 call option is to take advantage of an increase in Home Depot share price by building value in the call option to profit during the term of the option or be in the money at expiration. Your analysis of the potential for Home

Depot must match the objective, meaning that there is a reasonable probability that the underlying price will move the appropriate distance within the time frame of the option. The option we are demonstrating has only 62 days until expiration, so the stock must move quickly.

With only 62 days remaining, we would consider this a short-term option purchase, and I would recommend this type of option purchase for specific goals or events. If you are anticipating a significant event and you are not willing to risk the outright underlying stock, a purchased call option is a limited risk means of capitalizing the price movement. Short-term option purchases can be very successful, but time decay is much more aggressive under 60 days and will be working against your option value.

In Figure 4.3 we show a comparison of purchasing 100 shares of HD common stock and the purchase of a $20.00 call at expiration. In the figure the lighter line represents the 100 shares purchased outright, and the darker line is the option purchase with no time value remaining. You can also see how the option will not become equal

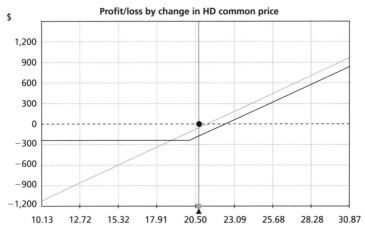

Figure 4.3 Underlying vs. call option comparison—Powered by Option Vue 6

to the outright stock purchase because of the $2.33 premium paid for the option as shown in Figure 4.1. However, once the option is firmly in the money, the value of the option will keep pace with the underlying at a 1 to 1 ratio once the delta of the option is 1.00.

You can see the limited risk of the option versus the underlying as the call option loss flatlines while the underlying price loss continues to deepen.

Analyzing Volatility

In Figure 4.4, we can see that the lighter grey line showing the implied volatility is around 58 percent.

This chart overlays the standard volatility shown by the black line in which we can see the current volatility for the underlying is above the volatility represented in our option purchase in Figure 4.1. But the implied volatility is just slightly lower and the average volatility over the past couple years is certainly lower than our current implied volatility. It is important to monitor the current volatility trend. With volatility charts, you look for the likelihood that a trend

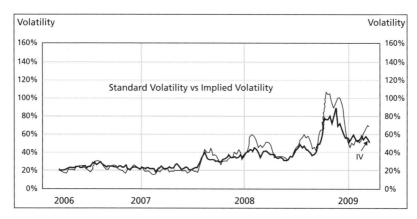

Figure 4.4 Home Depot volatility chart—Powered by OptionVue 6

of downward volatility will develop, thereby increasing the risk of premium loss on purchased options. The downturn in the last few days of trading before this option model was captured could be interpreted as a warning that you may be facing a reduction in implied volatility over time. If we remember back to our discussion of the Greeks, vega is the measure of sensitivity to volatility. The vega on this particular option is 2.90 so if volatility continues to fall, we could sustain a loss on the option of $2.90 per point of volatility change as well as the time value loss even if the underlying price remained unchanged. We need to be mindful of the potential for decreasing volatility in analyzing purchased option positions.

This is not to say that options cannot be purchased in periods of high implied volatility because the increased volatility may be a result of a long-term or permanent fundamental shift in volatility for the particular asset. However, the increased risk of buying in high volatility means that your analysis must be accurate for the sustainability of the volatility during the term of the option.

Volatility is relative to a particular point of view. If you look at the volatility chart again in Figure 4.4 and forget what you know beyond January 2008, you would be seeing a market in high volatility for the historical average. At this point, buying a call option would have been deemed to be high risk and may have not been recommended when in reality volatility nearly doubled, which would have increased the value of a purchased call option in relation to the underlying. In six months, the market may appear to be at low volatility when it is still significantly above the historical average.

The loss of time value and the loss of implied volatility are the main features of risk when you are buying options outright, especially at the money options with high premium that are at or out of the money and entirely made up of time value. The difficulty with purchasing call options is that you can be right with respect to the direction of the underlying market but have insufficient price movement to offset the loss of time value or volatility value.

Out-of-the-Money Calls

Another common call buying strategy is purchasing out-of-the-money call options because they are limited risk and less expensive than an at-the-money call or an in-the-money call. Purchasing out of the money can be very effective in a market with a potential for increasing volatility or a substantial increase in underlying price. The lower price of out-of-the-money call options often encourages traders to purchase multiple options in place of an at-the-money or in-the-money purchase. By purchasing multiple options, it is possible to achieve a higher total delta than the single at-the-money or in-the-money option. Let's look at an example (see Figure 4.5) and go through a comparison of risk versus reward on buying out-of-the-money calls.

Actuals	MSFT Common			Legend			
MSFT		18.33	+1.27	Symbol	Trade	Last	Chg

Options	JUL <116>						OCT <207>					
22.0 calls	Last	MIV	Delta	Gamma	Theta	Vega	Last	MIV	Delta	Gamma	Theta	Vega
21.0 calls	0.76	41.5%	32.7	7.97	-0.65	3.70	1.32	42.9%	40.1	6.13	-0.55	5.26
20.0 calls	1.10	43.4%	40.5	8.39	-0.75	3.97	1.71	44.7%	46.0	6.18	-0.59	5.40
19.0 calls	1.44	43.3%	48.7	8.43	-0.77	4.09	2.01	43.9%	52.0	6.08	-0.58	5.42
18.0 calls>	1.94	45.1%	57.1	8.09	-0.79	4.03	2.30	41.6%	58.0	5.85	-0.55	5.32
17.5 calls	..s..						..s..					
17.0 calls	2.47	45.7%	65.1	7.40	-0.75	3.79	2.65	39.0%	63.9	5.49	-0.49	5.09
16.0 calls	2.95	42.1%	72.5	6.45	-0.60	3.42	3.50	45.2%	69.7	5.02	-0.52	4.76
20.0 puts	3.15	50.0%	-59.6	8.39	-0.86	3.97	4.47	61.0%	-54.0	6.18	-0.79	5.40
19.0 puts	2.81	57.6%	-51.3	8.43	-1.01	4.09	3.85	61.5%	-48.0	6.08	-0.79	5.42
18.0 puts>	1.83	47.7%	-43.0	8.09	-0.82	4.03	2.75	52.2%	-42.0	5.85	-0.66	5.32
17.5 puts	..s..						..s..					
17.0 puts	1.55	53.4%	-34.9	7.40	-0.87	3.79	2.50	57.9%	-36.1	5.49	-0.70	5.09
16.0 puts	1.05	51.2%	-27.5	6.45	-0.76	3.42	1.69	51.4%	-30.4	5.02	-0.58	4.76
15.0 puts	0.85	56.0%	-21.0	5.38	-0.73	2.96	1.74	62.1%	-25.0	4.46	-0.66	4.32

Figure 4.5   Microsoft option chain—Powered by Option Vue 6

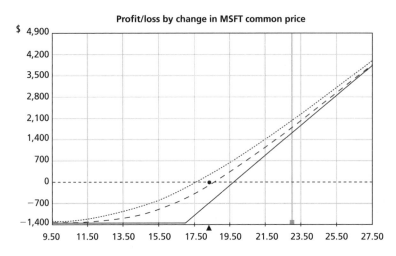

Figure 4.6 MSFT call option model—Powered by Option Vue 6

Using the option chain in Figure 4.5 let's look at two scenarios. We start by buying five Microsoft October 17.00 call options at 2.65 which represent 500 shares of Microsoft common stock. In this model the options have 207 days remaining until expiration. The call purchase costs of $1,325 plus costs of trading. Figure 4.6 shows the profit and loss scenario with the solid line representing expiration, the dashed line representing 100 days till expiration, and the dotted line representing the current day.

Figure 4.6 shows the profit of the option with the underlying MSFT rallying to 23.00 over 107 days. The estimated profit/loss on the 100 days until expiration is $1,815 profit on the 5-call purchase. This price change is well inside the historical and recent price movement for Microsoft at the time of this model. The maximum risk on the position remains the total premium paid plus costs of trading. The model is purposely demonstrated with extended time until expiration because of the reduced theta on the position. Now we can compare this to an out-of-the-money

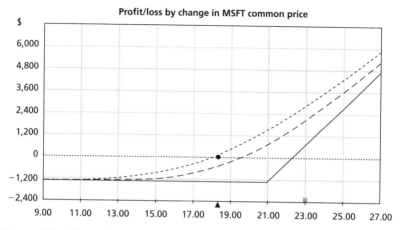

Figure 4.7 Microsoft multiple optionslt—Powered by Option Vue 6

purchase with nearly the same premium spent on an out-of-the-money trade buying two calls for each one in the previous scenario. In Figure 4.7 we show a model of buying 10 October Microsoft 21.00 calls at 1.32 each or a total premium of $1,320 versus $1,325 spent on the five options.

At the same point in time of 100 days remaining and the underlying price at 23.00 the 10-call purchase has a total profit of $1,960 or $145 more than the in-the-money option purchase. The profit and loss on the out-of-the-money call options has a steeper incline as price increases and will eventually outpace the 5-call purchase by two to one.

Where the multiple out-of-the-money call purchase advantage changes rapidly is in a shift in implied volatility. Looking back at Figure 4.5, we can see that the vega is slightly higher on the out-of-the-money calls, showing 5.26 normalized in dollars. The in-the-money call shows a vega of 5.09. If we calculate a 5-point downward shift in volatility over the time to the 100-day mark, we can assume that the in-the-money 17.00 call will gain about $127 less than in the zero volatility change scenario. Using the same 5-point drop in volatility on the purchase of the 10 October 21.00 call options, we would see them fail to gain about $263.00 compared to the original scenario. With the volatility shift the out-of-the-money calls have gained less than the in-the-money call purchase. The opposite would be true if the direction of the volatility shift was positive. The vega of the out-of-the money options would be multiplied by the number of options, thus giving a substantial boost to the value of the options. The out-of-the-money calls would profit substantially faster than the in-the-money call if the volatility were to shift 5 points to the positive.

The strategy of buying multiple out-of-the money options versus the at-the-money call or in-the-money calls is often referred to as delta positioning or delta trading. What you are trying to accomplish by delta trading is to achieve the desired long delta with similar premium costs that will compound as the market moves and builds more value. You can see from the example that in extreme market movement where the underlying asset moves far enough to place both strike prices deep in the money, the profitability of the option trade increases dramatically for the multiple option purchase.

Some traders will go further and use deep out-of-the-money options and buy several options instead of a smaller number of at-the-money or near to the money options. This strategy can certainly be effective in markets that move sharply up for call options or down for put options, but it is also a recipe for losing if the market enters a trading range over much of the life of the option. If too much time value elapses from the options, it will take an extreme market move to make up the lost premium much less put the options into a profitable situation.

Volatility is another significant consideration for multiple option strategies. Buying multiple options in low volatility and entering a period of increasing volatility is an excellent strategy for multiple options. When volatility is historically low, the most likely direction is up, and having several options to experience increases in premium value is certainly preferable to only one option. When volatility is high, the multiple option strategy has a great deal more to lose because the vega is basically the same; when volatility is low, the multiple option strategy will have several times the vega rate as a single option position.

To calculate the delta on multiple options as one position, we just add the deltas together. Then we can keep track of the positions as if they were a single position with a high delta. In the example in Figure 4.5 the 18.00 call has a delta of .58 per option or a total delta of 2.90. The multiple option strategy has an individual option delta of .40, but, when you combine the delta of 10 option the total delta equals 4.00. In the case of Microsoft stock, that represents 110 more shares worth of delta over the five-call purchase.

Call Options on Futures

Options on futures contracts work basically the same way as the equity call options we've been analyzing with a few differences. Futures contracts are leverage instruments in themselves in that a single contract represents a large quantity of a hard cash commodity, financial instrument, currency, or index share. Point values are represented in dollars per quantity of the hard cash item represented. If the futures quote on a soybean contract says 9.49, then that represents $9.49 per bushel of soybeans. The CBOT soybean futures contract represents 5,000 bushels of soybeans, which, if you are not familiar with soybeans, is over six tractor trailer truckloads of soybeans. The monetary value of a contract at $9.49 per bushel is over $47,000. Many of the financial contracts represent $100,000 cash value and the full Chicago Mercantile Exchange (CME) S&P futures contract represents a $250,000 portfolio. A single option or futures position represents a significantly larger amount of money than its equity counterpart in most cases. Let's look at a trade in which a July soybean call with the underlying at $9.49 per bushel is purchased. See Figure 4.8.

In Figure 4.8 we have highlighted a purchase in the July column of the 980 strike price. The premium shown is 67'0 which in this case represents .67 cents per bushel.

$$\text{Premium} \times \text{quantity} = \text{option premium (in dollars)}$$
$$\$0.67 \times 5,000 = \$3,350 + \text{costs of trading}$$

The option has a delta of .48 or 48 percent of the movement of the underlying and a gamma of .20; and theta and vega are normalized for dollars. Note that in Figure 4.8 the theta is significantly higher on the May option than the July option. This is another example of using time as a defensive position on purchasing call

Futures	MAY <42>			JUL <103>			AUG <136>			SEP <165>		
	952'0	+11'4		949'0	+8'4		932'4	+2'2		Last	Chg	Trade
Options	MAY <36>						JUL <99>					
1010 calls	MktPr	MIV	Delta	Gamma	Theta	Vega	MktPr	MIV	Delta	Gamma	Theta	Vega
1000 calls	28'2	39.8%	37.0	0.32	-31.4	56.4	60'0	41.2%	44.5	0.19	-20.3	97.6
990 calls	31'3	39.6%	40.0	0.33	-31.9	57.7	.....		46.3	0.20	-20.3	98.1
980 calls	34'7	39.4%	43.1	0.33	-32.3	58.7	67'0	40.8%	48.2	0.20	-20.3	98.4
970 calls	38'6	39.2%	46.4	0.34	-32.5	59.4	.....		50.1	0.20	-20.3	98.5
960 calls	42'6	39.0%	49.7	0.34	-32.5	59.6	74'4	40.5%	52.0	0.20	-20.2	98.4
950 calls>	47'2	38.9%	53.1	0.34	-32.3	59.4	.....		54.0	0.20	-20.0	98.0
970 puts	56'6	39.2%	-53.6	0.34	-32.5	59.4	.....		-49.9	0.20	-20.3	98.5
960 puts	50'6	39.0%	-50.3	0.34	-32.5	59.6	85'7	40.5%	-47.9	0.20	-20.2	98.4
950 puts>	45'2	38.9%	-46.9	0.34	-32.3	59.4	.....		-46.0	0.20	-20.0	98.0
940 puts	40'2	38.8%	-43.4	0.34	-31.9	58.8	74'3	40.3%	-44.0	0.20	-19.8	97.4
930 puts	35'4	38.7%	-40.0	0.33	-31.3	57.7	.....		-42.0	0.20	-19.6	96.5
920 puts	31'1	38.7%	-36.6	0.33	-30.4	56.2	63'7	40.0%	-40.0	0.20	-19.3	95.4
910 puts	27'1	38.7%	-33.3	0.31	-29.4	54.3	.....		-38.0	0.19	-19.0	94.0

Figure 4.8 Soybean call option chain—Powered by Option Vue 6

options. The more time until expiration, the slower the rate of time value decay. A quick calculation of the premium, adding the .67 to the 980 strike price, means that our breakeven is at 10.47 per bushel in July soybeans at expiration. In Figure 4.6 you can see the profit and loss model of the trade with the solid line representing expiration, the dashed line representing 30 days remaining, the dotted line representing 60 days remaining, and the top line represents the current situation. As with the equity call option, you can see that the maximum loss is the premium paid and, as the underlying gains price increases, the option profitability improves.

With futures the leverage of the underlying added to the leverage of the call option premium, the risk-to-reward ratio is exceptional as long as the underlying market rallies fairly quickly from the time of purchase. This model (shown in Figure 4.9) has no volatility increase or decrease built in and is showing only time decay and price as the risk factors. The time value decay on commodity options

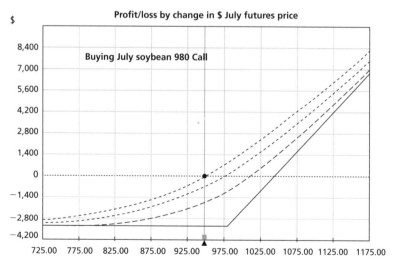

Figure 4.9   Soybean call model — Powered by Option Vue 6

can be substantial. If you look at figure, if the market were to move by $0.75 to around $10.25 within 30 days from purchase, you can see how the lower dotted line shows a profit of about $1,400, whereas if it took 60 days, the option would barely be breaking even.

Rolling your options forward is a possible strategy in derivative options as well; however, there are significant differences from equity options in this area. Futures have a delivery date which requires that the buyer of the contract pay for and take delivery of the underlying asset and that the seller must deliver the underlying asset or at least have a cash settlement that simulates the delivery system. As futures enter their notice period where contract writers are able to deliver the physical underlying commodity on purchased contracts, the holder of a contract is at risk of having to make this delivery. Futures usually have several delivery periods or contract months per year, and each of these contracts may be bid and offered at prices that differ from the underlying contract of the current options. As you roll forward, you will be rolling to an option that has a different underlying contract. This may cause you to experience a spread differential between contracts, which is called *basis*. In Figure 4.8 you can see how this may work in your favor from time to time as the August price is lower than the July price. This situation is considered to be an inverted market; in a normal market the contract should be factoring in the cost of storage and or interest on the cash underlying over the time period between contracts.

Futures Volatility

The increases in market volatility are more pronounced in futures markets than in any other market. The increase in volatility

dramatically increases the risk situation to option traders as well.
Let's look at the historical volatility of the soybean market over the
last few years.

You can see in Figure 4.10 that the volatility for the soybean market has steadily increased over the period captured in the figure
with the volatility peaking in late 2008. The future of this volatility trend is critical to the options buyer whether the position is an
outright investment or a hedge. If the volatility retraces 50 percent
of the increase from the 2007 level during the term of the option,
a significant loss of premium will occur. Let's look back at the theta
and vega and determine the premium loss assuming that 40 days
have elapsed until expiration and volatility contracts are 10 percent.
In this scenario we can estimate the theoretical option premium at
31 cents per bushel with no change in the futures price. We arrive
at this by multiplying the number of days elapsed by the dollar
figure represented in theta.

$$40 \text{ days} \times \$20.30 \text{ theta rate} = \$812.00 \text{ time value loss}$$

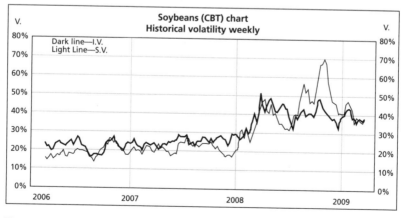

Figure 4.10   Soybean volatility—Powered by Option Vue 6

To see the volatility decay, take the vega rate and multiply it by the volatility change:

$$10 \text{ point change} \times 98.4 \text{ vega rate} = \$984.00$$

Now add the two figures together and divide by the per-point premium dollar value:

$$(\$984 + \$812)/\$50 = 35.92 \text{ points (rounded up, the result is 36)}$$

Subtract the 36 points from your initial premium outlay:

$$67.0 - 36.0 = 31.0$$

The theoretical value of the July 18.00 call option after 40 days and a drop in volatility of 10 points is 31.0 or $1,550.00. We initially paid 67.0 or $3,350 and now have $1,550 remaining with no change in market price. The same could be said if the volatility were to gain 10 points over the period. If you add the premium value from a volatility gain against the time value decay it will help offset the loss from time.

With the leverage represented in futures contracts, the monetary gain or loss from changes in volatility can be substantial and relatively quick. Historically speaking volatility tends to build slowly and disappear quickly, especially in futures markets. As a call buyer, you need to monitor the volatility of the market carefully when buying in high volatility. Derivative options can also vary in volatility from contract month to contract month, so you must monitor the volatility for the particular underlying contract as well as the front month volatility for changes in trends that could adversely affect your position. The obvious choice for derivative calls is to buy in low volatility and sell in increasing volatility, but it is not always possible to avoid a high volatility buy, especially if it is required by the investment objective as in the case in a hedge requirement.

Exercising Call Options

Exercising a call option comes down to dollars or cents, whichever applies. Some of the time you will not have any need to exercise a call option position because it will be out of the money which would automatically put you at a loss on your position. For example, if you purchase a 50-call option and the underlying is at 47, it would be silly to exercise the option to buy the stock at 50 when you can outright purchase the stock at 47 and then sell the option for whatever is left in premium, if anything.

It is possible that you may want or need to exercise a call option for two or three different reasons. For instance, when a purchased call option's delta has reached parity (delta 1.00), it may be advantageous to exercise the option into the underlying, but it will happen

Actuals	JNJ Common					
	JNJ		50.73	+0.09		
Options	MAR <4>					
65 calls	Trade	Last	MIV	Delta	Gamma	Theta
60 calls		0.04		0.00	0.00	0.00
55 calls		0.05		0.68	1.15	-0.27
50 calls>		1.10	32.0%	67.8	21.7	-8.11
45 calls		6.10		100	0.03	-0.03
40 calls		11.40		100	0.00	-0.02
55 puts		4.40		-99.3	1.15	-0.23
50 puts>		0.50	38.7%	-32.2	21.7	-10.1
45 puts		0.05		-0.01	0.03	0.00

Figure 4.11   Johnson & Johnson expiration—Powered by Option Vue 6

automatically if it remains in the money at expiration. Options usually achieve a delta of 1.00 only if they are deep in the money and there is little time remaining until expiration. This also occurs in periods with low interest rates because the value of the money leveraged with the option is hypothetically capable of gaining interest somewhere else in higher interest-rate conditions. Let's look at an example of some options at parity. In Figure 4.11 you can see a capture of March call options for Johnson & Johnson with only four days remaining until expiration.

You can also see that the 45 call option has a premium of 6.10 and a delta of 1.00 (100%) or at parity. If we exercise the option today, we receive the stock at 45.00 with a current market price of 50.73 so we lose .37 cents of premium over selling the call outright. If you are holding a bunch of these options, be careful in your analysis. Now let's look at the figure assuming you were holding the 50 call. The 50 call option has a premium of 1.10 and a delta of 67.8, not at parity at all, nor is it deep in the money. If you look carefully though, the numbers are almost the same as the 45 call The 50 call exercised would give 1.10 in premium but be .73 in the money, leaving a .37 loss of premium with only four days to go until expiration.

The need to exercise what? because of a deep in-the-money option is usually coupled with a liquidity problem in that the bid and offer are far too wide apart or there is insufficient quantity for the size of a trade you are trying to execute. Exercising the option cures the wide bid offer, and the investor can then hold or liquidate the underlying for the current value. This situation is more common in derivative trading as the option bids and offers on deep in-the-money options can be wide at times especially for sizable positions in nonindex or agricultural markets.

Derivative options near the money have a nasty habit of holding some value until the very last minute because of the volatility potential on the underlying futures, so you have to weigh the value of the option remaining against exercising the option. Unfortunately, it's a judgment call, and there is no real formula to apply other than keeping close tabs on the bid and offer while you are attempting to sell the option.

Make sure you are paying special attention to the risks associated with expiration and that exercising is not going to cause the trade to go beyond the risk suitability for your investment objective, especially if derivatives are involved. Derivative futures can have significant leverage for the margin required and create risk that may be beyond the trading objective for investor. Some investors buy options to avoid unlimited risk. When an option is exercised, that risk is limited only by the underlying price falling to zero.

Dividends are another possible reason for exercising an option ahead of expiration. We know that when a company pays a cash dividend, the value of that dividend is subtracted from the stock price on the ex-dividend date. Options on the underlying stock are affected as well because the underlying value changes. The option market is likely to price this into options prior to expiration. However, for the options that are expiring within the dividend period, you have to decide what is most financially advantageous.

Your option does not give you the right to the dividend payment, just the right to the stock. In order to be in line for the dividend, you must exercise your option ahead of the ex-dividend date. The situation comes down to cents for the most part—how much time value you will be giving up versus the dividend paid. If the option is at parity and the time value has completely eroded from a deep in-the-money option, then the exercise decision is a no-brainer;

however, if the option does have some time value, then we have to look at the expected dividend compared to the premium remaining. Let's look at a hypothetical example.

You own a 45.00 call option on XYZ, Inc., that expires in, say, a couple of weeks. The option is slightly in the money with the market trading at 50.00. XYZ announced an annual dividend of $1.00 per share. The dividend is to be paid in two days. The option is trading at 6.00. Do you exercise this option or sell your option and buy the equivalent shares of XYZ? If you exercise the option, you receive 100 shares of XYZ at 45.00 which is now trading at $50.00 per share, but essentially you have paid $51.00 for the stock because you have lost your $6.00 in premium. You will receive the $1.00 dividend, giving you a net purchase on the stock of $50.00. This exercise avoids the loss of $1.00 on the stock and the option by going ex-dividend.

If you were to sell your option at $6.00 and buy the stock at $50.00, you would gain the $1.00 from the dividend and retain the $1.00 in time value from the option. So you would end up with the stock at $49.00 after the dividend and time premium of the option.

In this case, it appears that selling the option premium and purchasing the underlying stock is a better choice, but it does not account for the fact that the option could be priced down for the dividend well ahead of time and bounce back after ex-dividend. Options often adjust to dividends well ahead of the ex-dividend date depending on the level of volatility. You should also make sure that you are consulting with your tax advisor concerning the ramifications of the dividend income and whether you are holding the stock for the correct amount of time after the dividend date.

You must also consider the interest that will be lost either because of the margin involved in buying the underlying stock or because your money is no longer gaining interest in your account.

When exercising an option, calculate the interest on the amount of funds required for the underlying once the option is exercised. If your margin rate is 6 percent and exercising the call option and holding the stock for the duration of the options life is 30 days then you must multiply .005 (6%/365 × 30) times the funds required for the purchase of the underlying. This cost must be subtracted from the amount of the dividend in order for you to properly evaluate the benefit of exercising prior to expiration. This situation is usually an issue only on a deep in-the-money option that would have little or no time value prior to the stock going ex-dividend. The interest would be less relevant than the time value in most cases.

Buying Put Options

When you are buying a put, you are buying the right to sell or be short an asset. The put option is a limited-risk right to be short the underlying at a particular price and time. A put option can be an independent investment or a hedge or cover for another asset.

Actuals	MSFT Common			Legend			
MSFT	18.33	+1.27		Symbol	Trade	Last	Chg

Options	JUL <114>						OCT <205>					
22.0 calls	Last	MIV	Delta	Gamma	Theta	Vega	Last	MIV	Delta	Gamma	Theta	Vega
21.0 calls	0.76	41.5%	32.7	7.97	-0.65	3.70	1.32	42.9%	40.1	6.13	-0.55	5.26
20.0 calls	1.10	43.4%	40.5	8.39	-0.75	3.97	1.71	44.7%	46.0	6.18	-0.59	5.40
19.0 calls	1.44	43.3%	48.7	8.43	-0.77	4.09	2.01	43.9%	52.0	6.08	-0.58	5.42
18.0 calls>	1.94	45.1%	57.1	8.09	-0.79	4.03	2.30	41.6%	58.0	5.85	-0.55	5.32
17.5 calls												
17.0 calls	2.47	45.7%	65.1	7.40	-0.75	3.79	2.65	39.0%	63.9	5.49	-0.49	5.09
16.0 calls	2.95	42.1%	72.5	6.45	-0.60	3.42						
20.0 puts	3.15	50.0%	-59.6	8.39	-0.86	3.97	4.47	61.0%	-54.0	6.18	-0.79	5.40
19.0 puts	2.81	57.6%	-51.3	8.43	-1.01	4.09	3.85	61.5%	-48.0	6.08	-0.79	5.42
18.0 puts>	1.83	47.7%	-43.0	8.09	-0.82	4.03	2.75	52.2%	-42.0	5.85	-0.66	5.32
17.5 puts												
17.0 puts	1.55	53.4%	-34.9	7.40	-0.87	3.79	2.50	57.9%	-36.1	5.49	-0.70	5.09
16.0 puts	1.05	51.2%	-27.5	6.45	-0.76	3.42	1.69	51.4%	-30.4	5.02	-0.58	4.76
15.0 puts	0.85	56.0%	-21.0	5.38	-0.73	2.96	1.74	62.1%	-25.0	4.46	-0.66	4.32

Figure 4.12   Microsoft puts—Powered by Option Vue 6

Let's look at an example of purchasing at-the-money puts on an individual stock. Figure 4.12 illustrates an option chain on Microsoft with July and October expirations showing.

In the figure let's look at the 18.00 put options in October. We can calculate the breakeven and profit-and-loss scenario of buying five of these October 18.00 puts at $2.75. We know that our out-of-pocket cost will be $1,390 including a $15.00 commission ($2.75 × 500 shares + $15.00) which will also be our maximum risk on the position. In Figure 4.12 you can see that the underlying MSFT stock is trading $18.33 and that this is an $18.00 put so it would be considered at the money. The breakeven can be quickly calculated for put options at expiration:

Strike price – premium – (costs of trading/number of contracts or shares) = breakeven
$18.00 − $2.75 − ($15.00/500) = $14.95 breakeven

When we place this position on a model, we can see how the option behaves with changes in the underlying asset. (See Figure 4.13.) You can see from the figure that as the price of Microsoft stock declines, the profitability of the put options increases. The solid line represents the options profit and loss at expiration, while the dashed line is about halfway to expiration, and the dotted line represents the day of the transaction. The maximum risk on the position occurs at an underlying price of $18.00 and above at expiration.

This option has a delta of 42.0, so it will gain $0.42 for each $1 the underlying stock price declines. Calculations for time value decay, volatility changes, and changes in the delta of the option are done in the same fashion as for call options. If the five purchased $18.00 puts experience 100 days of time value decay, then we

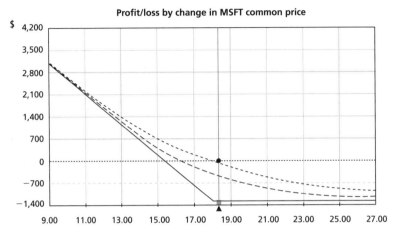

Figure 4.13   Buy MSFT 1,800 puts—Powered by Option Vue 6

would expect the options with a theta of .66 to have lost a total of $330 of the $1,390 premium in time value over the course of 100 days without including any movement of the underlying asset. A single point change in the volatility for Microsoft would equate to a change of $5.32 per option in value with the calculations normalized in dollars.

There are a few differences between call options and put options. The main difference is that the put option is a limited risk, but in a way it is also a limited gain. A call option can lose only the premium plus costs of trading, but can gain to infinity in price technically speaking. A put option is limited in risk to the premium plus costs of trading; however, it is limited in gain because the underlying asset can only fall to zero. Once the underlying asset has fallen to zero, the put option can no longer gain any value. Puts also differ in that they most generally have a little less volume, especially in derivative options, and they often have a bit lower implied volatility. This is not the case in Figure 4.12 but the overall market was in a period of high downside risk at the time of this model. Most generally, small investors have a lower comfort level with put options than with call options because of the theory of shorting the underlying, especially when the underlying is not already owned.

Large investors and funds use purchase put options regularly for protection against price movement on underlying asset purchases. A common strategy for buying put options is to use the put option as a presale for the underlying asset. If an investor has reached a trading goal and is ready to liquidate the underlying asset but is unable for tax reasons to accept the capital gain for the current tax year, a strategy might be to buy a deep in-the-money put option that has little or no time value. This option would not have to be exercised or liquidated until expiration and would give the investor the price desired without having to liquidate the underlying until a later date.

Put options are also excellent as an independent investment. If you are expecting a market to go lower but are not ready or willing to accept the unlimited risk of the outright short underlying asset, the put option offers an excellent vehicle for taking advantage of falling markets. It is often said that markets gain slowly and fall quickly. With a put option you can take advantage of the fast and hard market moves lower without having to come up with margin immediately for a short sale on the underlying.

Put options do not offer any downside protection against volatility changes. As volatility decreases, put options will lose premium or value just as their call option counterparts, and as volatility increases, put options will gain in value. Also just as with a call option, if the market moves in the correct direction to build value in the put option, both time and volatility are risk factors against premium gains.

Put Option Expiration

For the average investor, put options can often be confusing in that they give you the right to sell or be short the underlying asset. The situation becomes more complicated when a put option enters expiration. For equity options the expiration of a put option means that if the option is at or in the money, the investor must either have the underlying asset to sell in the amount represented by the put option or borrow the shares for a "short sale" from the brokerage house. Borrowing the shares means that the investor must be prepared for the margin required for the short sale from the brokerage house. The short sold underlying shares can be a substantial risk.

Investors who do not have the risk profile for short selling the market should be warned prior to expiration and liquidate the option position. There are usually transaction fees and margin fees associated with short selling that will go against any gains the option position might have made as well. The call option buyer who exercises the option must purchase the underlying shares for cash or on margin, but the underlying asset can only fall to zero thus requiring that the call buyer maintain some form of limited risk. This is because once a put option is exercised, the buyer is now short the underlying asset which has unlimited upside market potential and the risk must be margined accordingly.

Exercising put options is typically recommended only for substantial reasons such as a lack of volume that creates a wide spread between bid and offer or if the shares represented are already owned. In most cases liquidating the option is preferable to exercising the option.

Another method of liquidating a deep in-the-money put option where there is a need to exercise because of a lack of liquidity is to purchase the underlying shares represented by the put prior to exercising the option. Once the option is exercised, the shares will be offset and the position will be completed. The investor must have the cash or margin available to complete the purchase in order to accomplish this trade. For example, if the $18.00 Microsoft put options in the previous example were deep in the money and the market had fallen to $14.00 and the time value of the option had eroded, you would need to purchase 500 shares of Microsoft stock to lock in the value of the put. At expiration or if the option was exercised, then the 500 shares represented by the put option would be short against the 500 long shares.

This same strategy can be applied to derivative trading in order to liquidate a put option on a futures contract. When the option has a widespread between the bid and the offer and liquidating the option is necessary, you can purchase the underlying futures contract for each put option owned prior to expiration.

Purchased Option Strategy and Summary

As a general rule it is preferable to purchase options in periods of low volatility with the rationale being that there will be little or no change in volatility to affect the actual versus the projection. If the volatility does change, it will most likely be upward in low-volatility situations. The difficulty arises when volatility is already high and the objective calls for a purchased option position. The best defense for purchasing in high volatility is time. The sensitivity to changes in volatility decreases as time increases, so the longer the term of the option, the less effect you will see from minor changes in volatility.

The strategy of using time as a defense means that the option positions you should be looking for have extended terms until expiration. When purchasing options for an independent strategy, it is advisable to avoid options with less than 90 days until expiration. The theta and vega of these options is significantly lower, while the delta remains the same in relation to the underlying. As time passes, you will lose the advantage of reduced theta and vega, so you will want to be active in offsetting positions before theta accelerates, which usually occurs between 45 and 60 days until expiration.

A good defense is often a good offense, and aggressive position rolling can avoid significant time value decay and volatility sensitivity. When you are rolling positions forward, meaning selling the currently owned near-term option and purchasing one further out, it is important to remember the time value premium you will be adding to the original risk of the first purchased option. If you purchase a 160-day call option at $3.00 per share and after 60 days have $2.10 of the value remaining, you must add the $0.90 loss to the breakeven calculation of your rolled call option purchase. If the call option you are rolling into has a value of $3.00 once again, you must make your breakeven calculation with the new option as if you had spent $3.90 on the call, adding the $.90 from the previous option. The expenditure of additional cash may become impossible for the underlying price movement to overcome after a series of several rolls.

Another friend of the option buyer is intrinsic value. Intrinsic value is unaffected by extrinsic value changes like implied volatility or time. When you're in high-volatility situations where limited risk is the objective, consider using an option that is in the money. The option may have little or no time value risk, and the volatility risk typically degrades as options get further in the money. In addition the in-the-money option still has a limited risk profile in comparison to the cost of the underlying position, but there will be more out of pocket spent than with at-the-money or out-of-the money options. If, however, you consider the risk from the current underlying price to zero with respect to the cost of the call option to zero, there is a substantial difference.

Purchased Option Risk Management

The most important strategy when dealing with high volatility and when purchasing options is risk control. Options traders often become frustrated with losses because of a lack of understanding of time value, volatility, and risk control. Too many times options traders just allow purchased options to fall to worthless when there were clear indications of a need to exit a position earlier along the way. Let's look at strategies for dealing with purchased option risk through the use of stops, especially in high implied volatility situations. There are two basic forms of stops: hard stops and soft stops. *Hard stops* are those which can be placed in an order with your trading execution desk or broker. Soft stops are mental stops which must be managed manually. There are also other forms of stops:

- *Monetary stops:* This stop is based on the level of risk traders are willing to accept in liquidation value from the option purchase. Most options allow price stop orders, so this is a hard stop position. This is an effective method of controlling monetary risk; however, it does not account for any technical aspect of trading. Monetary stops allow you to maintain a certain level of capital regardless of the market movement. Retaining capital is the priority of the wise portfolio manager or investor in order to make dysfunctional capital available for other opportunities.

- *Price stops:* These are typically generated from technical analysis of the underlying asset. The methods for developing price stops vary as much as the traders themselves, but commonly professional traders use chart retracements, support and resistance, technical indicators and points based on the market closes and many other individual methods for developing price targets. Most important with price stops is to remain within your risk suitability for the investment. Price stops can be a hard stop or a soft stop. As a hard stop, the price on the underlying asset is determined through your own technical analysis and system of risk management on the underlying asset. Once you have the underlying price, calculate the theoretical option value at that price and place a good-till-canceled stop order in the market. This would be most efficiently done with option analysis software. The price stop has positive and negative aspects; it can be an effective means of controlling the risk of being wrong the market in that as the price of the underlying moves away from the option price, the value of the option will fall to the stop-out price and retain the remaining capital. Price stops can also be of help in defending against volatility changes and time value decay because there will be a physical stopping point for the loss. Unfortunately, this can also be a negative in that the underlying asset may not have reached the target support or resistance area set by your stop analysis, and your position will be liquidated regardless of the market movement or potential movement. If you use the price stop subjectively, such as if the underlying moves to a certain point, then you will liquidate the option. Subjective stops are fine, as long as you are able to pay close attention to the market and be alerted when the underlying reaches that point and you actually liquidate the option. Unfortunately, most traders using mental stops will second-guess their decision and not liquidate the position when they should or not be near the market when the stop should have been executed.

- *Time stops:* Time stops are an important function of option trading, especially in long-term options or high-volatility situations. Time value decay is constant on option positions, and theta accelerates as options move closer to expiration. To help avoid the risk associated with accelerated time value decay, you may roll options forward to longer terms. The time stop is a set number of days or a date in which the option position will be liquidated and, if still viable, rolled forward to a new expiration month. There is not a physical stop that can be placed on an order for a time stop, so the trade must be managed manually. It is important to evaluate the costs to roll forward versus the potential reward in the future. Time stops do not typically reduce the risk of volatility change other than that they limit the term of the trade to the period least affected by volatility in typical markets. Options with longer terms until expiration typically have higher vega than their short-term counterparts. When rolling forward, try to find options with implied volatility of the new option position equal to or lesser than the volatility of the liquidating option position.

- *Implied volatility stops:* Setting a stop based on changes in implied volatility is another method that cannot be placed in an order, but must be monitored by the investor or portfolio manager as a soft stop. Stock traders commonly use a volatility stop based on the average true range (ATR) over a set period of time, usually from 14 to 20 bars or periods on the chart, which provides a trailing price stop on the underlying stocks. The implied volatility stop is different in that it provides the benefit of the forward-looking power of implied volatility in options over the historical volatility of ATR or standard deviation.

  Most commonly we look at implied volatility changes with a retracement method that forms boundaries for the limits in changes in implied volatility (IV). If the implied volatility begins to fail on an option position, then the demand for the option is likely failing. If this is a call option, then the demand for call options has diminished, which may indicate a shift from buy signals to hold or sell on the underlying. If implied volatility reduces sharply over a period of time, this often means that the supply of options offered to the market has increased rapidly resulting from traders trying to liquidate premium and retain capital.

  With implied volatility stops, it is important to not focus on one single strike price but on an average of the strike prices around your option position in the same month. If there are a large number of strike prices available, then you may need to average several strike prices. The averaging is to smooth the data and deliver a more stable indication of overall implied volatility rather than just one strike price which may be skewed because of a market order or large volume of trades on a single bid or offer. The more strike prices you include, the more accurate your data will be. Traders often focus on individual strike prices as the underlying asset changes price, and they pick strike prices to try to "pin" the underlying price to, but by averaging, you are less likely to be affected by focused demand on a single strike price by a large hedger or fund. For example, if you have five strike prices each with a midrange implied volatility of 42 percent, 47 percent, 39 percent, 44 percent, and 49 percent, then you will add the five volatilities together and divide by 5. This will get a 44.2 percent average IV (221/5 = 44.2). From that amount, take a look at the underlying current volatility and a recent history of volatility for the underlying asset. If you have the data available, establish at least 90-day mean volatility average for the underlying asset. It will be difficult to get this information on the options, so we have to go with the underlying volatility. Hypothetically let's say that the current volatility (standard 20-day) is at 47 percent and the 90-day average volatility is 39 percent. There is an 8-point difference between the current and the mean volatility. You can use this figure as a stop out point for the options. If your average IV drops more than 8 percent, something is going wrong with the volatility picture and it is time to preserve capital. If you do not have all these data available, you can certainly set a target of no more than a 10 percent loss in volatility without the calculations. Remember to average the IV frequently so you know where you are.

• *Trailing stops:* An example of a trailing stop is that if you have purchased a call option and the market on the underlying rallies making the option more valuable, the stop is moved up to account for the increased value. With the trailing stop you have the opportunity to retain your original premium if the option value doubles or you will at least have more of the value retained through the course of the trade. The trailing stop does not move any farther than the original risk level for the trade. The downside to the trailing stop is that it will often not allow market fluctuation within a trend unless the stop is positioned a solid distance away in the first place.

The absolute most critical strategy to deal with risk in purchasing options is to have a strategy. Using a physical stop order in the market with a price—a hard stop—removes the subjective mental guessing game and limits an emotional response to a losing position. For the undisciplined or inexperienced trader, a hard stop is the most effective and necessary method of controlling risk. Nothing is worse than having a purchased option position slowly disintegrate into nothing and expire as worthless while the trader operates on hope that the market will recover. Even the most disciplined professional traders fall victim to hope-trading from time to time.

There are many strategies for dealing with volatility as we move into writing options and spreads and we will see significant advantages to these strategies in volatile conditions. However, if you are dealing with outright purchase options, you have limited choices so it is important to be paying close attention to the implied volatility and the volatility level of the underlying asset upon purchase and throughout the life of the trade.

Remember that implied volatility is the forward-looking volatility indicator and that you should consider that the change you might be expecting in the underlying asset may already be priced into the option you are purchasing.

Purchasing call and put options is an excellent strategy for low-risk profile investors or as hedging strategies for current or future positions. The key to success with purchased options is buying in low implied volatility and with lots of time for the market to make the move you are expecting.

Chapter 5

SELLING OPTIONS

Selling options is often referred to as writing or shorting options. All three terms have the same meaning although writing options is technically the correct term for offering the right represented by an option to the market. When someone writes an option, he or she is giving the right to the underlying at a specified price and specified time to the buyer. In exchange for the right to the underlying market, the option writer or seller is taking in a premium payment for that right. This is the premium paid by the option buyer. The option seller is assuming the risk that the value of the option will decrease over the term of the option and/or that the option will expire out of the money thereby allowing the seller to retain the entire premium as profit. Selling options is risk-oriented, while buying an option represents limited risk. The total gain potential for the option buyer is the risk for the option seller.

The risk in selling options is unlimited, and the profit potential is small in comparison to the risk, so what is the motivation for someone to sell an option premium? There are a few answers to this question:

- When you are selling options, you do not necessarily have to be correct about where the market is going to end up, just where it will *not* end up. Your analysis changes to deciding where the market is not likely to go and what conditions would cause the market to trade beyond your strike price. In essence, you are being paid for someone else being wrong.

- Option sellers have the advantage of the continuous time value decay that plagues the option buyers. As each day passes from the time an option is bought or sold to the last day of trading, the option seller has more of the premium that the buyer cannot recover. The market may move to regain the price, but the time value originally sold can not be recovered.

- It is often tossed around that a high percentage of options expire as worthless. Figures like 80 or 90 percent of all options held to expiration are at zero value on the day of expiration. This may fall under the category of market myth, but statistically speaking markets sometimes have more volume in out-of-the-money strike prices actively traded than those that are in the money. The nature of the average investor is to spend less on premium and buy limited-risk options, which means that more actual options may have no value early in the contract cycle and must be held to expiration because there is nothing left to do but wait. The actual number of strike prices trading in the money versus out of the money will be about 50/50 depending on the number of strike prices issued. This tendency for more options to expire as worthless increases the odds for the out-of-the-money call seller to have the option decrease in value or expire with no value.

There are two ways of selling options: covered and naked. A naked short option is one that has no cover trade either in the underlying asset or in an option at another strike price. A covered option is a short option that has a covering trade in either the underlying asset or another option position at a different strike price. In this chapter we discuss naked options in order to get down the basics of option selling and the key signals that identify options with the qualities for successful selling and risk management. We go into depth on the multitude of covered option strategies in Chapters 6, 7 and 8 on option spreads.

Selling Strategies

Option gurus and talking heads often go on about option selling being the best way to rake in the cash from the market, and they do so because, if done properly, option selling can be very successful. However, selling options is a game played with a higher percentage of successful trades gaining small amounts under high risk and can be disastrous if risk is not managed properly. When you are selling options, you can count on losing from time to time, but managing those losses is critical. The keys to successfully selling options and managing risk are completely contrary to those for buying options because you are looking for market conditions that signal an eventual reduction in volatility, a stall on a current trend, or a reversal in trend and options that have a relatively good probability of being out of the money at expiration.

Risk management is a significant issue in selling options as with any investment, and it is important to make certain that you are trading within your risk tolerance and trading objectives. If you are managing your own portfolio or you are a fund manger or financial advisor, your trading objectives and risk tolerance may or may not be that of a naked (uncovered) option seller. Consider risk carefully before selling naked option premium.

Elevated Implied Volatility

When we are looking for elevated implied volatility (IV), we are looking for IV that is above the mean volatility for the recent period. Ideally we are looking for candidates that have an underlying that is likely to decelerate in volatility or at least not increase significantly based on news for the individual underlying asset. We are looking for high implied volatility that has a respectable chance of staying within a certain trading range for a certain period of time or will begin to decrease over the term of the option. Herein lies the problem with selling options. Conventional market speculation and analysis have generated an elevated demand for the options in question for a particular reason; this is what has caused the high implied volatility. Therefore, as the option seller you are the contrarian; you must go against the conventional analysis in order to sell a naked high volatility option.

If a call option has generated high implied volatility, you must determine why it has high volatility. Are the call options in demand because the market is expected to go higher, or is there demand on the option because of hedge traders buying protection on their short underlying positions? The latter is very common and can often take the option seller by surprise. If a large number of funds or commercial traders are heavily short on a particular stock or especially commodity futures, they will often buy call options to limit the risk on their short positions. This can be an excellent opportunity to sell call premium because the demand will drive implied volatility higher; however, you will have to be keenly aware of the technical reversals in the underlying which might cause those same traders to short cover. In the process of the short covering, the option values for the calls that they bought, the same option you sold, will rise rapidly as each feeds the other.

Finding elevated implied volatility can be a daunting task, especially in equity markets where thousands of options are available. Many option software programs and Web-based applications have the capability to scan the market and find elevated implied volatility over the mean IV within whatever parameters the software has as a default; with many you can specify parameters. The most important thing to remember when dealing with software applications is that there is no intelligence built into the software to filter the stock options based on current events. For example, if we run a basic scan on Option Vue's latest analysis software, Option Vue 6, for elevated IV, we are given a list of options and strike prices with IV well above the mean IV. Many of these options look appealing but we do not want to use implied volatility as the only resource. Once you find high implied volatility, you must investigate why it is high, how long it has been elevated, and what the expectations are for the underlying asset in the near future.

The scan provided several current high-volatility options, including Autoliv (ALV) for a June $22.50 call with the underlying stock trading at $21.61. Figure 5.1 shows the option chain for this. The

Actuals	ALV Common			Legend		
		21.61	+2.52	Trade	Last	Chg
Options	JUN <79>					
25.0 calls	MktPr	MIV	Delta	Gamma	Theta	Vega
22.5 calls>	2.56	76.0%	49.0	5.18	-1.92	3.97
20.0 calls	3.80	79.6%	61.9	4.96	-1.88	3.71
17.5 calls	5.56		75.4	4.56	-1.37	2.96
22.5 puts>	3.33	67.9%	-51.0	5.18	-1.70	3.97
20.0 puts	1.87	65.7%	-38.1	4.96	-1.54	3.71
17.5 puts	0.98	68.5%	-24.6	4.56	-1.26	2.96
15.0 puts	0.50	75.3%	-12.8	3.10	-0.93	1.91

Figure 5.1   ALV option chain—Powered by Option Vue 6

figure shows the $22.50 call with the implied volatility at a staggering 76.0 percent; the delta is just shy of at the money at 49 percent; and it has a strong gamma at 5.18. Theta and vega are normalized for dollars. According to the scan, the option is 25 percent over the mean implied volatility. Although we have only a few strike prices to display, we can see that implied volatility on the call option is significantly elevated over the put options as well. What we should know about Autoliv without looking at anything but the option chain is that we may have some explanation for the elevated implied volatility in the underlying stock price movement, up 11 percent on the session. This is a first clue to starting the investigation concerning the history of option implied volatility to make certain that we are not looking at skewed volatility.

We can now review the fundamentals of Autoliv to see what is driving implied volatility on the at-the-money call to 76 percent. Just because you are looking to sell an option premium does not mean that your analysis of corporate fundamentals should be weak. It is essential to evaluate the stock just as you would for any underlying or purchasing options. Autoliv in this example is a mid-cap company with a stable history of price and regular dividends. Autoliv manufactures vehicle safety products for the automotive industry so its share price has likely been affected by a downturn in the auto industry. The company, before Figure 5.1 was captured, made a substantial offering of Treasury stock which caused a sharp downward fluctuation in the share price, but the new cash brought better analyst ratings of the cash position thus allowing the stock to recover. Take a look at the chart in Figure 5.2 for the recent stock movement.

From the chart we can see that Autoliv has fallen significantly from the June 2008 price. You can apply your own method of technical analysis to determine support and resistance here, but clearly the market has significant upside risk if the overall horizontal resistance is broken and held to the upside. You might also make an inverted head and shoulders chart pattern out of the late March activity.

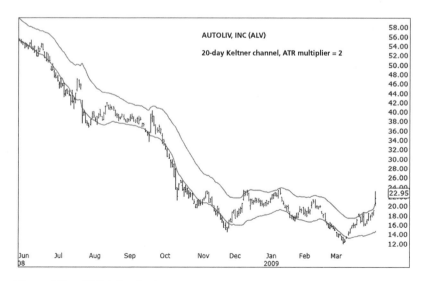

Figure 5.2   ALV daily chart

On this chart we only applied a 20-day Keltner channel with an average true range (ATR) multiplier of 2. Our implied volatility search was completed at the same time that the stock broke upward and closed above the channel on the last day displayed in the chart. This gives us further explanation for the increased implied volatility in the call options. The upside risk of the market and previous share prices would be tempting to call buyers who are unwilling to chance the outright long on the underlying and is an explanation for the demand for the call option or at least the risk aversion for call sellers. With the resistance areas on the chart and a promising uptrend, the increased implied volatility may also be a result of cover buying by short sellers in the underlying. By looking at the overall picture, we can see a definite upside risk if you were to consider selling call option premium, but the premium is excellent for the amount of the initial margin requirement.

Limited Time to Expiration

Selling options with short periods to expiration tends to boost the success probabilities of the trade. By limiting naked option positions to shorter time periods, you decrease the time for the underlying asset to make a substantial move that would place your short option in the money. As you look at options chains with Greeks, you will notice that theta increases as the number of days to expiration decreases. What you want is this accelerated theta in your corner. With shorter-term options the fundamentals of the underlying asset are somewhat clearer. You have at least some general idea of the upcoming dividends, earnings, Federal Open Market Committee (FOMC) meetings, and so on when you are trading within say 100 days of expiration. Ideally we are looking for something less than

100 days and preferably less than 60 days to capture premium. The key is to capture premium before the theta accelerates significantly so that it is still within a reasonably foreseeable set of fundamentals. Beyond 100 days you run the risk of an entirely new set of income and earnings data or, in the case of derivatives, a new set of production numbers. Your risk of an entire sector or even a whole market shift in one direction or another becomes greater. The downside to shorter-term option sales is that, in order to capture large chunks of premium, you must be closer to the money than if you trade in deferred options. You should be aware that the immediate risk is higher when you trade closer to the money so your risk control should be more aggressive. Consider a hard stop choice over a more subjective soft stop when the option delta is higher.

There is nothing wrong with shorting naked long-term options or even Long-term Equity Anticipation Security (LEAP) options in equities, but your strategy must be a bit different. Most often when we are selling long-term options, we are doing so with a hedge position of some sort in mind. In other words, we have something going against the option position and use the option position as a means to increase cash, but selling naked long-term options can be very profitable. When you are selling long term, you are looking to take advantage of a large chunk of time value and as much volatility value as possible. The best strategy for selling long term is to find options that are well out of the recent historical trading range and that have a high enough premium to be attractive.

Whenever you are selling an option premium, especially for longer-term options, you should be tracking the volatility trend of the underlying asset. Since we have no way of predicting volatility on extended terms, it will be important to track trends in current volatility and implied volatility to look for warning signs of increasing volatility against your short option position. If the underlying volatility appears to be on a long-term building trend, this could represent a threat to a deferred option position at some point down the road. Vega is often greater in deferred options over those with shorter expiration dates, so changes in volatility will have significantly more effect on the long-term options.

Runaway Markets

History has been rewritten in the area of market pricing in recent years, and it will be some time before we see many equity and commodity instruments trade outside their historical trading ranges again. If there is a lesson to be learned from the first decade of the twenty-first century, it is that markets can do the unthinkable and unimaginable and then put an exclamation point on it. The New York Mercantile Exchange (NYMEX) crude oil contract traded at over $140 per barrel, and some of largest U.S. banks traded for around $1.00 per share, all in a 12-month period.

Wild market swings are the Achilles heel of short option trading. For example, those who tried to capture premium on NYMEX crude at $50, $75, or $100 per barrel watched their premium evaporate along with tens of thousands of dollars more per contract if they held on to the summer of 2008. There are hundreds of examples of exceptional market pricing recently, and when a market is trending sharply higher, it is difficult to commit to risk control, believing that the market has to retrace soon. Inflated option premiums from spikes in implied volatility make these situations even worse. Be committed to your risk control on options positions. They are limited term instruments and term of the market moves against the position may be longer than your option expiration.

On the positive side, sharp market moves will create some of the best option premium selling opportunities you will find if your risk control is done properly. This is more common in commodities markets, but it happens frequently in equities as well. You can capitalize on the inflated premium levels, and as we move into option spreads, you will find several strategies for dealing with risk control in high-volatility trading.

Chasing a short call position to what seems like infinity happens to every short option trader at one point or another. By the time you lose faith in your correctness about a trade, you realize that you are several dollars in the money with little or no chance of regaining anything. It seems that everyone has to suffer it once before learning about risk control on short options and finding some discipline. The difficult thing to learn about options trading is trading with the trend just as you do with the underlying asset and maintaining risk control on naked short option positions.

Liquidity

Options are not necessarily traded in volume at every strike price. In fact, if you watch the open interest of options carefully, you will notice that certain strike prices will have very little volume or open interest. This means that there can be fairly wide differences in the bid and offer on a particular strike price. Be patient with selling options and wait for the buyer to come to you if the option has a wide bid offer or thin trading. If the buyer wants the option, he or she will eventually pay to get to it. As the seller, the less premium you receive, the more risk you have. If you use analysis software, take time to run a theoretical value and then check the current bid and offer for the particular strike price. If the values are weaker on the market, you might consider putting your offer in higher and allowing the bid to come to you. At times you may end up making the offer that gives you that little extra boost of premium. In doing this, be careful to avoid options that have little or no open interest unless you are really significantly above the theoretical value for the option in your offer. If there is little or no open interest in an option, then there is also no way for you to exit your position should you need to. You will then be at the mercy of the investor you sold your option to or a market maker who is there to take your money. Ideally, we are looking for strike prices that have fairly strong volume and open interest, thus giving you buying demand and ensuring your ability to trade out of the market as needed.

It is not uncommon for an option strike price with decent open interest to have periods when there are few offers or none at all, especially for derivative options. With these options you can set the price at which the option will trade unless someone else is willing to sell it cheaper. The only limitation to this strategy is your capital capabilities. Do not oversell your ability to provide margin for these positions. Some options have a daily limit in which the broker or computer system will not accept an order outside of the daily range unless it is a good till canceled order.

Letting the market come to you is a discipline that short options traders need to master. There usually is not a shortage of options buyers in most markets because purchased option strategies are better understood even with larger fund and portfolio managers. As an educated options seller, you have the ability to capitalize on the risk profile of other traders. Again, having the capital to maintain the margin on these trades is a requirement. If you cannot maintain the margin, especially if one or more of the trades go wrong at the same time, you lose all chance at profit or recouping a loss.

Selling Call Options

Let's demonstrate the ALV short call position as a trade and discover the profitability and breakeven on the position.

Actuals	ALV Common			Legend		
	21.61	+2.52	Trade	Last	Chg	
Options	JUN <79>					
25.0 calls	MktPr	MIV	Delta	Gamma	Theta	Vega
22.5 calls>	2.56	76.0%	49.0	5.18	-1.92	3.97
20.0 calls	3.80	79.6%	61.9	4.96	-1.88	3.71
17.5 calls	5.56		75.4	4.56	-1.37	2.96
22.5 puts>	3.33	67.9%	-51.0	5.18	-1.70	3.97
20.0 puts	1.87	65.7%	-38.1	4.96	-1.54	3.71
17.5 puts	0.98	68.5%	-24.6	4.56	-1.26	2.96
15.0 puts	0.50	75.3%	-12.8	3.10	-0.93	1.91

Powered by Option Vue 6

If we were to sell five of the ALV June $22.50 call options naked for $2.50, we would collect $1,250 minus the cost of making the trade. According to the analysis software, the margin requirement would be about $4,000; however, your rate may be lower or higher depending on your broker. If the underlying stock was below $22.50 at expiration, then the five options would expire as worthless and we would collect the entire premium in only 79 days. That is a return of 31 percent in 79 days on a $4,000 margin. That is the rosy picture of selling options, and often this is exactly what happens. If you are a portfolio manager and your risk profile allows you to have $5 million in short option risk, you can see the massive returns possible with the right options management program. The downside of this picture is what happens when a short option position goes wrong. Let's look at a profit-and-loss model on this trade and calculate the breakeven. (See Figure 5.3.)

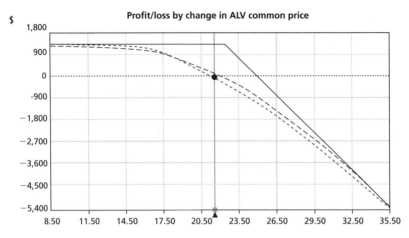

Figure 5.3   Selling five ALV $22.50 calls—Powered by Option Vue 6

In the option model our expiration line is the solid line, the dashed line represents 40 days until expiration, and the dotted line is the current market with zero time value decay. The maximum profit remains if the option underlying ALV stock stays below $22.50, but as the underlying stock price rises, the losses mount quickly. If the underlying stock price rallies back to $35.50, you can see that the loss is nearly $5,400 on only five options or 500 shares. Calculating the breakeven price for a short call option is fairly simple:

Strike price + premium captured = breakeven (minus costs of trading)

$22.50 + $2.50 = $25.00/share (minus costs of trading)

After our analysis of this short call position and the technical and fundamental picture for the underlying ALV stock, would this be a recommended short option position? If you're looking at the trade overall, the volatility has created an excellent premium opportunity, but at substantial risk. Given the technical picture, this would not be recommended for someone inexperienced in managing option risk. The volatility of the market and the potential for retracement off of the current rally on the chart gives you the sense that the probabilities are not too terribly bad. But if the market rallies substantially, you would need to be able to make adjustments or have defined risk control. If we punch in the general terms in to the probability calculator, we have a probability of around 50 percent that the market will remain below the breakeven at $25.00. There are a number of things on your side in this trade including the ever-present time value decay. The theta on this trade is not terribly high at the present time, but it will accelerate over the next 30 days. In the model you might notice the narrow width between the current 79-day and middle point 40-day marks. This a function of the weak theta at the present time. As time moves forward and closer to expiration, the distance widens between the 40-day line and expiration thus showing the acceleration of time value decay.

Another item on your side with this position is the high implied volatility and high underlying volatility. When volatility is extremely high, it certainly can go higher, but over time the chances of another big jump in volatility diminish, and the probabilities are that volatility is more likely to fall than rise. Volatility remains a risk; if the volatility were to move substantially higher, the effect on the option would still be significant. The vega on this option is $3.97, so if volatility were to gain 10 points tomorrow, the option would likely be worth around $290 representing about a $40 loss per option.

The main points to gather from this trade example is that, just because the software says that implied volatility is high and that the option is in an overvalued condition, it is not necessarily an appropriate trade. This particular trade demonstrates well how implied volatility is a function of the risk in the option position. As an option buyer you must pay for someone else to risk writing your $22.50 call option. As the seller, you want the buyer to pay as much as possible for the risk you are undertaking. This particular call option is not the greatest candidate for shorting the market because of the upside risk on the underlying asset; however, this option would be a fantastic candidate for the covered call strategy we discuss in spreads.

Selling Put Options

Using this same example let's flip our thinking 180 degrees. ALV stock has fallen dramatically in less than 12 months, and most if not all of the effect on share value was derived from outside forces in the overall market. We want to sell high implied volatility, but in the short call example we can see market risk that could cause a problem with the short call position. There is some demand for long call positions driving the volatility higher, which gives us additional clues about the future of ALV down the road. If we wanted to buy the breakout on ALV, but not take the immediate risk of being long the market with the risk of an immediate closure of the gap, we can look at alternatives for going long. One is to consider selling put premium. Selling put options means that you are selling the right to be short the underlying asset at a specific price and time. In this case you would be selling a put option on ALV to capture premium or obtain a better price on the long market position. If you look back again at Figure 5.1 (page 92), you can see that the implied volatility on the put options is lower than the call options, but this is still at an exceptional level of 65 to 70 percent. The at-the-money put would be considered the $22.50 trading at $3.33, and the $20.00 put is trading at $1.87. Since the $22.50 put is slightly in the money and has some intrinsic value and the $20.00 put is out of the money and totally made up of time value, let's look at an example selling the $20.00 put.

If we sell five ALV $20.00 put options at 1.85 (five-point pricing), we bring in a total premium capture cash value of $925 or $1.85 on 500 shares. Let's calculate the breakeven for a short put option.

Strike price – premium captured = breakeven (plus costs of trading)

$20.00 − $1.85 = $18.15 (plus costs of trading)

The margin calculation for five of these options looks to be about $3,300 depending on your brokerage situation, so with a $925 capture on $3,300 initial margin, the immediate risk to return is 28 percent in 79 days.

Short put options offer an interesting scenario for equity buyers. If your analysis determines that you want ALV stock in your portfolio or for your client, you can certainly purchase ALV at $21.61 outright and see if the breakout holds and the stock price begins to recover. The other choice is to sell the put premium in the number of shares intended for purchase. If you wanted to buy 5,000 shares of ALV, then writing 50 of the $20.00 put options in the example would bring in $9,250 in premium on $33,000 in initial margin. The capital required for the same purchase of the outright underlying is over $108,000 either in cash or cash and margin, which has an interest cost which must be factored in. In this example your initial capital requirement and have deferred the remaining $75000 for 79 days. Additional capital may be required for margin if the underlying asset's price falls. The worst case scenario for this type of buyer is that ALV falls below the strike price and the put seller must then buy the outright shares at $20.00 per share. In reality the purchase is made at $18.15 plus costs of trading because of the premium captured.

The downside to this strategy is that if ALV shares were to rally significantly over the period of 79 days, the put seller would miss out on the opportunity of the underlying shares but would have captured the entire premium. At the end of the term of the option if you end up with an expired option, then you can deduct premium captured to whatever price you make your purchase at. When we get into talking about spreads, we work on recapturing the upward market potential from selling naked put premium.

The concept of selling put premium as a supplement to or in place of equity purchases is not new, but in the current climate of volatility it deserves significant review. The strategy reduces your purchase price on long equity portfolio positions by adding cash value which can be applied to your net cost basis with a very simple strategy. In addition you are risking no more than the underlying shares you intend to purchase.

Selling Derivatives Options

As with buying options in derivatives, the leverage represented by futures contracts dramatically increases the risk of selling options. However, with risk comes the potential for reward. Option buyers spend significantly more money for options in most commodity markets than their equity counterparts; therefore, the seller is demanding more payment for the risk of selling. In derivative trading there is a tendency to go after extraordinarily high premium captures during volatile market trading. Futures generate high volatility on a regular basis, but when the overall market increases in volatility, premiums on futures options can become obscene.

A popular strategy for selling option premium is to sell when a market has been driven to the top end of a long-term trading range by technical or fundamental forces which have propelled price and volatility. This is a method of counter-trending without directly selling the underlying against the trend. When selling a call option, you can choose a strike price above the market and out of the money which allows room for the trend to continue over time without your necessarily suffering a loss on the position, or you can sell immediately as the market before volatility falls away completely. Counter-trending is risky, and you should be prepared to have additional margin available for the position, especially in high volatility markets. Counter-trending can also be very profitable for the options seller if the short option remain in the projected range for the period of the option. Let's look at an example of counter-trending using short calls in the gold market.

When markets go into a defensive mode, cash is moved from equity markets to safety areas, which are usually debt and currency reserves. Gold is a common safety zone for capital although gold as a government currency reserve has slowly dwindled over the years worldwide. Traders often consider gold to be a protection mechanism against falling interest rates, devalued currency, and inflation. Let's look at the COMEX gold chart for the June 2009 contract. (See Figure 5.4.)

The gold chart shows us a history of a recent push higher nearly equal to the rally midway through 2008. It appears that there is resistance to the gold market holding above $1,000 per ounce. In this snapshot we have highs in the gold market at just over $1,012 and a downward trend in the recent trade. We added the statistical and

Figure 5.4 Commdity Exchange, Inc. (CMX or COMEX) gold chart — Powered by Option Vue 6

Futures	JUN <57>		AUG <120>		OCT <181>	
	927.70	+7.40	928.80	+6.10	938.90	+13.90
Options	JUN <56>				AUG <119>					
	MktPr	MIV	Delta	Gamma	Theta	Vega	MktPr	MIV	Delta	Gamma	Theta	Vega
970 calls									44.8	0.21	-30.8	210
965 calls	30.90	32.0%	38.7	0.34	-40.3	140						
960 calls	32.50	31.8%	40.3	0.35	-40.3	142	60.10	34.8%	45.7	0.21	-30.9	211
955 calls	.....		42.0	0.36	-40.6	143	.....		46.8	0.21	-30.7	211
950 calls	35.10	31.0%	43.7	0.36	-39.9	144	63.50	34.5%	47.8	0.21	-30.6	211
945 calls	37.80	31.4%	45.4	0.37	-40.6	144	.....		48.8	0.22	-30.5	211
940 calls	39.90	31.4%	47.2	0.37	-40.8	145	67.50	34.4%	49.9	0.22	-30.5	211
950 puts	58.60	31.8%	-56.3	0.36	-41.0	144	84.40	34.4%	-52.3	0.21	-30.5	211
945 puts	55.40	31.7%	-54.6	0.37	-41.0	144	.....		-51.3	0.22	-30.5	211
940 puts	52.40	31.5%	-52.8	0.37	-40.9	145	78.50	34.3%	-50.2	0.22	-30.4	211
935 puts	49.40	31.4%	-51.0	0.37	-40.8	145	.....		-49.2	0.22	-30.3	211
930 puts>	46.30	31.1%	-49.1	0.37	-40.4	145	72.30	34.0%	-48.1	0.22	-30.1	210
925 puts	43.30	30.9%	-47.3	0.38	-40.0	144	69.60	33.9%	-47.0	0.22	-29.9	210
920 puts	40.70	30.9%	-45.4	0.38	-39.7	144	66.60	33.8%	-45.9	0.22	-29.7	209

Figure 5.5 Gold option chain — Powered by Option Vue 6

implied volatility to the chart to show where volatility is in relation to the market movement. In this case, gold experienced the highest volatility as the market fell from the 2008 rally and then decreased, but remained elevated over historical levels in the early 2008 level shown on the chart. Given the current chart and volatility, let's look at the call options available (see Figure 5.5).

The option chain for June gold shows that we have 56 days remaining in the option. Our upper level of resistance on this market is just above $1, 000 per ounce, so ideally we would like to get close to that level with our breakeven. Implied volatility at around 32 percent is not as high as it has been for this market, but it is elevated over the standard mean implied volatility. If we look specifically at the 965 call options in June gold, we can see a market price of $30.90 with the underlying trading at 927.70. Selling the 965 call option with a premium of 30.90 gives us a breakeven of $995.90 on the June futures.

$$965.00 + 30.90 = 995.90$$

The breakeven price is below the contract high for June gold. It is in what we consider to be a defendable area, since there is a recent high on June above the currently selected strike price and time is on your side with fairly aggressive time value decay. The option model for this trade (see Figure 5.6) shows the profit-and-loss projection of selling five June gold 965 calls at 30.90.

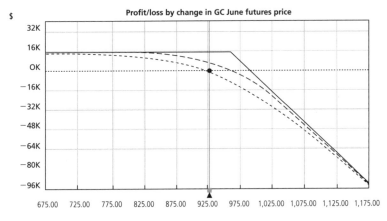

Figure 5.6   June gold option model—Powered by Option Vue 6

With this trade we have captured a premium of 30.90 with multiplier for gold options at $100 per point. The total premium captured would be $3,090 × 5 options equaling $15,450. You can see in the model that we maintain maximum premium below the price of $965 on the underlying and that the solid line does not cross the breakeven until 995.00. Beyond that point, the losses on just five gold call options can add up to substantial amounts of money quickly. If a sharp move higher was to happen shortly after the trade was applied, the position would lose quickly as you can see from the dotted line representing zero time value decay. As time moves forward and the position has roughly 30 days left (represented by the dashed line), the point where the option position breaks even is higher on the underlying futures, but again the position can begin losing quickly without risk control.

There are some important lessons to be learned from this gold trade. Selling a call premium in high implied volatility in this market during 2008 would have been the wrong choice. When volatility was the highest, the market was near the low points for the year in price. As volatility began to decrease, the futures market rallied significantly and the volatility trend continued downward. Volatility is not an indicator of price; it is an indicator of price fluctuation.

Short Option Risk Management

Short options have a high risk profile because the risk is not limited. When you are taking small gains from the market, you cannot afford to have large losses, and proper management can help keep the inevitable short option loss to a minimum. There are some management techniques for risk that are different from purchased options:

- *Monetary stops:* With the unlimited risk of selling an option premium, it is important to know how much you are willing to risk for the premium you have captured. If are selling an option for $500 per option, it is ludicrous to risk $5,000 for that $500 maximum profit. Who would do that? It happens all the time, and unfortunately some short option traders lose and lose big for a very small profit potential. Most often a monetary stop of two to four times the premium sold is recommended. If that amount is outside your risk profile for the option sale, you should not be naked short trading the option.

   A monetary stop of some sort is recommended for all short option positions as a safety valve unless you have a hard price stop for technical support or resistance. Decide your monetary risk and stick to it with a hard stop.

- *Volatility stops:* Follow the volatility stop guidelines laid out previously. In working with volatility stops on short options, you are going to be protecting against increases in implied volatility.

- *Price stops:* As with long options, you can determine a price stop on your option based on the trade of the underlying futures. If you are selling a call option and the underlying futures have a resistance level above your position that would be considered a change in trend or breakout, then use that price to calculate a theoretical value for the option at that price. It is best to do this assuming zero time value decay and zero negative volatility change. The price stop should be physically placed in the market as an order unless you are using a monetary stop as your safety net. If you are selling a put premium, unless you are willing to risk to an underlying price of zero, place a hard price stop on the option. The same rules apply. Use your analysis of the underlying asset to determine a price based on support levels, and calculate theoretical value for the option assuming zero time value decay.

With a short option premium, the key is to eliminate an emotional response to losing by using a hard stop position. Preserving capital and margin for the next position in high-percentage trading is far more effective than letting the losers ride until they win. What you are losing when you hold a small profit potential short option through large margins is opportunity. The cost of lost opportunity resulting from capital being tied up just amplifies a loss that may not be recovered.

Summary

The best way to analyze selling an option is to force yourself to think of a couple reasons why you would buy the option you are looking to sell. You will be forced to explain why you wouldn't buy the option; if it is a bad buy, it is a great sell. Sometimes you have to take the mathematical probability analysis out of the picture and use common sense.

Option traders often price by implied volatility rather than by market trading price, but in doing so they must not be dissuaded from paying attention to the fundamental rules of the underlying asset.

Investors will often complain of the risk of shorting options while they are trading the underlying in the same quantity or more. This is a lack of understanding of options trading. It is not uncommon to find fund managers with the same opinion, again a lack of understanding. A short option can never have more risk or margin than the underlying asset being traded outright in the same represented quantity. One hundred shares of the stock carries the same risk as one short stock option, no matter how you slice it. The same goes for an option on a futures contract.

Chapter 6

BASIC OPTIONS SPREADS

Spreads represent combinations of the underlying asset and purchased or short options or combinations of purchased and/or short options. The purpose of a spread is to reduce cost basis and premium cost, enhance profitability, capture premium, or take advantage of high- or low-volatility situations in the market. In this chapter we discuss the risk and reward of options spreads and the uses for each kind of spread for the small investor or fund manager.

Remember, one of the initial risks of any option spread on top of the premium risk or market risk is the commissions developed from executing multiple options within one trading strategy. Each position, especially in futures trading, can generate significant commission costs. Most of the time the reward potential for this type of spread more than offsets the risk of the commission outlay, but it is something to factor into your breakeven calculation. Commissions are often overlooked as part of a trading risk, so make certain you are adding your current rate for the type of trade you are employing into your software, or be vigilant in your paper calculations. Let's look at why we employ options spreads, and then we'll take a look at examples of each type of spread and how it can be beneficial as an investment vehicle or as a means for offsetting risk in another position.

We use option spreads for several reasons:

- Spreads offer the benefit of applying other people's money to offset some or all of the cost of a debit premium position or underlying asset position.
- Some spread strategies can capture premium in the market with limited risk.
- Option spreads can help reduce margin requirements on underlying spreads.
- Spread strategies can help improve risk-to-reward ratios over individual option strategies.

Options spreads can be created as credit or debit spreads. A *credit spread* is one in which the premium amount of short option positions is larger than the premium outlay for purchased option positions. A *debit spread* is just the opposite in that the amount of premium paid for purchased option positions is larger than the premium captured by any short option positions.

Many spread strategies can help us deal with trading in high volatility by capturing volatility against positions at other strike prices and or expiration periods. There are three categories of option spread combinations:

- *Vertical spreads:* These spreads contain options with the same underlying asset and expiration month, but the strike prices are different. Vertical spreads can also be spreads combining underlying asset and options. In commodities, you would have a vertical spread if the underlying asset and the option were in the same contract month.

- *Horizontal spreads:* These spreads contain options with the same underlying asset and strike prices, but the expiration date is in a different expiration month or contract month.
- *Diagonal spreads:* These spreads are a combination of vertical and horizontal spreads. Options in the diagonal spread will have the same underlying asset, but different strike prices and expiration dates.
- *Intermarket spreads:* These spreads are combinations of option spreads in which options are used in different underlying markets. An example would be a seasonal spread between corn and wheat. This spread would normally be done on the underlying futures, but it can be accomplished with options positions. Many of these spreads are not recognized as official spreads with respect to reduction of margin requirements for short options.

Covered Calls

The basic covered call strategy is created by holding a long position in an underlying asset and selling the call premium against the position or by creating the position simultaneously by buying the underlying asset and selling the call premium in the same trade order. This strategy was popular enough among professional traders to cause the CBOE to develop an index on the covered call strategy for the S&P 500 in 1986. This index is called the Buy Write Index. In recent years it has gone from an option trader's strategy to a fixed one-click strategy on many online trading platforms. The covered call is a very commonly executed strategy among more advanced equity and derivatives traders.

The objective of the covered call is to bring premium against the cost basis of the underlying so as to improve profitability and reduce risk. Let's look at an example of a covered call strategy using Caterpillar, Inc. (CAT). To keep things simple, we use a one-lot example, meaning 100 shares of CAT and a one-call option. In actual trading, regardless of whether you are using 100 or 10,000 shares, the strategy remains the same other than that a high volume of options will be subject to liquidity and availability of options. Furthermore, commission costs in equities will be divided by your commission rate per number of shares.

For our hypothetical trade let's assume that you've completed your analysis and you've decided to upgrade CAT from hold to buy. Figure 6.1 shows the price history and volatility on a weekly basis.

You will notice a couple things from this weekly chart. First Caterpillar has a small upward trend moving from the March 2009 low, volume has increased dramatically, and the market has strong statistical and implied volatility. It is a nearly ideal condition for covered call trading in high volatility. Hypothetically, let us assume a channel support of 28.00 on the current daily chart and resistance at 34.00. Let's look at the option chain (Figure 6.2) and put this trade together.

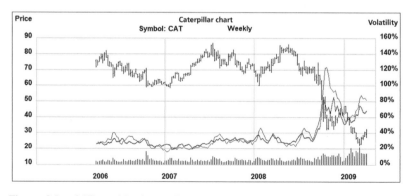

Figure 6.1 CAT weekly chart—Powered by Option Vue 6

Actuals	CAT Common			Legend							
		32.15	+0.61	Trade	Last	Chg					
Options	MAY <41>						AUG <139>				
35 calls	MktPr	MIV	Delta	Gamma	Theta	Vega	MktPr	MIV	Delta	Gamma	Theta	Vega
34 calls	1.83	64.3%	44.9	6.47	-3.28	4.15	3.55	59.7%	52.4	3.67	-1.66	7.70
33 calls	2.26	65.9%	51.1	6.34	-3.43	4.23	3.99	60.7%	55.9	3.56	-1.69	7.70
32 calls>	2.76	67.9%	57.2	6.04	-3.53	4.23	4.46	61.8%	59.3	3.42	-1.71	7.64
31 calls	3.30	69.6%	63.1	5.60	-3.55	4.14	4.94	62.6%	62.6	3.26	-1.71	7.52
30 calls	3.90	71.7%	68.6	5.07	-3.51	3.98	5.49	63.9%	65.9	3.09	-1.70	7.35
29 calls	4.55		73.3	4.13	-3.42	3.77	6.09	65.6%	69.1	2.90	-1.70	7.13
35 puts	4.72	62.8%	-61.3	6.19	-3.05	3.98	6.70	57.3%	-51.1	3.76	-1.56	7.64
34 puts	4.10	64.6%	-55.2	6.47	-3.28	4.15	6.20	59.6%	-47.6	3.67	-1.64	7.70
33 puts	3.49	65.2%	-48.9	6.34	-3.38	4.23	5.60	60.2%	-44.1	3.56	-1.65	7.70
32 puts>	3.02	67.7%	-42.8	6.04	-3.50	4.23	4.99	60.1%	-40.7	3.42	-1.64	7.64
31 puts	2.57	69.9%	-36.9	5.60	-3.55	4.14	4.52	61.6%	-37.4	3.26	-1.66	7.52
30 puts	2.17	71.9%	-31.4	5.07	-3.51	3.98	4.01	62.0%	-34.1	3.09	-1.63	7.35
29 puts	1.83	74.0%	-26.7	4.13	-3.41	3.77	3.62	63.8%	-30.9	2.90	-1.63	7.13

Figure 6.2 Caterpillar option chain—Powered by Option Vue 6

You can see in the figure that CAT stock is trading at 32.15 and there are option chains displayed for May with 41 day remaining and August with 139 days remaining. You will also see that implied volatility on both calls and puts is high with a slightly better IV in the May options than the August option.

If we were to purchase 100 shares of CAT at 32.15, we would have a capital outlay of $3,215 plus costs of trading either in cash or cash and margin. If we were to sell the May 33 call option against the purchase for $2.25, we would collect $225 minus costs of trading against the cash outlay for the purchase. Our theoretical cost basis on the underlying has now been reduced to $29.90 per share (not including the costs of trading on each) on our $32.15 purchase. To calculate your maximum profit potential on a covered call position, we need to determine the distance between the current underlying and the short call strike price and then add the premium captured:

$$\text{Strike price} - \text{underlying current price} + \text{option premium} = \text{maximum profit}$$
$$\$33.00 - \$32.15 + \$2.25 = \$3.10$$

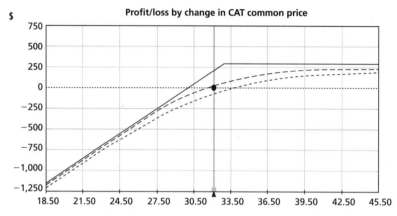

Figure 6.3 CAT option model — Powered by Option Vue 6

Now let's look at a model of the profit and loss of this position (see Figure 6.3). In the figure you can see that the short call limits the upside potential of the underlying CAT stock, but it also reduces the breakeven point to the theoretical cost basis of $29.90 which is where the solid line crosses the 0 line. The underlying shares also eliminate the risk of the short call. The underlying 100 shares have a combined delta of 1.00 versus the 51 percent delta of the 33.00 call option (shown in Figure 6.2). This means that the underlying can gain on the option prior to expiration as you can see from the midpoint lines in the model.

Figure 6.4 shows you the difference at expiration for the trade without the short call option. Figure 6.4 is on a slightly different scale from Figure 6.3 in order to present a wider look at the price advantage on the trade breakeven by selling the call option. We know that with either the outright position or the covered call the market should fall from current levels, so we must have a risk control stop below the market at some point depending on the risk tolerance.

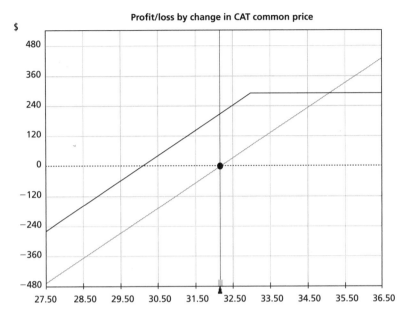

Figure 6.4 CAT outright vs. covered call—Powered by Option Vue 6

Given this hypothetical situation, we said support was around $28.00. You can see from Figure 6.4 that if the position was to be stopped out near expiration at about $27.50, we would have a loss of over $470 on the outright and just over the $260 mark with the premium from the short call applied. Our total profit potential on the position with the outright 100 shares of CAT is unlimited. With the short call it is $310 through the period of the option's life, although the model has withdrawn $30.00 for commissions between the stock and option trades. Commissions and trading fees are something to consider, remember to add each option commission charged to your breakeven position.

If the market is below $33.00, the option will expire worthless, and you will retain the premium from the option and maintain the long 100 shares of CAT. If the market is above $33.00 at expiration, the short call will be exercised into 100 shares short of CAT stock and the two positions will offset each other.

It is possible to retain the CAT stock even if the $33.00 call is in the money. Once the time value of the option has eroded to zero and the delta of the option is 1.00, you can consider rolling the option forward to a new expiration month. Let's look back at the August options in Figure 6.2. If you are near the expiration of the May contract (let's say 40 days have expired), we can estimate what the August $33.00 call option would be worth. To keep it simple, lets assume that CAT is priced at $33.00 so we have little change in premium to account for a delta of 55 percent, and $0.85 in upward movement in the underlying would add about 45 cents to the August option price and give us a total value of 4.44. Now we would have to deduct the time value in the amount of $69 (1.69 × 41 days) from the value. This gives us an estimated value at expiration of the May option of 3.75 (399 + 45 − 69 = 375). This is a method of calculating future options value without an advanced option calculator. This scenario was run through two different calculation programs with the same parameters; one came up with a future value of 4.05; the other, 3.85. The quick add-and-subtract method was close.

If at or near the option expiration for the May option the underlying is around $33.00 and we do not want our position offset, we can buy back the May $33.00 call for a minimal amount and sell the Aug $33.00 to pick up another 3.85 in premium against the cost of the underlying to continue the covered call position.

Imagine if you were able to do this roll against the underlying asset several times. By applying the profits from short call option positions to your actual cost basis, you can have a theoretical cost basis that is significantly reduced. You should check with your tax consultant on the ramifications of selling an option premium compared to your cost basis for the underlying.

What happens if CAT has a strong market rally during the term of the short call option? Your profit is limited to the $310 maximum profit minus trading costs regardless of the upside movement unless you make a change in the option such as rolling it up or out to another month.

Covered calls are best done in markets in which you already intend to buy and risk capital or in which you already currently hold positions. Selling call premium against your underlying held stock, index, ETF, or futures position can reduce the risk of changes in volatility and market direction because you are applying other people's cash to your position to smooth the rough spots. Cover calls can increase your profitability on long market positions substantially in a short period of time.

Cover calls are referred to by a couple other names. Sometimes they are called a buy-write strategy; they can also be referred to as a synthetic short put. The actual synthetic short put would be your buying the underlying shares or futures contract and selling the at-the-money call. Any synthetic short call would mean selling the underlying asset and selling the at-the-money put.

There is debate among traders as to the value of doing a covered call versus selling the at-the-money put option. On average they likely work out about the same, but it is possible that one strategy will outperform the other if the implied volatility is heavily skewed to one side of the option chain. If there is substantially higher volatility on the call side, then the covered call will have a better premium. If the implied volatility is better on the put options, then the premium would likely be better to that side of the equation. Shorting the at-the-money put option versus the covered call spread also eliminates one commission charge.

Covered calls are an excellent strategy for high-volatility market conditions, especially those with trading range markets or lower trending markets. Covered calls tend to outperform the outright stock in both bearish and neutral market conditions, but they underperform in upward trending and bullish markets. Using covered calls in high-volatility markets increases the premium captured and can increase the effectiveness of the position.

Covered Puts

The covered put is a much less commonly utilized strategy than a covered call because the put involves short selling a stock or futures position. To create the covered put, you would sell the underlying asset and sell a put option to capture the premium of the short put or limit the upside exposure to a short sale on the underlying asset.

Let's look at an example of a covered put position. Using the CAT option chain in Figure 6.5, let's assume a hypothetical short

Actuals	CAT Common			Legend							
	32.15	+0.61	Trade	Last	Chg						
Options	MAY <41>						AUG <139>				
	MktPr	MIV	Delta	Gamma	Theta	Vega	MktPr	MIV	Delta	Gamma	Theta	Vega
35 calls												
34 calls	1.83	64.3%	44.9	6.47	-3.28	4.15	3.55	59.7%	52.4	3.67	-1.66	7.70
33 calls	2.26	65.9%	51.1	6.34	-3.43	4.23	3.99	60.7%	55.9	3.56	-1.69	7.70
32 calls>	2.76	67.9%	57.2	6.04	-3.53	4.23	4.46	61.8%	59.3	3.42	-1.71	7.64
31 calls	3.30	69.6%	63.1	5.60	-3.55	4.14	4.94	62.6%	62.6	3.26	-1.71	7.52
30 calls	3.90	71.7%	68.6	5.07	-3.51	3.98	5.49	63.9%	65.9	3.09	-1.70	7.35
29 calls	4.55		73.3	4.13	-3.42	3.77	6.09	65.6%	69.1	2.90	-1.70	7.13
35 puts	4.72	62.8%	-61.3	6.19	-3.05	3.98	6.70	57.3%	-51.1	3.76	-1.56	7.64
34 puts	4.10	64.6%	-55.2	6.47	-3.28	4.15	6.20	59.6%	-47.6	3.67	-1.64	7.70
33 puts	3.49	65.2%	-48.9	6.34	-3.38	4.23	5.60	60.2%	-44.1	3.56	-1.65	7.70
32 puts>	3.02	67.7%	-42.8	6.04	-3.50	4.23	4.99	60.1%	-40.7	3.42	-1.64	7.64
31 puts	2.57	69.9%	-36.9	5.60	-3.55	4.14	4.52	61.6%	-37.4	3.26	-1.66	7.52
30 puts	2.17	71.9%	-31.4	5.07	-3.51	3.98	4.01	62.0%	-34.1	3.09	-1.63	7.35
29 puts	1.83	74.0%	-26.7	4.13	-3.41	3.77	3.62	63.8%	-30.9	2.90	-1.63	7.13

Figure 6.5 CAT option chain—Powered by Option Vue 6

sale on the CAT underlying stock at $32.15, and this time we will sell the at-the-money put option with the assumption that CAT remains range bound. If we sell the May $32.00 put option for a premium of 3.0, then we have a maximum profit of $3.15 minus the costs of trading with a result of $315.00 per 100 shares. The risk on this position is unlimited, unlike the covered call in which the stock can only go to zero, the covered put is truly an unlimited risk. The breakeven can be calculated by:

Strike price + premium captured = breakeven

$32.00 + $3.15 = $35.15 (minus costs of trading)

When considering short selling in any market, be sure you are clear on the risk orientation of the trade and whether it is appropriate for your objectives.

Let's take a look at the profit and loss model for this position. You can see in Figure 6.6 that the covered put option has limited

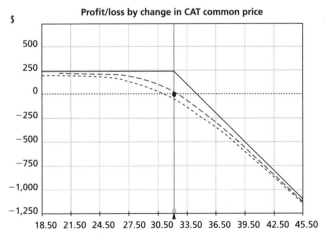

Figure 6.6 Covered put model—Powered by Option Vue 6

profit potential and unlimited risk. The trade we've created here is hypothetical and CAT is based on the same model as the short call option, not a technical recommendation of downside potential. Make sure that you are following your fundamental and technical analysis for short market opportunities when choosing markets for a covered put. When using covered put options, you want to find companies or futures markets that have found a high trading range rather then those floundering on the bottom of a major downward shift.

The covered put is an excellent method for bringing in premium to help you survive the process of the market finding a top. If you suspect a market has begun to top or that a market is in the middle of a topping chart formation, the use of the cover put strategy can insulate your short market position until the market confirms a defined pattern. We will often use an at-the-money put option in this situation where we are bringing high premium at a 50 percent delta against 1.00 delta short per position. We have reduced the delta of the underlying and brought premium against the upside risk to the amount of the premium captured.

This is also a position that can be used as a short hedge in both equities and commodities where a short-term cover for delta is necessary. This strategy is becoming more popular with agriculture and livestock hedgers as they take advantage of high implied volatility premiums against short hedge risk. The 1:1 movement of the underlying versus the put option is attractive to those wanting an immediate downside but a more subdued risk profile.

The downside to covered puts, especially in futures trading, is that markets tend to go down faster than they go up. If you are using a covered put strategy to reduce risk or margin, just be aware of the potential to miss the downside because the short put will eventually offset the entire delta of the underlying or be victim to a breakout to the topside in which the premium will be exhausted before the underlying actually tops.

A common strategy prior to expiration of the covered short option position is to consider rolling out, out and up, or out and down. *Rolling out* means making a horizontal trade of the current options for options of the same strike price in a deferred contract month. When rolling out and up or down, you are making a diagonal trade, liquidating the current option and selling one closer or farther away from the current market, up or down depending on whether you are long or short the underlying. Rolling is best done very close to expiration of the option position unless the option is deep in the money and has no time value.

Traders will also roll when a position becomes in the money prior to expiration and the time value has faded. They do this to try to capture more time from another option. This can be a roll up or down in the same month (vertical), horizontal, or diagonal to a new contract month.

There are a couple of additional risks when you're rolling to new premium against the underlying. If you are rolling because the position has gained significant value from your staggering investment prowess and you are looking to protect your profits, this is a good reason to roll, but look carefully at the total range of the underlying first just to make sure it is not time to take some profit and run.

If you are rolling to further insulate a losing position from more losses, just remember that most losing positions get worse, not better, and that selling all of the premium on the board won't help some positions get better. In fact it will just set you up for a fast moving reversal against the new premium, and you have just locked in a substantial loss because with the new closer in premium sales, the underlying value cannot recover to the original level against the new short premium.

Covered Call and Put Strategy and Summary

The covered call and put spreads are popular strategies and are excellent methods of bringing in option premium and opposing delta against existing positions to reduce costs or margin requirements by bringing premium cash against the position. Covered call and put positions have the same risk profile as the outright underlying or a naked short option position because of the unlimited risk of the position.

Risk management for covered call and put positions should be the same as for any outright stock or futures position. With the covered call, to avoid secondary exposure to the short option, consider using an order-triggers-order type for exiting the positions. If the underlying position is stopped out, the option position should be liquidated according to your instructions.

Be careful not to overleverage because of the premium captured in short options. The reduced margin from the covered call frees up capital, but make certain that you are not beyond the total margin available should the options expire and the underlying is left outright.

Bull Call and Bear Put Spreads

Bull call and bear put spreads are vertical limited-risk spreads that are excellent for offsetting time value and decreasing volatility risk. Each spread is created by purchasing an option closer to the current market and selling an option farther away from the market on a one-to-one ratio. The purpose of the spread is to create a position in the market that has a window in which it can make a profit and have completely limited risk exposure.

Bull Call Spread

Let's look at an example of a bull call spread used in the CBOT corn market. Futures markets make excellent examples for many option spread positions because of the overall market volatility and leverage. In Figure 6.7 you can see the option chain for CBOT corn options for July with 85 days remaining and September with 141 days remaining. For our bull call spread example, we will use the September options. If you are new to futures trading, you will notice that the quote prices are different. The corn options in this option chain are quoted in whole numbers representing 1 cent per bushel and then $^1/_8$ cents after the apostrophe. CBOT corn is a 5,000-bushel contract with each cent of option value representing 1 cent per bushel or $50. So the September 420 call

Futures	MAY ‹28›		JUL ‹89›		SEP ‹151›	
	404'4	0'0	414'6	0'0	423'4	0'0
Options	JUL ‹85›					SEP ‹141›				
480 calls	MktPr	MIV	Delta	Gamma	Theta	Vega	MktPr	MIV	Delta	Gamma	Theta	Vega
470 calls	15'7	43.7%	31.2	0.41	-9.13	35.5	29'0	44.2%	38.8	0.40	-7.99	51.1
460 calls	18'1	43.3%	35.0	0.48	-9.43	37.0	32'7	45.0%	42.3	0.41	-8.26	51.8
450 calls	20'7	43.1%	39.2	0.50	-9.71	38.3	36'0	44.6%	46.1	0.43	-8.27	52.3
440 calls	23'7	42.7%	43.8	0.52	-9.88	39.2	39'4	44.4%	50.0	0.43	-8.25	52.4
430 calls	27'2	42.4%	48.6	0.53	-9.93	39.8	43'2	44.0%	54.2	0.43	-8.15	52.3
420 calls	31'3	42.2%	53.7	0.53	-9.93	39.9	47'0	43.5%	58.4	0.43	-7.96	51.7
410 calls	35'7	42.2%	58.8	0.52	-9.80	39.4	52'0	43.6%	62.7	0.42	-7.84	50.8
400 calls›	40'7	42.2%	64.0	0.50	-9.54	38.4	57'0	43.6%	66.9	0.40	-7.62	49.4
440 puts	49'1	42.7%	-56.2	0.52	-9.87	39.2	56'0	44.3%	-49.8	0.43	-8.22	52.4
430 puts	42'4	42.5%	-51.4	0.53	-9.95	39.8	49'6	44.0%	-45.7	0.43	-8.14	52.3
420 puts	36'5	42.2%	-46.3	0.53	-9.93	39.9	43'7	43.8%	-41.5	0.43	-8.02	51.7
410 puts	31'1	42.2%	-41.1	0.52	-9.80	39.4	38'4	43.6%	-37.2	0.42	-7.85	50.8
400 puts›	26'1	42.2%	-36.0	0.50	-9.54	38.4	33'5	43.7%	-33.0	0.40	-7.65	49.4
390 puts	21'4	42.0%	-30.9	0.46	-9.09	36.8	29'1	43.6%	-28.8	0.38	-7.36	47.6
380 puts	17'4	41.8%	-26.0	0.42	-8.52	34.6	25'0	43.8%	-24.8	0.35	-7.05	45.5
370 puts	14'2	42.2%	-21.5	0.37	-7.95	32.0	21'4	44.0%	-21.0	0.31	-6.71	43.0

Figure 6.7 Corn option chain—Powered by Option Vue 6

option is 47'0 cents per bushel or $2,350. You will often see grain options quoted without any designation for whole points rather than ⅛ points so if the 420 call was quoted as 470, the result would be the same. If the option was quoted at 47'4 (or 474) it would be 47½ or $2,375.

Assume a hypothetical purchase of the September 420 call at 47'0. Then to create the bull call spread, we sell the September 470 call at 29'0. We have spent $2,350 on the purchase of the 420 call option, and by selling the 470 call option, we capture premium in the amount of $1,450 giving us a net purchase price of 19'0 or $950.

The bull call spread is limited risk because if the underlying futures remain below 420 at expiration, then both the 420 and 470 call options would remain out of the money and expire as worthless. If the market is above 470 at expiration, then both options would be in the money, and the long futures obtained from the exercise of the 420 call would be offset by the short created when the 470 is exercised.

The maximum profit potential of the position is the difference between the spread prices and the original premium and costs of trading.

$$\text{Upper strike price} - \text{lower strike price} -$$
$$\text{premium paid} = \text{maximum profit}$$
$$470 - 420 - 19 = 31 \text{ or } \$1,550$$

We paid 19 cents for the trade, so as with any purchased option, add the premium paid to the purchased strike price for the breakeven on the trade; in this case that would be 439 on the underlying futures.

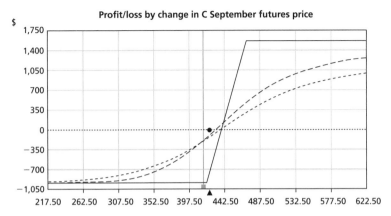

Figure 6.8 CBOT corn bull call spread option model—Powered by Option Vue 6

Now look at Figure 6.8 for the profit and loss model on the bull call spread.

You can see that this model has both a limited risk and a limited profit potential. The total maximum profit potential is the $1,550 we calculated previously, and the maximum risk is the net option premium spent on the position. Also notice that the profit and loss occurs slowly at intermediate time frames represented by the dashed and dotted lines. This slow growth in premium is a result of the decreased delta of the spread. This is a disadvantage of the bull call spread. With the long 420 call having a delta of 58.4 percent and the short 470 call having a delta of 38.8 percent, the net long delta movement against the underlying futures is only 19.6 percent. This delta will increase slowly as the 420 call becomes in the money; but the net gamma it is nearly completely offset meaning that the change in the delta will be very slow as the market moves higher. The bull call spread will not return quick profits. The spread is designed to allow time decay to work on the short call option premium through the remaining life of the option. In the model you can see this delta effect in the intermediate time lines. Even if the underlying market was to gain a full $1.00 per bushel and both options were firmly in the money, the option spread would gain only around half the maximum profit potential.

The bull call spread is designed for upward-trending or trading-range markets with an upward tilt. The advantage to the bull call spread is that the short call premium sold above the market has the potential to offset portions of two risk factors in the purchased option—time decay and volatility risk. If the market trends sideways, the short call will lose time value at a pace nearly equal to the long call position, at least to the point where the short call premium is exhausted. The extrinsic value of the higher call option is reduced to a small amount prior to expiration from either negative market movement or time value decay.

The bull call spread is an excellent technique to use in volatile markets. If a significant change in implied volatility were to occur, then the long and short call options would be affected in equal proportions to their respective vega, at least until the short call premium was exhausted. When purchasing call options in a high volatility market that has the potential for a sharp decline in volatility, consider the bull call spread as an excellent tool.

A follow-up strategy to the bull call spread is that once the time decay has weakened the value of the short call option, it is possible to break the spread and purchase back the short call option. This strategy leaves the long call outright with a reduced overall cost. The profit you obtain from buying back the short call option can be subtracted from the total premium of the purchased call option, and you can consider it a reduced cost long position that is free to gain if the market runs higher.

We normally recommend purchasing back low value or worthless short positions on bull call spreads because it improves the potential of the trade should the market finally make a move or recover from a period of weakness that reduced the value of the short call option.

Bear Put Spreads

The bear put spread represents the opposing position to the bull call spread. In the bear put spread we are purchasing a put option closer to the underlying market and selling a put option farther away in order to create a limited-risk short position We will use 30-year U.S. Treasury bonds as an example, and, as with any short market position, your analysis should show a definitive reason to be short the underlying. The chart in Figure 6.9 shows risk in either direction, although the general bias would be negative in the long term. Volatility is down-trending so selling uncovered option premium in this market may not be out of the question, but the safer bet at this point is to consider a limited-risk position.

Using the option chain in Figure 6.10, we can put together the bear put spread using the purchase of the June CBOT U.S. Treasury bond 127 put option and the sale of the June CBOT

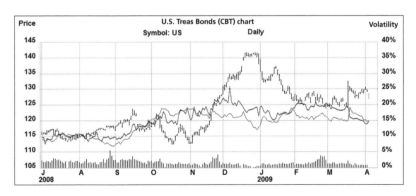

Figure 6.9 30-year U.S. Treasury bond chart — Powered by Option Vue 6

U.S. Treasury bond 122 put option. The underlying futures contract is $1,000 per point and represents $100,000 in U.S. T-bonds and the option are quoted in sixty-fourths. The 127 put option is $2^{48}/_{64}$ or $2,750, and the 122 put option is quoted at $1^{07}/_{64}$ or $1,109.38. There are a couple of items to note in the Treasury option chain. The implied volatility for T-bond options is low in comparison to other markets we have looked at so far, and there is not a May underlying futures contract to go with the May options. The implied volatility (IV) for bonds is fairly low all the time, which is why it is important to look at the history for each individual contract, equity, or index for it's own historical volatility. You cannot assume that because one is 40 percent IV and one is 14 percent IV, that the IV on the 40 percent market is high. Historically speaking 14 to 18 percent IV for Treasury bonds is very high volatility, making the trade above 18 percent exceptional.

Our net purchase price on the spread is roughly $1,610 plus the costs of trading. The same scenario exists for the bear put spread. Our maximum profit is the distance between the two strike prices

Futures	JUN ‹59›		SEP ‹151›		DEC ‹242›	
	126'315	-2'070	125'220	.....	124'180	.....

Options	MAY ‹22›						JUN ‹50›					
	MktPr	MIV	Delta	Gamma	Theta	Vega	MktPr	MIV	Delta	Gamma	Theta	Vega
134 calls												
133 calls	0'120	14.1%	8.94	3.69	-16.4	52.7	0'440	14.1%	19.2	4.50	-18.2	129
132 calls	0'190	14.1%	13.2	5.06	-21.6	67.9	0'570	14.0%	23.9	5.15	-20.3	145
131 calls	0'290	14.2%	18.9	6.55	-27.3	84.4	1'090	14.1%	29.2	5.72	-22.5	159
130 calls	0'420	14.0%	26.1	7.96	-32.0	100	1'290	14.3%	35.0	6.16	-24.6	172
129 calls	0'610	14.2%	34.5	9.03	-37.0	113	1'520	14.3%	41.2	6.42	-25.9	181
128 calls	1'210	14.3%	43.7	9.56	-40.0	122	2'150	14.4%	47.6	6.49	-27.0	186
127 puts›	1'530	14.7%	-46.9	9.45	-41.9	124	2'480	14.6%	-46.0	6.36	-27.5	187
126 puts	1'250	14.9%	-37.8	8.74	-41.3	121	2'190	14.7%	-39.8	6.04	-27.4	185
125 puts	1'050	15.4%	-29.6	7.62	-40.1	113	1'590	15.1%	-33.9	5.58	-27.1	179
124 puts	0'520	15.9%	-22.5	6.29	-37.1	102	1'390	15.4%	-28.6	5.02	-26.2	170
123 puts	0'390	16.4%	-16.8	4.97	-33.4	89.2	1'210	15.7%	-23.8	4.41	-25.0	159
122 puts	0'290	16.8%	-12.3	3.78	-29.0	76.6	1'070	16.1%	-19.6	3.79	-23.6	147
121 puts	0'220	17.4%	-8.96	2.80	-25.4	64.9	0'590	16.5%	-16.0	3.19	-22.0	134

Figure 6.10　Treasury bond option chain—Powered by Option Vue 6

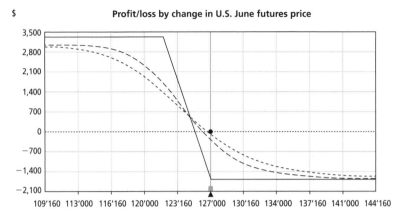

$

Profit/loss by change in U.S. June futures price

3,500	
2,800	
2,100	
1,400	
700	
0	
−700	
−1,400	
−2,100	

109'160 113'000 116'160 120'000 123'160 127'000 130'160 134'000 137'160 141'000 144'160

Figure 6.11   Treasury bond option model — Powered by Option Vue 6

of $5.00 and $5,000 with a total maximum risk of the premium and fees. The delta of the bear put spread also shares the same issue as the bull call spread in that the offsetting premium significantly reduces the net short delta of the trade. You can see in Figure 6.11 that the intermediate time-frame lines, represented once again by the dashed and dotted lines, have a slow growth rate in premium.

Figure 6.11 shows the profit-and-loss model for the bear put spread. The pattern in the model is opposite of the bull call spread. As the underlying futures price on the horizontal axis falls, the spread eventually reaches maximum profitability. As futures prices rally, the trade falls to its maximum potential loss. As with the bull call spread, portions of the time value decay on the purchased put option are offset by the put being sold at a lower strike price. The same applies for changes in volatility with the offsetting short put premium slowing the rate of increase or decrease in volatility.

The strategy of using bull call and bear put spreads is effective for conservative direction positions that do not rely on a sudden market move. Either spread will react quickly with a low delta represented in the trade. Ideally, bull call and bear put spreads should be used in situations where the volatility is higher on the out-of-the-money options giving any decrease in volatility a better offsetting position.

Bull call and bear put spreads do not necessarily need to be placed as spreads although, if you are placing the orders separately for the purchase and the sale, you must be aware that one side of the transaction may not fill and could place the other position at risk until it is filled. These spreads also do not have to be liquidated as one spread although the same risk applies as when placing the order in that one side or the other may not receive a fill, thereby leaving the other option outright and exposed to additional risk.

It is most preferable to have a bull call or bear put spread that has a one-to-three risk-to-reward ratio or greater, although that is increasingly difficult to find with the more advanced options analysis in today's market. The trades demonstrated have risk-to-reward ratios of around one to two, which is common in heavily traded options markets.

Risk Reversal

The term *risk reversal* is used in a couple of different ways in trading. In foreign-exchange trading, risk reversal is the difference in delta and volatility between similar call and put options. In options trading outside of FOREX (Foreign Exchange Market), risk reversal is an aggressive vertical trade that can be done long or short in the market. When doing a risk reversal long the market, you are selling a put option and buying a call option in the same expiration month. If you are doing a short risk reversal, you are selling a call and buying a put option in the same expiration month. In equity trading, risk reversals are also called synthetic long or short.

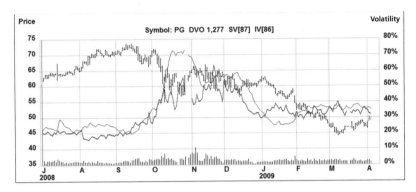

Figure 6.12 PG daily chart—Powered by Option Vue 6

Long risk reversals are excellent trades for taking a fairly aggressive long position in the market without being directly at risk of owning the underlying outright. Risk reversals are a benefit under high-volatility conditions because they provide the upside potential of the underlying asset but allow for a trading range in the underlying during the term of the option.

Using the chart for Procter & Gamble (PG) (see Figure 6.12), we can see that the company has found a short-term bottom in the last month or so of trading. Let's assume that our hypothetical analysis has PG as a good long-term buy. You would like to have PG in your portfolio, but you are concerned about buying the market too high and having a retest of the recent lows against your position. You have a couple of choices with this type of scenario. With the volatility as it is currently, you have a call option that is not too unfairly valued given the recent volatility. However, from a historical standpoint looking back to the summer of 2008 and before, the current volatility is elevated, meaning that the outright call option premium may be overvalued or priced too high for estimated market movement to offset time decay and volatility risk. You could purchase the outright PG stock and risk to the support level of your choice. You can also take a long risk reversal which would be to sell a put while purchasing the call option so as to provide the strong delta of the position and reduce the premium outlay. In doing so, you would create a low point where the stock would be exercised into the underlying stock at a better price. You would also be creating a long call position that would increase to delta 1.00 if the market continued higher.

Looking at Figure 6.13, we have the PG option chain where we can see that the implied volatility is not as high as on some other assets we have looked at, but it still gives cause for concern on deflating volatility over the term of a call option. The bull call spread is not aggressive enough in delta, so you are looking for ways to offset the volatility and time value risk to the trade, with the strong upside potential of the underlying stock.

The risk reversal can accomplish several goals for this position. It can allow you to enter the market with a short put and long call position with an aggressive delta and the potential to exercise either option into your desired long-term long.

In Figure 6.13 we have the option model for PG puts and calls and the underlying Procter & Gamble stock trading at 49.63. If we consider going out of the money a little to reduce option premium

Actuals	PG Common		Legend		
	49.63	+0.21	Trade	Last	Chg

Options	JUL <106>						OCT <197>					
57.5 calls	MktPr	MIV	Delta	Gamma	Theta	Vega	MktPr	MIV	Delta	Gamma	Theta	Vega
55.0 calls	1.05	29.0%	27.2	4.85	-1.15	8.31	2.07	29.4%	37.6	3.99	-0.99	13.0
52.5 calls	1.89	31.3%	39.2	5.32	-1.48	9.83	2.90	30.1%	46.9	3.95	-1.09	14.0
50.0 calls>	2.97	33.0%	52.1	5.18	-1.65	10.5	4.09	31.9%	56.2	3.69	-1.18	14.3
47.5 calls	4.40	35.6%	64.3	4.51	-1.73	10.2	5.49	33.6%	64.9	3.25	-1.21	13.9
45.0 calls	6.10	38.5%	74.8	3.55	-1.70	9.11	6.94	34.6%	72.7	2.73	-1.16	12.9
52.5 puts	5.10	26.9%	-60.8	5.32	-1.20	9.83	6.50	30.4%	-53.1	3.95	-1.04	14.0
50.0 puts>	3.70	29.2%	-48.0	5.18	-1.43	10.5	5.11	31.6%	-43.8	3.69	-1.12	14.3
47.5 puts	2.60	31.3%	-35.7	4.51	-1.49	10.2	3.96	32.9%	-35.1	3.25	-1.14	13.9
45.0 puts	1.80	33.6%	-25.2	3.55	-1.43	9.11	3.03	34.6%	-27.3	2.73	-1.11	12.9
42.5 puts	1.25	36.4%	-17.1	2.44	-1.29	7.62	2.25	36.0%	-20.6	2.14	-1.03	11.5

Figure 6.13   PG option chain—Powered by Option Vue 6

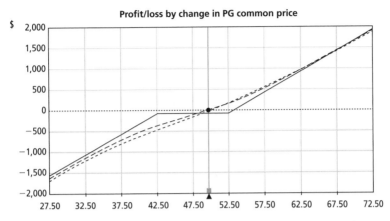

Figure 6.14 PG long risk-reversal model — Powered by Option Vue 6

costs and buy the October PG 52.50 call for 2.90, we achieve a long delta with the call option of 46.9 percent. Outright this would be a limited risk position with a breakeven at 55.40 on the underlying. If we sell the October PG 42.50 put for a premium of 2.25, we have at total net premium debit of .65 per option spread and we have an additional long delta of 20.6 percent. The total combined delta on the position is 67.5 percent long the underlying stock.

Now let's look at the model for this trade as shown in Figure 6.14. The risk reversal has a similar angle to the underlying with the profit building sharply as the market rises and losing sharply as the market falls. The important point to the risk reversal is the breakeven points on each side of the trade. There is a flat area on the model where both options expire as worthless and the total loss is the premium paid for the spread. Unlike the outright purchase of the underlying market, however, the risk reversal does not start losing significantly at expiration until it reaches $42.50, while the underlying would start losing immediately.

Calculating breakeven for the risk reversal depends on whether the spread is applied for a debit or credit. If it's a debit spread, we must add the cost of the position to the long call strike price to see the breakeven point at expiration:

52.50 call option + .65 = 53.15 breakeven on long call side

If the spread had been applied to a credit, we could subtract the amount from the long call position to find the underlying breakeven point, and we would have a breakeven on the short put slightly below the strike price in the amount of the credit.

For risk control on a risk reversal, consider using the methods outlined in outright selling options, or as you would with the outright underlying position. The risk reversal is an aggressive position that should be monitored carefully.

Short risk reversals are commonly done in place of actually short selling outright equity and futures positions. Often the margin requirement for a short risk reversal will be less than that of the outright short position, which makes it attractive to traders seeking to retain cash. In addition, short risk reversals can be applied to a position as a cover trade for volatile market conditions, reports, or unexpected fundamental changes. One of the things to look for in a short risk reversal is any type of advantage that might be gained through differences in implied volatility between the puts and the calls. The ALV (Autoliv, Inc.) option chain we demonstrated earlier is an example of the disparity in volatility that could be capitalized on with a risk reversal. A call option with high implied volatility will provide more premium toward the cost of the purchased option and reduce time value and volatility value risk.

A risk reversal is also an excellent method of hedging a future sale on held stock or reducing the cost of protective put options on held stock positions. We can look at an example using a commonly

Figure 6.15   Exxon Mobil chart—Powered by Option Vue 6

held energy stock. The energy market experienced tremendous profits through 2007 and early 2008, and the stock value of Exxon reached up into the $90+ range, but with falling energy prices your trading goal is to retain as much Exxon stock value as possible, and you want to add low cost hedge security to your position.

You can see from Figure 6.15 that the underlying has traded above $60.00 for the past few years. Hypothetically, lets say your cost basis is $60.00 and you do not want to risk much below that price. The volatility appears to be trending higher on a weekly basis, and there is a risk of the market having additional volatility but returning to the uptrend over time. Some of your choices are to place a hard stop in the market and risk being stopped out prior to a market rally, purchase a protective put option, sell a covered call, or combine the latter two and use a short risk reversal. Let's look at the Exxon option chain in Figure 6.16

If you purchase the Exxon Mobil October 60.00 put option outright for $3.70, your breakeven price on the underlying stock will be $56.30 which is below your cost basis, but this does not limit the upside on the underlying. If you add the sale of an out-of-the-money call option to create the short risk reversal, you can

Actuals		XOM Common		Legend			
		70.44	+0.19	Trade	Last	Chg	

Options		JUL ‹106›					OCT ‹197›				
	MktPr	MIV	Delta	Gamma	Theta	Vega	MktPr	MIV	Delta	Gamma	Theta	Vega
85 calls	1.69	32.5%	26.0	2.84	-1.85	12.1	3.44	34.2%	35.6	2.28	-1.65	18.7
80 calls	3.22	34.1%	40.7	3.27	-2.35	14.5	5.20	35.6%	46.5	2.32	-1.85	20.2
75 calls	5.47	36.2%	56.6	3.13	-2.58	15.0	7.48	37.2%	57.5	2.18	-1.95	20.2
70 calls›	8.53	38.9%	71.1	2.51	-2.51	13.5	10.26	38.8%	68.0	1.88	-1.90	18.9
65 calls												
80 puts	11.62	32.6%	-74.0	2.84	-1.82	12.1	13.58	34.0%	-64.4	2.28	-1.54	18.7
75 puts	8.05	33.6%	-59.3	3.27	-2.27	14.5	10.31	35.2%	-53.6	2.32	-1.75	20.2
70 puts›	5.31	35.7%	-43.4	3.13	-2.50	15.0	7.61	36.9%	-42.5	2.18	-1.86	20.2
65 puts	3.36	38.2%	-28.9	2.51	-2.42	13.5	5.44	38.6%	-32.0	1.88	-1.82	18.9
60 puts	2.01	40.8%	-17.8	1.61	-2.07	10.8	3.70	40.3%	-22.9	1.47	-1.66	16.5

Figure 6.16 Exxon option chain—Powered by Option Vue 6

reduce your premium outlay while still maintaining some upside potential on your position. If we were to consider selling the 80 call option for $3.44, we would reduce our premium outlay to .25. The breakeven on the option position would now be 59.75 which at expiration, if the option was in the money, the underlying stock would be offset at 59.75 minus the costs of trading. The advantage here is that you have eliminated most of the premium outlay for the trade thus making your protective position costs virtually nothing. If Exxon returns to the upside over the term of the option, it is possible that the shares value could exceed $80 per share, at which point you would need to decide if the option should be allowed to be exercised and offset your outright long positions or rolled to a deferred contract month with a higher strike price and additional premium. A trade above $80 per share would result in the option position slowly offsetting the gains until the option position reached a delta of 1.00 where there would be no further gains on the underlying position.

Let's look at a model of the outright risk reversal without the underlying first. (See Figure 6.17.) Then we can study how the hypothetical hedge works.

If we add to this position a hypothetical purchase of 100 shares of Exxon Mobil at a cost basis of 60.00, the model changes to look

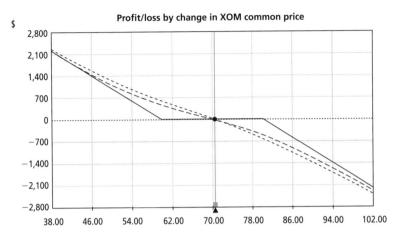

Figure 6.17 Exxon short risk-reversal model—Powered by Option Vue 6

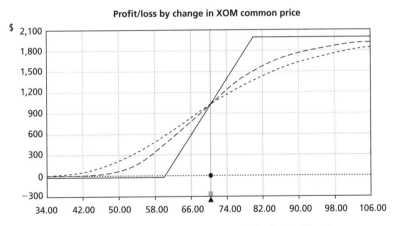

Figure 6.18 Exxon hypothetical trade—Powered by Option Vue 6

something like a bull call spread with a zero risk. (See Figure 6.18.) You can see that at expiration we have terminated the trade if the market trades below the breakeven of 59.75. We also have limited the profit potential to $80 per share minus the cost of the risk-reversal position.

There are some volatility risks to the risk-reversal position, especially if the gain in volatility is asymmetrical on the short option.

If volatility increases the premium value of the short option position in a flat market movement, you can have losses on the option position that may not be offset by the long market position. The same can be true for the long put. If the volatility drops substantially, the purchased option may lose value against the position regardless of underlying market movement.

Synthetic Long or Short

The synthetic long or short is a risk reversal, but, technically speaking, an actual synthetic position is a risk reversal made up of the at-the-money options. Using the Exxon example one more time, if we were to sell the October 70 put for the price listed at 7.61 and buy the October 70 call option for 7.48 as shown in Figure 6.16, we would actually come out with a very slight credit of .13. Synthetics placed for a credit are not terribly common, but it does happen when the volatility is inflated on one side over the other. The purchased call option has a long delta of 57.5 percent, and the short put option has a long delta of 42.5 percent, giving us a combined delta of 1.00 equivalent to the underlying 100 shares of stock. The synthetic will trade the same as the underlying, so why pay two commissions? The simple answer is leverage. The margin on the option position is typically 20 percent of the value of the underlying shares, while the underlying itself has a typical cash requirement of 100 percent or a margin of at least 50 percent. So in the case of the Exxon shares represented, 100 shares would have a cash requirement of $7,044 or a $3,522 margin. The synthetic long would have margin of $1,408 minus the small credit of $13 plus the costs of trading.

All of that looks very attractive and in theory works exactly as does the underlying. The risk to the synthetic is that you have two options that must be liquidated in order to exit the trade. There is always the possibility of variance between the bid and the offer for the individual option positions or for the spread itself. Liquidity can also be an issue in some markets from time to time, but usually we would offset the synthetic long with a short sale on the underlying and vice versa for the put.

The synthetic short is a way to simulate a short sale on protected stocks on the "no-short" list, but you should check regulations for any new rules on short option positions on these stocks. The regulations regarding short selling are likely to be in flux for some time to come.

Sell-Buy-Sell

The sell-buy-sell strategy or covered risk reversal is a strategy that combines the risk reversal with an additional short option premium to reduce costs and risk. In many cases the sell-buy-sell can be applied as a credit spread depending on how narrow the range is. In equity or commodity markets where volatility is extreme and option premiums are very high and overly risky because of inflated premiums, the sell-buy-sell strategy can reduce time decay risk, volatility risk, and market range risk. To help demonstrate this, we can look at a stock with high share value and a relatively stable growth history that builds high premium around the at-the-money options—IBM. (See Figure 6.19.)

If you look at the October 100 call options, which are the at the money calls in this scenario, the premium is 11.99 and implied volatility is 38 percent. The premium of the 100 call option is proportional to the stock value; however, it is still a large investment if you are trying to trade any significant lot size. To obtain upside range and reduce option premium, we could create the

Actuals												
	IBM Common			Legend								
	102.22	+1.40	Trade	Last	Chg							
Options			JUL <106>						OCT <197>			
130 calls	MktPr	MIV	Delta	Gamma	Theta	Vega	MktPr	MIV	Delta	Gamma	Theta	Vega
125 calls	1.15	32.3%	15.4	1.47	-1.84	12.1	2.80	32.5%	25.7	1.50	-1.86	22.3
120 calls	1.95	33.4%	22.8	1.78	-2.46	15.7	4.00	33.6%	32.6	1.59	-2.19	25.4
115 calls	3.14	34.8%	31.6	2.03	-3.10	18.8	5.49	34.7%	39.8	1.61	-2.48	27.8
110 calls	4.75	36.2%	41.4	2.11	-3.59	20.9	7.30	35.9%	47.3	1.58	-2.70	29.2
105 calls	6.88	37.9%	51.5	2.04	-3.94	21.8	9.49	37.1%	54.8	1.49	-2.85	29.7
100 calls>	9.49	39.6%	61.2	1.85	-4.05	21.5	11.99	38.4%	61.9	1.36	-2.89	29.1
115 puts	16.48	35.5%	-68.4	2.03	-3.12	18.8	19.08	34.9%	-60.2	1.61	-2.37	27.8
110 puts	13.05	36.6%	-58.6	2.11	-3.57	20.9	15.96	36.3%	-52.7	1.58	-2.61	29.2
105 puts	10.11	37.9%	-48.5	2.04	-3.88	21.8	13.14	37.5%	-45.3	1.49	-2.76	29.7
100 puts>	7.77	39.9%	-38.8	1.85	-4.02	21.5	10.65	38.7%	-38.1	1.36	-2.80	29.1
95 puts	5.80	41.7%	-30.0	1.57	-3.92	20.0	8.55	40.2%	-31.5	1.20	-2.78	27.7
90 puts	4.26	43.6%	-22.5	1.27	-3.64	17.8	6.80	41.8%	-25.6	1.03	-2.67	25.6
85 puts	3.11	45.9%	-16.6	0.94	-3.28	15.2	5.38	43.6%	-20.3	0.86	-2.52	22.9

Figure 6.19 IBM option chain—Powered by Option Vue 6

more conservative limited risk bull call spread by buying the 100 call and selling the 120 call option for a net premium of 7.99. To achieve a more aggressive delta, we can combine the bull call spread with the higher risk profile of the risk-reversal spread and sell a put below the market in a combined spread. In this way we can further reduce premium costs and improve the long delta of the position.

As an example, if we were to sell the 85 put option with the buy of the 100 call option and the sale of the 120 call, we capture premiums of 5.38 and 4.00 for a total of 9.38. The 11.99 purchased option premium minus the 9.38 capture premium gives us a net cost on this at-the-money call of only 2.31 and an upside market breakeven point of 102.31.

$$100 \text{ strike price} + 2.31 \text{ premium} = 102.31$$

This is in contrast to the 111.99 premium with the outright call purchase. This premium capture changes the premium outlay risk to reward ratio of nearly one to eight. However, with the short put

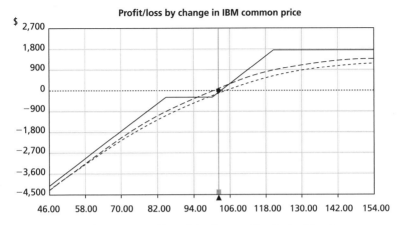

Figure 6.20 IBM sell-buys-sell model—Powered by Option Vue 6

option the overall risk to the downside is limited only by the stock going to zero.

Look at Figure 6.20 to see the profit and loss scenario of this trade. The short put premium will need appropriate risk control for a naked short put option or outright underlying stock position. Ideally this type of position should be used in a scenario in which the expectation is for stable to decelerating implied volatility. There is a substantial amount of short option premium in the position and a large increase in implied volatility would significantly increase risk on the the short put premium. As a result volatility gains in the long call premium may be partially or completely offset until expiration. You can see from the model that this trade is designed for a market uptrend, and the maximum profit is $1,800 on one option spread. The spread will gain or lose value fairly slowly in the intermediate time frames because the delta is reduced from the underlying position.

This example is on a longer-term option position, but these trades work very effectively in short expiration options because the dual short options help offset rapid time value decay on purchased option positions.

The sell-buy-sell can be created as a short position by selling an out-of-the-money call option, buying a closer-to-the-money put, and selling an out-of-the-money put.

Summary

Basic option spreads offer the trader an opportunity to use premium, volatility, and time value offsets from options with the same underlying and expiration. These spreads are the most common spreads executed on the market and the most well understood. As an investor or trader in today's volatile climate, some back to basics in option trading is very appropriate. As we move forward into the volatility of the future, being able to limit risk and control exposure to deflated premium without getting overly complex in option strategy is going to be very attractive to retail traders. In addition, the leverage gained from using option spreads over even their outright counterparts will help you increase your market position rapidly with limited or reduced risk to the trades. Always monitor your risk carefully on any uncovered option premium be it long or short, and make sure you are trading within your risk tolerance and suitability.

Chapter 7

ADVANCED SPREADS

Advanced option spreads add another dimension to options trading. With advanced options spreads we are bringing an additional dimension of ratios to the basic option spread and beginning to work with neutral delta trading strategies.

Ratio Spreads

Ratio spreads are an evolution of the bull call or bear put spread. They combine long purchased options with multiple short options. Ratio spreads bring an additional short option premium to purchased options to reduce the premium outlay, protect against time value decay, and insulate long options from significant reductions in implied volatility.

For an example of a ratio spread we will look again at Caterpillar, Inc. (CAT) options with a few more out-of-the-money options selected on both calls and puts. We are using CAT again because of the inflated implied volatility on the out-of-the-money call options.

Call Ratio Spread

Call ratio spreads are excellent spreads for high implied volatility conditions where there is a significant risk of a dropin implied volatility. In the model in Figure 7.1, we have placed the at-the-money 32 call and put options together to demonstrate the range of a ratio spread. As an example of a call ratio, we can consider purchasing the May CAT 32.00 call option for 2.76 while selling two of the May CAT 36 call options for 1.14. The total premium captured with short of two calls is 2.28 while we're spending 2.76 on the purchased option position for a net debit on the spread of .48.

The ratio spread changes the net on the Greeks because the multiple shorts do more to offset the single long position. Even though we are purchasing call premium, we will end up with a short delta on the spread. The long option has a delta of 57.2 percent long, while the shorts combined will have a total delta of 66.4 percent, leaving us with a net short delta of 9.2 percent. Theta will be calculated as a positive, so time decay will be working in favor of this trade. Theta on the long option of -3.36 will be offset by the

Actuals	CAT Common		Legend									
	32.15	+0.61	Trade	Last	Chg							
Options			MAY <43>						AUG <141>			
38.0 calls	MktPr	MIV	Delta	Gamma	Theta	Vega	MktPr	MIV	Delta	Gamma	Theta	Vega
37.0 calls	0.89	58.9%	27.9	5.64	-2.41	3.49	2.45	56.5%	42.0	3.88	-1.50	7.42
36.0 calls	1.14	59.8%	33.2	5.91	-2.67	3.82	2.78	57.3%	45.5	3.85	-1.55	7.59
35.0 calls	1.46	61.4%	38.8	6.26	-2.93	4.07	3.14	58.2%	49.0	3.79	-1.60	7.70
34.0 calls	1.83	62.6%	44.9	6.46	-3.12	4.25	3.55	59.2%	52.5	3.71	-1.64	7.75
33.0 calls	2.25	64.2%	51.1	6.32	-3.26	4.33	4.00	60.4%	56.0	3.59	-1.67	7.75
32.0 calls>	2.76	66.1%	57.2	6.02	-3.36	4.33	4.46	61.4%	59.4	3.45	-1.69	7.69
32.0 puts>	3.02	66.1%	-42.8	6.02	-3.34	4.33	4.99	59.7%	-40.6	3.45	-1.62	7.69
31.0 puts	2.57	68.2%	-36.9	5.58	-3.38	4.24	4.51	61.0%	-37.2	3.29	-1.63	7.57
30.0 puts	2.17	70.2%	-31.4	5.05	-3.34	4.08	4.01	61.6%	-33.9	3.11	-1.61	7.40
29.0 puts	1.82	72.2%	-26.6	4.12	-3.25	3.86	3.61	63.2%	-30.7	2.92	-1.60	7.18
28.0 puts	1.53	74.6%	-22.5	3.59	-3.12	3.59	3.19	64.1%	-27.7	2.71	-1.56	6.91
27.0 puts	1.28	77.2%	-18.9	3.09	-2.97	3.29	2.84	65.6%	-24.8	2.46	-1.53	6.60
26.0 puts	1.04	79.0%	-15.7	2.62	-2.74	2.98	2.51	66.9%	-22.1	2.25	-1.48	6.25

Figure 7.1 CAT option chain for ratio spreads—Powered by Option Vue 6

−2.67 doubled for the two options creating a favorable theta of 1.98. Vega will behave the same way with a volatility decrease, although it will work against the position aggressively if the volatility rises significantly. The vega of the long position is 4.33, while short calls combined have a vega of 7.64 leaving a net short vega of 3.31.

Figure 7.2 shows us the profit-and-loss model for the ratio spread. The model shows the limited risk of the call ratio spread. Should the underlying price fall, the only loss would be the premium outlay plus the costs of trading. The trade generates profit in a window at option expiration between the long and short strike prices. In this example we used May options with only 43 days to expiration.

The intermediate time-frame lines show that if the underlying asset rallies quickly, the long call will not be able to make up for the delta of the short call options and will create a loss that will increase and eventually become a delta of 1.00 short. In order to find breakeven at expiration, you will need to take the lower strike

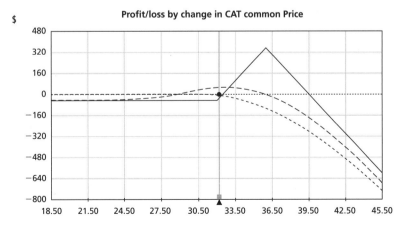

Figure 7.2 CAT ratio spread model—Powered by Option Vue 6

price and add the premium spent to find breakeven on the long call side:

$$32.0 + .48 = 32.48 \text{ lower breakeven}$$

For the breakeven on the upper side of the trade, you must add the difference in the spread between the long and short calls to the short call strike price and subtract the premium spent:

$$36.00 \text{ short call strike price} - 32.00 \text{ long call}$$
$$\text{strike} = 3.00 \text{ difference}$$
$$3.00 \text{ difference} + 36.00 = 39.00$$
$$39.00 - .48 \text{ premium} = 38.52 \text{ breakeven}$$

If the ratio spread premium is a credit rather than a debit, you will have to flip around the breakeven calculations and subtract the premium credit from the long call strike price to find the lower breakeven. For the upper breakeven you will need to once again add the difference between the strike prices and then take the premium credit, divide it by the number of short options, and add that figure to the short call strike price.

The advantage to the ratio is a reduction in the premium outlay and the capture of offsetting risk to the time value and volatility. The ratio call spread provides a means to place a short-term option position to capitalize on an anticipated trend increase in price. By doing a ratio spread in short-term expiration options, we have less time for the underlying asset to rally beyond the window of profit potential and we have advanced time decay on the out-of-the-money short call options. Ratio call spreads can be very effective long-term spreads as well. The key to success in purchasing ratio spreads with extended time to expiration is choosing short options that have elevated implied volatility if possible and that have a wide spread between the purchased options and the short options. The wider the spread, the more the range of opportunity at expiration.

When using ratio call spreads for the long term, your goal is to pick markets that have a long-term upside but with some expectation for range trading to work the time value out of the short call options. The best scenario is for the market to climb very slowly because without time or volatility decay, a sharp market rally will adversely affect the trade.

The ratio call spread has some disadvantages:

- Ratio call spreads have a very low long delta if not a small short delta and will not gain significantly in a sharp market rally.
- Ratio call spreads have a defined window of market opportunity and unlimited risk beyond the breakeven.
- Ratio call spreads have multiple commission charges which can significantly affect the profitability of the position.

Ratio Put Spread

In Figure 7.3 you can see that the ratio put spread is a mirror image of the ratio call spread. Using the CAT option chain, we created the ratio put spread by purchasing the May CAT 32.00 put option for 3.02 and selling two of the May CAT 28.00 puts for 1.53. This spread differs from the call spread in that we created it for a very small credit of .04:

$$3.02 \text{ purchased premium} - (1.53 \times 2) \text{ premium}$$
$$\text{credit} = .04 \text{ credit}$$

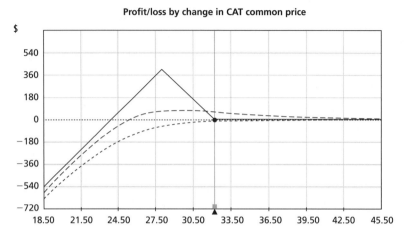

Figure 7.3   CAT put ratio model — Powered By Option Vue 6

In real trading this credit would be eaten up by commissions, but it shows you the advantage of placing ratio spreads on as small a premium as possible in trading range markets. If CAT prices increase, the spread will lose value to zero fairly quickly because of the short term of the option positions. Breakeven calculation for the ratio spread functions the same way as the ratio call spread only in reverse for put options.

If at expiration all option strike prices are out of the money, then each option will expire worthless and the gain or loss will be the premium credit or debit resulting from the placement of the position. The spread is designed for the ideal scenario being the market ending up between the two strike prices which would cause the long call or put option to be exercised into the underlying asset, CAT in this case. At expiration it is important to have risk control in place for the underlying asset or liquidate the option position prior to expiration.

If at expiration all the strike prices are in the money, each will be exercised into the underlying asset. In the CAT example, the long call will create a buy on the underlying of 100 shares per option while the two short calls will create a short sell of 200 shares of CAT stock leaving a net short sell of 100 shares, which will develop margin that the investor must be prepared for. The inverse would occur for the put spread: the short sell from the long put would offset one of the long purchases from the short puts leaving 100 shares of purchased CAT at the short put strike price of $28.00.

Risk control on ratio spreads can be very subjective because such spreads have limited risk on one side. Time value is always on your side, and the temptation is to allow the spreads to run regardless of market movement because of the remaining time value. The best risk control for ratios is a soft stop technique using the value of the underlying because it is difficult to predict the spread value with any degree of accuracy for a hard stop. If the underlying asset price breaks resistance or a change in the volatility trend occurs, the ratio spreads should be monitored for liquidation. These spreads have a tendency to get out of control quickly in rapid market movement despite the low delta, and the trades should be monitored carefully; they are not set-it-and-forget-it trades like a bull call spread or outright option purchase.

Double Ratio Spread

The *double ratio spread* is a ratio spread on both sides of the market. The double ratio can be difficult in its risk-to-reward ratio unless the spread is constructed on both sides as a credit or at least a very small debit. In addition, a double ratio generates six commissions, so use caution when trading advanced multiple options spreads that generate a lot of commissions. These spreads are used frequently, but they are not often placed simultaneously. Let's look at a model of the double ratio using the two previous ratio spreads

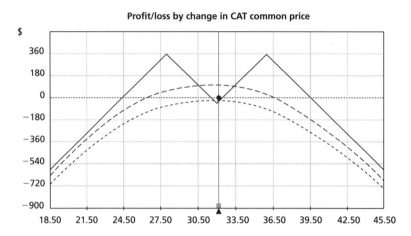

Figure 7.4   Double ratio model—Powered by Option Vue 6

(call ratio and ratio put) which have a small debit premium combined, not including costs of trading.

You can see from Figure 7.4 that the trade has a very wide window of profit opportunity, except for the small area in the middle where both purchased options would be at the money and would expire with little or no value. The trade has almost no potential for gain until expiration when all the time value is retired. Just as with the individual spreads themselves, you can see the unlimited risk on the outside of the short strike prices once the short premium is exhausted.

Ratio Diagonals

Ratio spreads can be done as diagonal spreads using options in different expiration months. The risk of doing a calendar or diagonal ratio is that the earlier expiration options could be in the money and cause an exercise of the option into the underlying asset and change the delta of the spread. The most common diagonal ratio is to use a purchased option in a longer-term expiration month while selling options in a short-term expiration month to take advantage of the advanced time value decay on the short-term options. If you look a back at Figure 6.21, we could construct a ratio using the Aug expiration 32 call for 4.46 while selling two of the May expiration 35 calls for 1.54 each. The net premium would still be a debit of 1.54; however, the advantage is that if CAT stock remains below 35 for the term of the May options, then the entire premium of the May short calls of 2.92 is applied to the breakeven of the August 32 call which would remain an outright call option.

Should the CAT price rise above 35 at expiration of the May option, then two short 35 calls would be exercised into 200 shares or a short delta of 2.00 against the long August call option delta of 59.4 percent, leaving a net short delta of about 140 percent. This would develop significant margin.

Diagonal or calendar spreads can be very effective at reducing costs on long-term options; however, the risk tolerance for the trade should be that of a net short or long position depending on the construction of the trade.

Ratio spreads in general do not have to be one to two; they can be any ratio. It is common to have one to three or more depending on the implied volatility of the position. Ratios of this nature are best done at maximum implied volatility because the short options will increase in delta and vega quickly.

Back Spreads

A *back spread* is essentially an inverted ratio spread. When constructing a back spread, you are selling an option closer to the underlying market or even an in-the-money option while purchasing an out-of-the-money option premium at a ratio to the short option. The back spread is designed for a low implied volatility scenario with the expectation of increasing implied volatility over time. Back spreads are not short-term trades. They should be created as long term as possible and is even a potential for Long-term Equity Anticipation Security (LEAP) options. As an example we can look to Alcoa, a manufacturer of aluminum products. This is not a trade recommendation, but the situation has similarities to favorable conditions for using back spreads. An economic downturn and falling aluminum prices cause a rapid decline in the stock price which is likely recoverable in a reasonable period.

Let's look at Alcoa (AA) in the chart in Figure 7.5. You can see the sharp drop in price in AA stock over the course of the weekly chart, so what we are looking for is a return to the long-term uptrend and a breakout of the channel to the upside.

Figure 7.5   Alcoa weekly chart—Courtesy of CSM Futures Group

To create the back spread, we will buy two out-of-the-money calls, and we will sell one at-the-money call. Look at the option chain in Figure 7.6 For this example we are using a slightly larger lot size. We consider selling 10 of the October AA 6.00 call options for a premium of 3.20 while simultaneously purchasing 20 of the October 9.00 call options at 1.60. The net premium on this option spread is zero plus the costs of trading.

As we mentioned earlier, ideally you want this purchase in low implied volatility or at least average volatility on the short call option over the long call options. In this case Alcoa has fairly high implied volatility because of its rapid decline, but the premium scenario, chart, and implied volatility relationship make it eligible for a back spread.

The breakeven calculation for the back spread with zero premium means that any price above 9.00 at expiration will be profitable, while any price below 6.00 will result in no gain or loss. Between 6.00 and 9.00 is where the loss potential occurs on this spread. You are short the 6.00 call with no coverage until 9.00, so if the value of the 9.00 calls is no longer equal to the 6.00 call premium, you have a loss.

Actuals	AA Common		Legend		
	8.17	-0.01	Trade	Last	Chg

Options	JUL <106>						OCT <197>					
15.0 calls	MktPr	MIV	Delta	Gamma	Theta	Vega	MktPr	MIV	Delta	Gamma	Theta	Vega
12.5 calls	.....		22.0	9.82	-0.44	1.22	.....		33.1	9.29	-0.38	2.06
11.0 calls	0.58	80.0%	34.0	11.3	-0.59	1.56	0.96	76.3%	43.5	9.46	-0.45	2.30
10.0 calls	0.82	82.1%	43.5	11.5	-0.66	1.70	1.25	78.7%	51.1	9.15	-0.48	2.37
9.0 calls	1.18	85.9%	53.8	11.7	-0.71	1.75	1.60	81.4%	59.3	8.98	-0.49	2.36
7.5 calls>	1.87	91.8%	69.9	9.44	-0.70	1.61	2.27	86.5%	71.6	7.27	-0.48	2.15
6.0 calls	2.79		83.0	5.66	-0.59	1.23	3.20		82.3	4.71	-0.42	1.75
10.0 puts	2.70		-56.5	11.5	-0.66	1.70	3.12		-48.9	9.15	-0.47	2.37
9.0 puts	2.03	85.9%	-46.2	11.7	-0.71	1.75	2.47	81.4%	-40.7	8.98	-0.48	2.36
7.5 puts>	1.24	92.5%	-30.1	9.44	-0.70	1.61	1.65	86.5%	-28.4	7.27	-0.47	2.15
6.0 puts	0.66	100%	-17.0	5.66	-0.58	1.23	1.00	93.1%	-17.7	4.71	-0.41	1.75
5.0 puts	0.40	108%	-10.5	3.70	-0.47	0.92	0.67	98.6%	-12.0	3.33	-0.35	1.39
4.0 puts	.....		-5.79	2.11	-0.33	0.61	.....		-7.35	2.12	-0.27	1.02

Figure 7.6 Alcoa option chain—Powered by Option Vue 6

At expiration the distance between the two strike prices of 3.00 is the maximum risk plus costs of trading. If this was a debit spread, you would have to add the premium paid to the 3.00 maximum risk plus costs of trading. If the spread was created for a credit, the premium amount would be deducted from the 3.00 plus costs of trading.

Now let's look at this trade on a model as shown in Figure 7.7 The model shows us graphically the loss potential of the trade at expiration, but the back spread is one few option spreads in which you are not trying to accomplish time value decay. You can see in the intermediate timelines that, as time passes, the breakeven increases on the horizontal price line. The more time decay there is from the purchased options, the more the AA price is required to gain value. You can also see the maximum loss at expiration price of 9.00 where the 6.00 call is fully in the money by 3.00 and where the 9.00 calls would be at the money and worthless.

The advantage to the back spread is that it is a limited risk trade with an unlimited upside potential that gains delta very quickly as

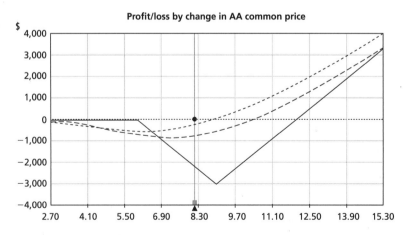

Figure 7.7 AA call back spread—Powered by Option Vue 6

the price increases to a delta of 1.00 for low premium costs. Back spreads will often be created with the short option premium in the money, but still having time value remaining on the short option to improve the premium captured and reduces the cost of the long option premium positions. This may also reduce the risk in that the distance between the strike prices may be smaller.

We used this AA example with the higher implied volatility to allow some room to show the risk of changes in implied volatility to an options spread like the back spread. Back spreads and ratio spreads are very vulnerable to implied volatility and in Figure 7.8 we have adjusted the implied volatility of the AA call back spread to account for a 25-point reduction in implied volatility from the current level on the spread.

With the change in implied volatility the intermediate time frame dashed line now does not cross the breakeven point until above 11.40 on the model, whereas before the dashed line representing the same time value decay crossed just over 10.00 on the

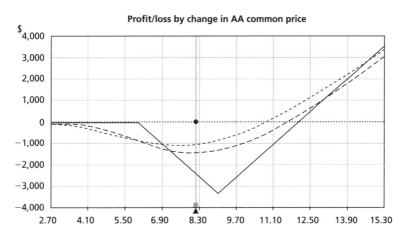

Figure 7.8 AA call back spread minus 25 percent volatility—Powered by Option Vue 6

chart. This strong reduction in implied volatility is possible where volatility is high. Changes in implied volatility can work in favor of an options spread as well.

In Figure 7.9 we demonstrate the same AA back spread with a 25-point increase in implied volatility. In this model we can see how the implied volatility change has benefited the spread with the intermediate time-frame line crossing breakeven just over the 9.00 mark. The goal with a back spread is to buy at low volatility and have both price and volatility increase during the term of the option position.

It is important to note that since a back spread is limited risk to the downside, traders frequently make the mistake of holding the spread too long. Time value is a significant problem to back spreads, and the best risk control for time value on this spread is early withdrawal. You can roll a back spread forward by liquidating options and applying a new spread so as to avoid the risk of time value.

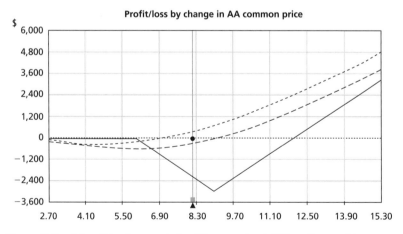

Figure 7.9 AA call back spread plus 25 percent volatility—Powered by Option Vue 6

Credit Spreads

Credit spreads are option spreads created to capture premium from the market with limited risk. They are created by selling a premium closer to the current market and purchasing a covering option below or above the short position, depending on whether it is a call or put. Credit spreads are best done in periods of high implied volatility where the volatility is skewed to the at-the-money options. For an example of a credit spread position, we turn to the New York Mercantile Exchange (NYMEX) market and look at the crude oil options. Crude oil has had significant swings in price over recent months, and these swings have built the implied volatility significantly. We can start with the crude oil chart shown in Figure 7.10.

In the chart you can see that the implied volatility decreased somewhat recently but that it is still well elevated above the 2008 level. The chart shows the decline in prices, and a trading range develops for a short period. Toward the end of the chart capture there is a slight uptrend to the market. Premium levels in the NYMEX crude oil contract make it attractive for selling a premium,

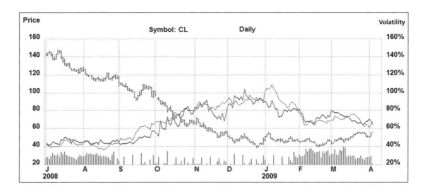

Figure 7.10 June NYMEX crude oil daily—Powered by Option Vue 6

but the market is highly volatile and is known for wild market swings. To avoid the unlimited risk and high margin requirements of the market, we can look at the credit spread for capturing this premium.

Credit Call Spreads

The NYMEX crude oil contract (Symbol: CL) represents 1,000 barrels of crude oil, so each 1.00 movement in the underlying contract equals $1,000. Let's look at the option chain for the July contract of NYMEX crude oil. (See Figure 7.11.)

With the risk of significant changes in crude oil pricing, we focus on the shorter expiration contract, which is the June options. Implied volatility is elevated above the underlying and the mean average for crude oil and elevated on the call option side of the market. The at-the-money volatility is slightly higher than the out-of-the-money calls.

If we were to look at selling the June 58 call option for 3.25 and purchasing the June 60 call option for 2.35, we would capture a total premium of .90 cents or $900 minus costs of trading. If in 43 days the underlying June contract for crude is below 58 dollars per

Futures	JUN <47>		JUL <81>		AUG <110>		SEP <140>		
	54.57	+0.25	56.37	+0.51	57.44	+0.49	Last	Chg	Trade
Options	JUN <42>				JUL <76>				
61 calls	Last	MIV	Delta	Gamma	Theta	Vega	Last	MIV	Delta	Gamma	Theta	Vega
60 calls	2.35	61.8%	33.5	2.94	-51.4	69.9	4.55	59.0%	48.4	2.70	-39.7	102
59 calls	2.94	62.4%	36.5	3.64	-53.3	71.5	4.89	59.3%	51.0	2.68	-40.1	102
58 calls	3.25	62.8%	40.0	3.82	-54.6	72.7	5.29	59.6%	53.6	2.65	-40.3	102
57 calls	3.60	62.9%	43.7	3.94	-55.3	73.5	5.60	59.5%	56.2	2.60	-40.1	102
56 calls	4.04	63.4%	47.5	4.01	-56.0	73.8	6.19	60.1%	58.7	2.55	-40.2	101
55 calls	4.50	63.8%	51.5	4.04	-56.2	73.6	6.49	60.4%	61.3	2.48	-39.8	99.9
54 puts	4.45	64.5%	-44.5	4.01	-56.3	72.9	5.30	61.3%	-36.1	2.41	-39.7	98.2
53 puts	4.39	65.3%	-40.4	3.94	-56.0	71.7	4.84	61.6%	-33.7	2.33	-39.0	96.1
52 puts>	3.73	65.8%	-36.4	3.81	-55.1	69.8	4.40	61.9%	-31.2	2.24	-38.2	93.6
51 puts	3.41	66.5%	-32.4	3.63	-53.9	67.5	4.00	62.2%	-28.8	2.14	-37.3	90.7
50 puts	2.90	66.8%	-28.8	3.02	-52.1	64.7	3.54	62.7%	-26.5	2.02	-36.2	87.5
49 puts	2.39	67.3%	-25.7	2.69	-50.0	61.4	3.28	63.2%	-24.3	1.90	-35.1	83.9
48 puts	2.05	67.9%	-22.8	2.49	-47.8	57.8	2.96	63.7%	-22.2	1.79	-33.7	80.1

Figure 7.11 July crude oil option chain—Powered by Option Vue 6

barrel, then each option in the spread would expire as worthless and the entire premium would be captured. Breakeven can be calculated by adding the premium capture to the short option strike price, making the breakeven 58.90 minus costs of trading. Between 58.90 and 60.00 is the risk area of the spread of 1.10 or $1,100. Look at the model on this trade shown in Figure 7.12.

The model shows the limited profit and limited risk on the credit spread. This particular spread is unusual in that the risk-to-reward ratio is unusually narrow. Credit spreads often require risk of 1.5 to 2 times the amount of the premium captured. This spread is an example of the advantage gained by the volatility variance between at-the-money and out-of-the money call options.

You can see from the intermediate timelines that the credit spread is designed mostly for profit at expiration. The trade will not significantly gain value during the term of the option unless the underlying crude oil market significantly falls. If the underlying market rallies, the spread will slowly gain premium value up to the maximum loss of $1,100.

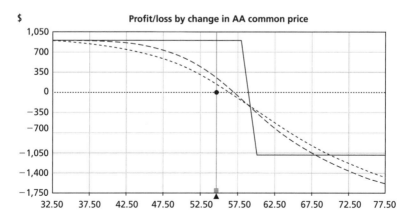

Figure 7.12 June crude oil call credit spread—Powered by Option Vue 6

Credit Put Spreads

The credit spread can be completed on the opposite side of the market with put options as well. Using the same June crude oil options from Figure 7.11, we can sell the June 50 put for 2.90 and the June 48 put option for 2.05 for a net premium of .85 or $850. The breakeven for the put spread is subtracted from the 50 put strike price, thus creating a breakeven of 49.15.

In the model shown in Figure 7.13 the trade shows a less than desirable risk-to-reward ratio of over 1:2, but this is not uncommon.

Equity markets often have narrow premium spreads to allow for a reasonable credit spread premium. Equity credit spreads can often exceed 1:2 in risk to reward, but they can be successful as a part of your trading objective to capture option premium while still maintaining a limited risk profile on the short options. In Figure 7.14 we show the option chain for Exxon Mobil.

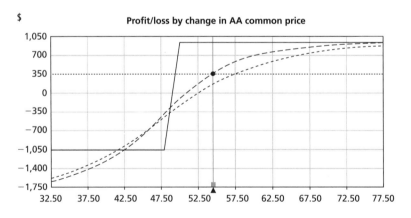

Figure 7.13 June NYMEX crude credit put spread—Powered by Option Vue 6

In this example we look to sell five of the July 65.00 put options at 3.35 while buying five of the July 60 put options for 1.85 giving us a net premium capture of 1.50 per share. With the XOM stock

Actuals	XOM Common		Legend		
	70.44	+0.19	Trade	Last	Chg

Options				JUL <106>						OCT <197>		
	MktPr	MIV	Delta	Gamma	Theta	Vega	MktPr	MIV	Delta	Gamma	Theta	Vega
90 calls												
85 calls	0.82	31.4%	16.4	2.07	-1.28	9.11	2.22	33.3%	26.9	1.97	-1.38	16.5
80 calls	1.69	32.5%	27.5	2.79	-1.85	12.4	3.44	34.2%	36.5	2.22	-1.65	18.9
75 calls	3.22	34.2%	41.7	3.14	-2.36	14.6	5.20	35.6%	47.0	2.25	-1.86	20.2
70 calls>	5.47	36.2%	56.9	2.97	-2.58	15.0	7.48	37.3%	57.7	2.11	-1.95	20.2
65 calls	8.54	38.9%	70.7	2.41	-2.51	13.6	10.27	39.0%	67.8	1.83	-1.91	18.9
80 puts	11.53	31.9%	-72.6	2.79	-1.75	12.4	13.60	34.0%	-63.6	2.22	-1.55	18.9
75 puts	8.02	33.4%	-58.3	3.14	-2.25	14.6	10.31	35.1%	-53.0	2.25	-1.75	20.2
70 puts>	5.31	35.7%	-43.1	2.97	-2.50	15.0	7.61	36.8%	-42.3	2.11	-1.85	20.2
65 puts	3.35	38.2%	-29.3	2.41	-2.42	13.6	5.42	38.6%	-32.2	1.83	-1.82	18.9
60 puts	1.85	39.4%	-18.5	1.58	-1.96	11.0	3.30	37.9%	-23.3	1.44	-1.53	16.6
55 puts	.....		-11.3	1.03	-1.78	8.22	.....		-16.2	1.06	-1.51	13.6

Figure 7.14   Exxon option chain—Powered by Option Vue 6

trading at 70.44 per share, the amount of premium captured with 106 days of risk could be considered a bit disproportionate.

This spread is only $5 and change from the current trade of the underlying and is capturing 1.50 in total premium. The risk reward is not totally out of line, but the proximity to the current market and the total risk makes this trade on the border. Let's look at the model in Figure 7.15

Profit/loss by change in XOM common price

Figure 7.15   Exxon credit spread—Powered by Option Vue 6

The risk to reward on this position is 1:2.4 risking $1,750 if XOM falls through 60.00. On the positive side of this trade we can look back at Figure 6.15 to the Exxon chart and see that the 60–65 mark is a short-term support for the market and that the short put is a potentially valid risk as we used this same point as a hedging point in the previous Exxon example. At expiration on the credit spread, if the stock price is above 65.00, all options will expire worthless and the entire premium will be captured.

Implied volatility changes are less significant on credit spreads than they are on outright short options. As with bull call and bear put spreads, the cover option provides an offsetting premium, and also offsetting values to delta, theta, and vega. This means that the trade will be less reactive with the movement of the underlying as well as experience significantly less effect from changes in implied volatility. The vega of the Exxon credit spread example is reduced to 2.60 from 13.6 for the outright short 65 put option. This works quite in your favor in the event of a major increase in implied volatility, but it reduces the ability to capitalize on reductions in implied volatility prior to expiration.

At expiration, if the underlying market is above 65, then all options will expire worthless and the maximum premium will be captured. Between 65 and 60 the breakeven would be the 65 strike price minus the premium captured. If the underlying market is below 60, then all options will expire in the money and offset with the maximum loss.

Strangles and Straddles

When you are looking for the ultimate method of capitalizing on changes in implied volatility, there is no better strategy than strangles or straddles. Options strangles and straddles are created by selling or buying calls and puts on both sides of the market.

Strangle and straddle strategies are the basis for a number of delta-neutral trading strategies. Because you are buying or selling call and put premiums on both sides of the market, the delta of each option offsets its counterpart on the opposite side of the market. For example:

- *Straddle*. A straddle is created by selling or buying a call and put option with the same underlying asset, the same contract month, and the same strike price. For example, buying the Exxon 65 put and 65 call would be a straddle

- *Strangle*. A strangle is created by selling or buying a call and put option with the same underlying asset and with the same contract month, but with different strike prices. For example, buying the Exxon 70 call and 60 put would be a strangle.

Straddles and strangles can be long or short, and each has its own advantages and disadvantages. Let's look at some examples of these strategies and how the new market volatility affects delta-neutral trading.

Long Straddles

The *long straddle* is created by buying a put and a call with the same underlying, at the same strike price, and in the same contract month. The options being bought at the same strike price create an automatic delta-neutral situation, and typically these options are bought either at the money or somewhat close to the money. The delta of any call and put at the same strike price should always end up being a delta of zero until market movement skews the delta to one side or another. With the options at zero delta, they should experience slow premium change until the market movement creates a strong delta to one side of the position or the other.

The purpose of the long straddle is typically to capitalize on anticipated market movement that has an unpredictable direction, such as a market prior to a major report or an individual stock prior to a significant news announcement. As an example, straddles are often used to trade pharmaceutical companies prior to drug announcements which can have a significant impact on the underlying stock price.

In the long straddle both options are being purchased, so the risk of the position is limited to the premium paid for both options plus the costs of trading. There are significant risk implications to using straddles in the higher volatility of the new market. The long straddle has a very dangerous combination of double time value and volatility value which can cause significant losses if left unmonitored. The long straddle seems very attractive to traders who believe that they can capitalize on the market regardless of which direction the market moves. The reality of actually profiting from a straddle can be much more difficult and requires a careful selection process before any investment is made.

There are key points you would want to see in a long straddle position:

- *Extended time value.* A long straddle involves purchasing options on both sides of the market that are mostly or entirely of extrinsic value. To protect against accelerated theta on a position, it is critical to purchase straddles as far out as affordable or that fit into the trading plan. The longer the term of the option position, the lower the rate of theta. We normally recommend that straddles be beyond 100 days to expiration, even if you are trading short term on the position. Straddles are not typically recommended under 60 days to expiration unless your trading objective is for very short-term trading. When using straddles in futures, you must account for basis differences between nearby contracts and deferred contracts when trading long-term options. As an example, the fundamental picture for December live cattle can be much different from the picture for June live cattle. If you are buying a straddle for an anticipated December price change using deferred options such as the June Live Cattle to avoid time value decay, you may be subject to significant differences in how the market reacts between December and June.

- *Low implied volatility.* We would like to have low implied volatility (relative to the current and historical volatility levels) that remains steady or trends higher from the current level during the term of the straddle. The straddle has significant implied volatility risk, and large decreases in implied volatility can cause premium values in a straddle to become unrecoverable, meaning that the underlying may not have the price range to make up for volatility loss. The best friend of the straddle trader is a sharp increase in implied volatility early in the life of the trade. Straddles are sensitive like an individual purchased option only with double the risk because the option premium on both options will react together either positively or negatively to changes in underlying volatility. The implied volatility can become skewed to one side, but your risk analysis should count on a bilateral reaction.

Let's look at an example of the long straddle in Figure 7.16. In the figure we show the option chain for AT&T (Symbol: T) with the current stock price at 26.83 and implied volatility averaging around 40 percent. If we consider buying the October AT&T 27 call option for 2.60 and the October 27 put option for 3.70 for a combined total premium of 6.30, we create a long straddle. The maximum risk for the position is the 6.30 premium spent on the trade.

Figure 7.17 is the model that shows the excellent qualities of the straddle for a significant market move to either side of the market, especially early in the trade. With the current timeline represented by the dotted line assuming zero time value decay, the straddle can provide significant profit potential for a major price change. As time passes halfway to expiration, represented by the dashed line, the line crosses the zero breakeven line at much wider points on the horizontal price scale. This highlights the necessity to avoid time value decay with long straddles.

AT&T is a perfect example of the implied volatility difficulty that traders will face in the future. Several months before this book was

Actuals	T Common		Legend								
	26.83	+0.29	Trade	Last	Chg						
Options	**JUL <106>**						**OCT <197>**				
31 calls	MktPr	MIV	Delta	Gamma	Theta	Vega	MktPr	MIV	Delta	Gamma	Theta	Vega
30 calls	0.74	36.2%	30.0	7.72	-0.79	4.55	1.38	38.0%	35.9	5.80	-0.67	6.87
29 calls	1.03	37.4%	37.2	7.90	-0.90	5.06	1.73	39.2%	41.4	6.31	-0.73	7.19
28 calls	1.40	38.9%	44.6	7.81	-1.00	5.41	2.12	40.4%	47.3	6.35	-0.77	7.41
27 calls>	1.85	40.5%	52.0	7.46	-1.08	5.58	2.60	42.1%	53.3	6.21	-0.81	7.50
26 calls	2.38	42.5%	59.1	6.89	-1.12	5.55	3.10	43.5%	59.3	5.91	-0.83	7.46
25 calls	3.00	44.9%	65.7	6.19	-1.15	5.36	3.64	44.8%	65.1	5.48	-0.84	7.29
29 puts	3.90	35.2%	-62.8	7.90	-0.82	5.06	4.89	36.7%	-58.6	6.31	-0.64	7.19
28 puts	3.23	36.2%	-55.4	7.81	-0.91	5.41	4.28	38.0%	-52.7	6.35	-0.69	7.41
27 puts>	2.66	37.6%	-48.0	7.46	-0.98	5.58	3.70	38.9%	-46.7	6.21	-0.72	7.50
26 puts	2.16	39.0%	-40.9	6.89	-1.02	5.55	3.17	39.9%	-40.7	5.91	-0.74	7.46
25 puts	1.74	40.5%	-34.3	6.19	-1.02	5.36	2.73	41.3%	-35.0	5.48	-0.75	7.29
24 puts	1.38	42.0%	-28.2	5.40	-0.99	5.02	2.27	41.8%	-29.5	4.94	-0.73	7.01
23 puts	1.09	43.6%	-22.8	4.67	-0.93	4.57	1.91	43.2%	-24.5	4.02	-0.71	6.63

Figure 7.16 AT&T option chain—Powered by Option Vue 6

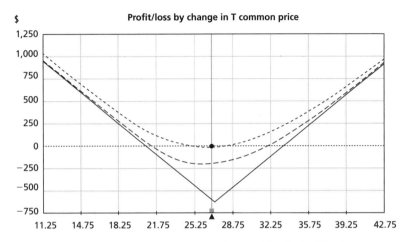

Figure 7.17   AT&T long straddle model—Powered by Option Vue 6

published, AT&T had implied volatility well in excess of 70 percent, and historically the volatility had been well below 30 percent. As options traders in today's market, we can no longer make base assumptions regarding the implied volatility range of a particular security. The market has set a new range, and all we can do is be prepared for change and understand the effect of volatility changes on positions prior to trading.

As an example, if we adjust this price model for a 15-point reduction in implied volatility, you can see the disadvantage in the price chart. In the model shown in Figure 7.18, you can see that the current time-frame dotted line is at a significant loss per 100 shares before any time value decay because of the shift in implied volatility. The dashed line, representing 99, days remained shifted downward, but the volatility is less significant as time passes. Volatility does not affect the option pricing at expiration.

Straddles can be very effective if they are placed prior to reports such as an earnings report where immediate market movement is

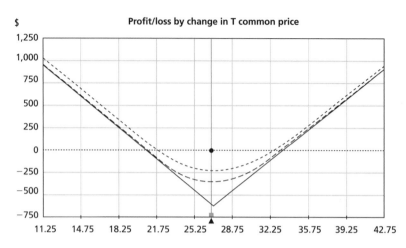

Figure 7.18 AT&T long straddle minus 15 percent volatility—Powered by Option Vue 6

likely to occur or prior to a major grain or livestock report in commodities trading. The key to success in straddles is not getting caught in a volatility trap in which implied volatility drops rapidly after an announcement or event. This ensures that your probabilities match your profitability. If your probability analysis shows that the underlying has 25 percent or less chance of reaching outside the V shaped range of the straddle model in the intermediate time frame, then it is possible that you may be buying at too high a volatility or that the underlying may not show the range necessary to build value in a straddle.

Long straddles and other delta-neutral strategies can be complicated in risk control because they are limited risk. Just because the risk is limited on the spread does not necessarily mean low or no risk. The underlying asset can move in either direction and reverse back and forth through the straddle thus eroding time value and possibly reducing volatility. The difficulty with a long straddle is your exit strategy. How you take profits and how you avoid losses. First we have to look at what will really happen when the underlying begins to change the straddle. If we look back again at our first AT&T model, Figure 7.17, the hypothetical simulation shows that if AT&T stock moves up to around 33.00, we might anticipate a gain of around $250 on the entire straddle. Looking at the delta of the individual options, it would appear that in this scenario the 27 call would have a value of around 7.00 and that the 27 put would have a value of around 1.80 for a total value of 8.80; we paid 6.30. Now what?

- You can liquidate the straddle, take your money, and run. The old saying is, "You don't go broke taking profits."
- You can let your winner run here if you believe that the market movement will continue, and you can possibly apply a stop on the spread premium if your brokerage house allows it. You do not, however, want to see the underlying reverse direction and return to the midpoint or lower. You will likely lose time value and potentially volatility premium if the market fails on any technical upturn.
- You can liquidate and roll up the long put option. Take your 1.80 back from the 27 put and roll up to a higher strike price to protect profits in the trade. If the market turns around, you will have a higher delta put option to protect the premium gained on the call. This assumes that there will be no volatility shift because of the market reversal; however, be aware of slight changes in volatility. This strategy also increases time value decay because you have now increased the overall theta by bringing in a higher strike price put option.

- You can liquidate the short put and sell a call. This option tends to be our favorite for protecting the long-term trend, insulating the long call option from a market failure, and recovering premium from a short call. If we take back the 1.80 from the original put option and are able to sell maybe another 1.50 in premium from the short call option out of the money, then we now have a bull call spread with a cost basis of 3.00 minus the costs of trading. The straddle is now successful with remaining potential for the bull call spread, and we can eliminate most of the remaining risk with a stop at 3.00 on the bull call spread. If the market retreats, the bull call spread will be offset by the original premium being intact.

- You can trade the underlying against your straddle. If your straddle has gained enough to push the delta on one side of the trade to an acceptable profit level, you may consider trading the underlying against the spread to preserve the premium. You will lose the remaining time value in the spread if you hold the underlying and the option position until expiration, but the 1.00 delta of the underlying against the straddle automatically locks in your profits on that side of the trade. Using the AT&T example again, Figure 7.17, if the underlying has moved to 33.00, you could sell the underlying and liquidate the put option. You would at least have the six points from the intrinsic value of the call option from 27 to 33 plus whatever premium you are able to recover from the put option. The underlying now covers any downside risk to market losses on the 27 call and locks in the profitability. Be aware that you may be required to margin the underlying asset until the cash value of the 27 call is recovered through liquidation. This can be fairly hefty, especially in futures trading.

Long Strangles

Long strangles are created by purchasing both call and put options with the same underlying asset and same expiration month but with different strike prices. Most of these options are at similar or equal distances from the current market unless there is a specific hedge purpose involved. The long strangle differs from the straddle in that the options are usually out of the money and at a significantly lower premium, but it is not unheard of to buy an in-the-money strangle. We focus here on the out-of-the money strangle because it's the most common, but remember that the major risks of straddles and strangles are time and volatility, so an in-the-money position can help avoid portions of that risk.

Refer back to the AT&T option chain in Figure 7.16 on page 170. Assume a hypothetical purchase of the October AT&T 30 call option for 1.38 and the October AT&T 24 put option for 2.27 giving us a total premium outlay of 3.65. This outlay is nearly half the premium outlay for our straddle example. Because the options are both of equal distance from the at-the-money strike price, the combined delta of both positions is zero.

Like the straddle the long strangle is designed to achieve a significant market move in either direction in order to add value to an option on one side of the market. The goal is to see eventually the premium change skewed to one building value faster than the other side loses, thus leading to an eventual delta on one side of 1.00. We can see a model of this trade in Figure 7.19.

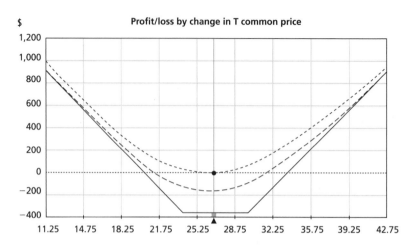

Figure 7.19   AT&T long strangle model—Powered by Option Vue 6

The long strangle looks very much like the long straddle only the deep V shape is replaced with a flat line of limited risk between the two strike prices. You will also notice that the trade has just slightly weaker profitability than does the straddle, but they are very close to the same profit capability on each side. However, the long strangle will usually have less premium risk. What the strangle has in increased risk over the straddle is the potential for a change in implied volatility that may be unrelated to the underlying volatility and more substantial than the at-the-money options. This is not necessarily quantifiable in an equation because it is subjective to the market demand for the out-of-the money options. If analysts suddenly believe that the range trade for a particular security is weaker than previously thought, the implied volatility may drop substantially on the out-of-the money options.

In addition, the strangle has a much larger area for the maximum loss between the two strike prices, represented on the model by the flat area at the bottom. The total premium outlay for the strangle is less, but the pricing area for loss is larger. The farther out of the money the strangle options are, the less profitability potential there is at expiration.

A strangle may benefit more or less than an at-the-money straddle from changes in implied volatility depending where the demand shows up for option premium. If the pricing is centered on the closer-in options, the implied may not rise as much on the out-of-the-money premium. In futures trading, the opposite is usually more common where out-of-the-money call and put options will see the increase in volatility at the money positions. Usually this is an effect of premium costs for at-the-money positions more than any other reason. Lower cost options can develop higher demand in certain markets.

Long Neutral Delta Summary

At expiration the long straddle and strangle options will be treated as any other purchased option position. With the straddle, one of the options will be in the money; one will not. The option would be exercised into the underlying position at the straddle strike price unless the option offset prior to expiration. The strangle may or may not have any options in the money at expiration in which case both would expire as worthless, but if one side is in the money, the other will expire and the in-the-money option will be exercised into the underlying at that option's particular strike price.

We've discussed risk control with directional options strategies, but long neutral delta trading strategies like the straddle employ some different risk controls:

- *Monetary stops.* Monetary stops are universal in options trading strategies. For long neutral delta strategies like straddles and strangles, you will need to decide a spread premium in which to liquidate the spread and place the order with your brokerage house.

- *Volatility stops.* Monitoring implied volatility is critical in long neutral delta trading. Check the current volatility of the underlying asset regularly, and average the implied volatility of the options on both sides of the market to monitor for changes in the implied volatility for the option. Your risk tolerance to decreasing volatility is a personal preference, but we typically recommend no more than 20 percent of the current underlying volatility. So, for example, if current volatility is 40 percent on the underlying asset, then we would be looking at no more than an 8-point drop in implied volatility as a trigger for at least minimal rechecking of the probability calculation. We also recommend placing a hard stop for the spread based on the theoretical value of the option spread at that price, depending on the risk tolerance of the investor.

- *Avoid a volatility trap.* This risk control is a pre-trade risk management technique. Before considering a neutral delta strategy ahead of a market event, news, or report, take the time to investigate the history of implied volatility on the underlying and the options prior to making your trade. If you see a significant increase in volatility in the days or weeks leading up to the event you are expecting, then others may have already priced any changes into the options market ahead of time. It is not uncommon for expected earnings, dividends, or fundamental news for a market to be priced into the options well ahead of the event. If you are looking at a long straddle as a potential portfolio hedge position, be very cautious because the overall market may be way ahead of you. If you place a long straddle or strangle position after the event is prepriced into the market, the result is not likely to be favorable for your position. It is not uncommon to see volatility significantly decline just after major reports or news, especially if the news is neutral to the market or within analysts expectations for the numbers. In agriculture and energy markets, reports are frequently prepriced based on the expected numbers from analyst estimates, and the only significant changes in the market occur when the numbers are on the extreme fringes of the range. Call options are often the most susceptible to prepricing because small investors frequently use outright out-of-the-money call options ahead of market news. Portfolio managers may be buying call options as a hedge on short market positions ahead of reports. This demand will drive up the implied volatility only to have these traders reduce their exposure to time value or delta after the report.

- *Time limits for spreads.* There is no method for pricing based on the movement of the underlying on long neutral delta since both sides of the market have potential, but with time value always working against the position, you can decide that, if the underlying price remains within a certain range in a certain period of time, then your probability for success on the long strangle or straddle has been significantly reduced. Include a time stop or time limit to the spread before you liquidate or roll ahead to a new contract.

- *Define spread objectives.* The most important risk control on long straddle and strangle positions is to clearly outline why you are placing the trade. If the trade is designed as a hedge or an outright investment on short-term market fundamentals, then make the trade based on that event. If you are not satisfied with the outcome of the fundamental news and the market doesn't react as strongly as expected, there is one rule that applies—take your small loss and get out. Years of trading have demonstrated clearly that the bad trade usually gets worse and very rarely gets better. Preserve capital and live to fight another day. You can hold a bad trade until it wins in the underlying stocks, bonds, and futures. You cannot do so with a time-sensitive and volatility-sensitive instrument like an option or a long option spread. While you are waiting for the value of the options to recover, time is ticking away at your investment. If you are willing to risk the entire premium, then by all means set the trade and forget it; let it ride and see what happens. If you do not have that trading profile, then don't be afraid to admit that a trade is not working and move on. When you are stuck in a bad trade, it can feel like you have an anchor hanging from your neck, and it is very difficult to see the market with the correct perspective. Liquidating clears the air and opens up new opportunities. Avoid holding obvious losing trades, as you will likely miss a better opportunity.

Short Straddles

Then you sell or short a straddle, you are selling a put and a call with the same underlying in the same contract month. Selling a short straddle takes all the disadvantages of the long straddle position and turns them to your favor. You also accept all the advantages of the long straddle as risk. The short straddle puts the inevitable time value decay on your side as well as any chance for collapsing implied volatility, but the risk factor is the potential for a major price change on the underlying asset or a major upward spike in implied volatility.

To demonstrate the short straddle, let's look at the option chain for McDonalds, Inc. (MCD) in Figure 7.20. In the option chain we can see that the underlying market is trading at 56.64, which makes the at-the-money call and put option at the 57.5 strike price. In contrast to the long straddle positions, short straddles are ideally done with fewer than 100 days before expiration, thus providing increased theta over the longer-term options. Long-term straddles offer substantial premium, but the fundamental changes to the underlying company or instrument and wholesale market changes are more difficult to predict. These trades can be also done just days before expiration or as a volatility capture ahead of a report, news announcement, or other fundamental event that may have inflated implied volatility in advance.

If we sell five of the 57.5 put options for 5.76 and five of the 57.5 call options for 4.08 in the June expiration, we capture a total

Actuals	MCD Common			Legend								
	56.64	+0.29	Trade	Last	Chg							
Options	MAY <43>						JUN <78>					
	MktPr	MIV	Delta	Gamma	Theta	Vega	MktPr	MIV	Delta	Gamma	Theta	Vega
70.0 calls							0.92	27.7%	20.6	3.36	-0.81	9.50
67.5 calls	..s..											
65.0 calls	0.45	27.0%	15.6	4.01	-0.97	5.50	1.36	28.1%	28.5	3.72	-0.99	11.7
62.5 calls	0.90	28.3%	26.2	5.09	-1.42	7.78	2.04	29.3%	37.2	3.86	-1.18	13.5
60.0 calls	1.60	29.4%	38.9	5.50	-1.80	9.52	2.97	30.7%	46.1	3.77	-1.35	14.6
57.5 calls>	2.69	31.7%	52.0	5.22	-2.11	10.3	4.08	32.1%	54.9	3.50	-1.46	15.1
57.5 puts>	4.01	31.6%	-48.0	5.22	-2.08	10.3	5.76	31.4%	-45.1	3.50	-1.37	15.1
55.0 puts	2.86	33.3%	-35.8	4.45	-2.15	10.1	4.56	32.9%	-36.9	3.10	-1.42	14.9
52.5 puts	2.01	35.4%	-25.6	3.48	-2.08	9.18	3.61	34.6%	-29.5	2.63	-1.42	14.1
50.0 puts	1.40	37.9%	-17.7	2.43	-1.89	7.83	2.81	36.2%	-23.2	2.15	-1.37	12.9
47.5 puts	.....		-12.1	1.70	-1.65	6.37	.....		-17.9	1.70	-1.28	11.4

Figure 7.20 MCD option chain—Powered by Option Vue 6

combined premium of 9.84. Breakeven on the call side of this position is calculated by adding the total premium to the 57.5 strike price:

$$57.50 + 9.84 = 66.34$$

The put side breakeven is reached by subtracting the total captured premium from the strike price:

$$57.50 - 9.84 = 47.66$$

Now let's look at the model in Figure 7.21 to see how the profit and loss of a short option position looks. In the figure we can see the profit and loss of the MCD 57.5 short straddle. The model is the inverse of the long straddle in that your profitability is between the two breakeven points we just calculated. Time value also works in your favor; the dashed line takes a fairly good distance of market movement before crossing breakeven into negative territory. The pinnacle of the triangle is of course the strike price of both options.

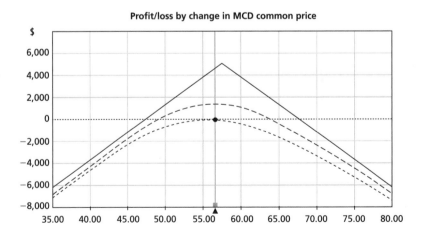

Figure 7.21 MCD short straddle—Powered by Option Vue 6

This would occur if the underlying asset was to expire at a price of 57.5 leaving both options in the money.

The nice thing about a straddle is that the amount of premium captured can create a significant range on the chart between breakeven points. To put this into perspective, look at the MCD daily chart in Figure 7.22. In the shaded area we have displayed the approximate area between the breakeven points on this straddle.

The chart represents over one year of daily movement for the underlying stock, and the straddle premium breakeven is nearly outside the entire market range.

Short Strangles

The *short strangle* is created by selling put and call options with the same underlying contract and in the same expiration contract, but with different strike prices. The strangle has the same risk profile as a straddle and the goal of the strangle is to capitalize on

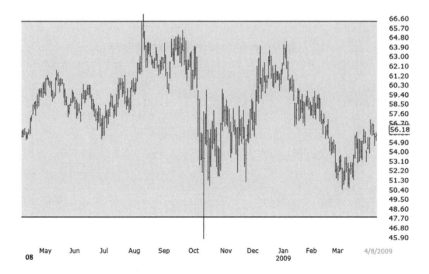

Figure 7.22 MCD daily chart

volatility and time value decay while having a position farther away from the current market than the straddle. Unlike the long strangle, you would not want to be utilizing in-the-money positions for the short strangle. The trade needs to be entirely extrinsic value and be typically the farthest away from the current market so that you can achieve a reasonable premium.

Let's look at a model of the short strangle using MCD Options again. (See Figure 7.20 above.) If we consider selling five of the June MCD 65 call options and five of the June MCD 50-put options for a combined premium of 4.17. We take in a total premium of $2,085. We can calculate our breakeven by adding the combined premium to the call option strike price of 65, so the upside breakeven is now 69.17. On the downside the breakeven is 45.83, leaving us a range in which the trade has profitability minus trading costs between these two points. If we look at the model for this trade in Figure 7.23, we can see a similar pattern to the short straddle with the familiar flat area between the two strike prices.

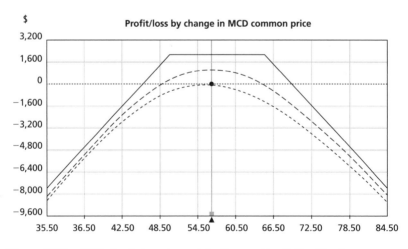

Figure 7.23   MCD short strangle model—Powered by Option Vue 6

You can see the maximum profit represented in the expiration line between the two strike prices and decreasing profits on each side of the market. The dashed line, representing halfway between expiration and inception, and the dotted line, representing no time value decay, show clearly that the trade could quickly go against your position and increase in value. The strangle strategy has unlimited risk on the call side of the trade, and risk that is limited only by the underlying asset trading to zero on the put side of the equation.

Short Neutral Delta Summary

As with every trade, the short neutral delta trading strategy has negative aspects. The risks of upward changes in implied volatility are significant. In addition, when placing short straddles or strangles based on trading ranges like those demonstrated in the MCD examples, the trading ranges are meant to be broken, and the short straddle or strangle trader will have to make quick decisions regarding the risk of the trade and the probability of success.

Some of the important points to consider when trading short straddle and strangle positions include:

- Short neutral delta positions function most effectively in the accelerated time value of short-term expiration contracts. Long-term positions are certainly acceptable as long as the premium captured justifies the risk undertaken for the term of the contract.
- Elevated implied volatility relative to the recent historical volatility is preferred for short option positions, especially neutral delta short option positions. Changes in implied

volatility against the position can quickly skew the premium thus offsetting time value decay and creating losses for the position.

- Short neutral delta strategies are not guaranteed winners from time value alone, just like the individual options themselves. The risk of the underlying trading quickly outside the trading range is significant during the term of the option position. The trading range demonstrated by the MCD chart, Figure 7.22, could be easily penetrated at any time to either side without warning from fundamental or wholesale market changes.

- Successful short option trading relies on good research into the underlying asset and potential changes that could affect the security in price and volatility as well as issues that could affect the entire sector of the market pertaining to the option in question. When trading individual stocks or futures with short neutral delta strategies, the individual security is susceptible to broad market risk as well.

Risk control for short neutral delta strategies varies depending on the risk tolerance and trading expertise of the seller. Some of the strategies we covered for long neutral delta are valid for the short side of the market as well. In addition:

- *Monetary stops.* Decide what premium increase your risk tolerance will allow. Set a spread premium stop at that point.
- *Volatility stops.* Your stop in this case will be based on a volatility increase rather than a decrease.
- *Underlying asset price.* Because the short neutral delta strategies have unlimited risk based on the underlying asset

movement, we can consider utilizing a stop position based on pricing or delta. The delta of the position at placement is designed to be delta-neutral or delta-zero. If the delta on one side of the position becomes significant, then the entire premium is at risk. We can look at the gamma of the underlying asset and add the gamma amount to the delta for each dollar of price movement in order to achieve a rough estimation of the new delta for each option as the price moves. Remember this is compounded, not simple addition. You are adding the gamma amount to each new delta calculation. If the delta of one side of the trade crosses 70 percent, there is not likely to be much premium remaining in the opposing option. If the market continues to move toward that side of the equation, the delta will eventually reach 1.00 against your position.

- *Rolling options.* The next step in risk protection on neutral delta strategies is commonly taught as the best method for managing neutral option risk. Rolling options in fact is an advanced strategy which requires constant market attention, advanced options analysis, and low trading rates. We'll begin discussing rolling options for short neutral delta strategies with a warning about the risks of rolling options to maintain neutral delta. When you place a straddle, strangle, or other neutral delta strategy variation such as the condor or butterfly spread we will be demonstrating, you have placed multiple positions in the market, sometimes at a ratio to one side or the other. In order to maintain a neutral delta in a changing market, the options must be adjusted or rolled to offsetting delta positions. In the MCD short straddle example, Figure 7.23, we have neutral delta to begin the trade, and if the market were to fall significantly, the delta of the 57.5 put option would increase at a significant rate. The 57.5 call option would lose value and delta against the 57.5 put option. The delta of the position would become skewed to the short side fairly quickly and increase rapidly as the market fell. To maintain the offsetting delta, the 57.5 call option would have to be liquidated, and a lower call option would have to be sold to return to neutral delta, or both options would have to be liquidated and replaced with lower strike prices. You have your original two transaction commissions, and now you have added four more—two to liquidate and two to originate the new spread. We are up to six commissions and are likely in the hole on the total premium unless volatility drops significantly. Let's say you go ahead and roll down in steady volatility and replace the 57.5 strike prices with a 50.0 strike price straddle. You are now back to neutral delta, and we'll say hypothetically that you regained your original premium level by the transaction. If MCD fell to 46, would you add an additional four commissions to the total costs of trading and maybe retain your original premium? The risk would be substantial to do so. If the market returns to the uptrend in conditions of increasing implied volatility rolling back the other direction to maintain neutral delta continues to increase the number of commissions and you would have to be able to react fast enough to roll back the other way and maintain the constant delta neutral. In decreasing implied volatility conditions, the chances of maintaining the premium level are very small. By the time you add up the brokerage commissions and what is likely to be some losses from the option positions you could have a substantial loss from a position with limited profit potential. If you are going to attempt advanced strategies such as rolling spreads, quality analysis software is absolutely necessary. This assessment is not a discouragement of rolling as much as a warning to be aware of the risks of traders and experts telling that it is a simple and easy risk protection in short option trading. Large capital and floor traders do not necessarily pay the same level of commissions that a retail or smaller level trader may incur. This leaves the small investor with a false sense of the costs involved in rolling positions when looking at hypothetical or simulated trading results or even actual results from professional option traders.

- Of all these strategies, we most often recommend a monetary stop with small investors. And if rolling trades are going to be a risk control method, we want to be rolling in steady or increasing volatility conditions to improve the premium captured with each roll. The monetary stop is often used in neutral delta trades as a percentage of the premium captured. In other words, if the spread premium captured on the short spread increases by 50 or 100 percent or more, the spread would be subject to liquidation for risk control. For example, if we capture $2.50 a share from a short spread, liquidation point on a 200% stop would be when the premium exceeds $5.00 per share. This is often referred to as a *double the premium stop*. The monetary stop method significantly improves the control for the small investor. It is typical that if a short option spread doubles against you, there is a significant change in trend in the market that may be counter to neutral delta trading.

Chapter 8

WINGSPREADS

W*ingspreads* are an advanced adaptation of some of the spreads we discussed in Chapters 6 and 7. These spreads are called wingspreads because, when you lay out the spread, you are creating two options close together that make up the body of the spread and two options on the outside that become the wings to the spread. Wingspreads are part of the neutral delta or nondirectional family of spreads and are designed to take advantage of ranges of market trading, volatility, and time value decay.

Butterfly Spread

There are several variations on butterfly spreads traded today. Butterfly spreads vary slightly in design from equity options trading, interest rate trading, and commodity option trading. We focus on a couple of common option variations of the butterfly. Butterfly spreads are not specifically neutral delta spreads, but they are frequently very close to neutral delta with a very small long or short delta depending on the spread.

Long butterfly spreads are created by purchasing a premium close to the current market while selling a ratio to that premium on an out-of-the-money strike price, creating a ratio spread of one long to two short. To finish the butterfly, the ratio is covered by another purchased option that is an equal distance from the short strike prices. The long butterfly creates a window of profit potential with limited risk and low premium exposure. Let's look at an example to help you understand the construction of the butterfly spread.

Using the option chain shown in Figure 8.1, let's assume a hypothetical purchase of five of the July IBM 100 call options at 9.44 along with the sale of ten July IBM 110 call options for 4.75 and finally the purchase of five July 120 call options for 1.93, giving us a total combined option premium of 1.87. The combined delta of the position is approximately 1.2 percent long, very near neutral delta.

Calculating breakeven on a long call butterfly spread is accomplished by taking the total premium of the spread and adding it to the closer-to-the-market long call strike price:

$$100 \text{ strike price} + 1.93 \text{ premium} = 101.93 \text{ underlying breakeven}$$

Actuals	IBM Common			Legend								
	102.22	+1.40	Trade	Last	Chg							
Options	JUL <106>						OCT <197>					
130 calls	MktPr	MIV	Delta	Gamma	Theta	Vega	MktPr	MIV	Delta	Gamma	Theta	Vega
125 calls	1.15	32.3%	15.4	1.47	-1.84	12.1	2.80	32.5%	25.5	1.47	-1.86	22.4
120 calls	1.93	33.3%	22.8	1.77	-2.45	15.7	4.00	33.6%	32.3	1.59	-2.20	25.4
115 calls	3.14	34.8%	31.6	2.03	-3.10	18.8	5.49	34.8%	39.7	1.63	-2.48	27.8
110 calls	4.75	36.2%	41.4	2.11	-3.59	20.9	7.30	35.9%	47.3	1.61	-2.70	29.2
105 calls	6.89	37.9%	51.5	2.04	-3.94	21.8	9.49	37.2%	54.8	1.52	-2.85	29.7
100 calls>	9.44	39.4%	61.2	1.84	-4.03	21.5	11.99	38.4%	62.1	1.39	-2.89	29.1
105 puts	10.16	38.1%	-48.5	2.04	-3.90	21.8	13.14	37.4%	-45.2	1.52	-2.75	29.7
100 puts>	7.77	39.9%	-38.8	1.84	-4.02	21.5	10.65	38.7%	-38.0	1.39	-2.81	29.1
95 puts	5.80	41.6%	-30.0	1.57	-3.92	20.0	8.55	40.2%	-31.2	1.22	-2.78	27.7
90 puts	4.25	43.6%	-22.5	1.27	-3.64	17.8	6.80	41.7%	-25.2	1.04	-2.67	25.6
85 puts	3.11	45.9%	-16.6	0.95	-3.28	15.2	5.36	43.5%	-19.9	0.85	-2.51	23.0
80 puts	2.20	48.0%	-11.9	0.71	-2.81	12.5	4.14	45.3%	-15.5	0.68	-2.29	20.1
75 puts	1.53	50.3%	-8.39	0.51	-2.33	9.88	3.11	46.8%	-11.9	0.53	-2.01	17.2

Figure 8.1 IBM butterfly option chain—Powered by Option Vue 6

Since we created a ratio spread and covered the outside with a call option, we now have limited risk, but also limited profit potential. The top side breakeven for the market is calculated by subtracting the captured premium from the outside purchased call options:

120 strike price − 1.93 premium = 118.07 underlying breakeven

Essentially the butterfly is a combination of a bull call spread and a short credit spread with the short options at the same strike price.

We can see a model of the profit and loss for this trade in Figure 8.2. Remember that this trade is a five lot, so the maximum risk is the 1.93 premium paid multiplied by the five contracts. The triangle in the center of the figure represents the maximum profit on the position, which is substantial given the premium risk. In this case the risk to reward is 1:4. Anywhere between the two breakeven points the butterfly spread has profit at expiration with the maximum occurring at the 110 strike price.

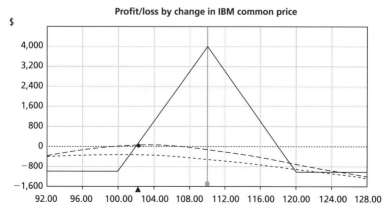

Figure 8.2 IBM long call butterfly model — Powered by Option Vue 6

Butterfly spreads are designed for expiration; this is not a spread you can expect to be seeing an immediate return on investment. You are establishing a window for the market to expire in a certain range, and you have profit potential within that range. If you look at the dotted line representing no time decay and the dashed line which represents the midpoint to expiration, you can see that little change in value can be expected until the time value has eroded from the short option position.

Butterfly spreads can be adjusted, but you must consider that you just paid four commissions per spread in applying the trade. Rolling options positions will add commission charges as well as any premium additions to the breakeven. You would have to have a specific reason for considering rolling a butterfly where some assurance of the projected expiration of the market would justify the expense. The spread is designed to take your best analysis of the future of the market price and give you a range in which right as in correct the market.

It is not uncommon, however, to leg out of a butterfly spread, especially if the options are significantly in the money or out of the money. In the IBM example above, let's just assume that IBM stock has radically dropped and that the short 110 call options are just a few cents in value. You can make the decision to buy these two options back and still maintain your limited risk profile. With the 100 call options bought back, you can subtract the profit gained from the purchase liquidation of the short call options from the total premium spent on the long call options and give the underlying stock or futures position an opportunity to come back and build value in the long option positions. It is best to consider this only when the majority of the premium has been extracted from the short call option position and when it will not substantially increase the overall premium outlay.

Long Put Butterfly

The long put butterfly creates the same window of opportunity as the long call butterfly, only on the short side of the market. To create the long put butterfly, you are purchasing a put option close to the current market, selling a 2:1 ratio of out-of -the-money put options and buying a further out-of-the-money put option at an even distance from the short put options. With the put butterfly, your short option strike price should be selected to provide a credit to apply to the cover put position.

Let's go back to the IBM option chain and create the long put butterfly. This model (shown in Figure 8.1) is created on a one-lot basis and demonstrates the risk versus reward. Remember, it doesn't matter if the purchase is 1, 100, or 1,000 options; the model remains the same with profit and loss adjusted for quantity.

If we purchase one July IBM 100 put option for 7.77 while selling two of the July 90 put options for 4.25 and then purchase one July IBM 80 put option for 2.20, we have a combined spread premium of 1.47.

Calculating breakeven for the spread, you take the combined premium and subtract it from the at-the-money put option. This gives you an initial breakeven of 98.53 on the underlying IBM stock:

100 put strike price – 1.47 combined premium = 98.53

And on the lower end you add the combined premium to the lowest purchased strike price which is the 80 put:

80 put strike price + 1.47 = 81.47

Like the long call butterfly, the long put butterfly is designed to work toward expiration, and significant gains are not likely until the time value of the short put options is reduced.

In the model shown in Figure 8.3, we can see the same profit window with the underlying price decreasing on the horizontal axis. The maximum risk to the spread is established on both ends with the time value decay and market price reduction maximizing at the 90 strike price at expiration.

The advantage to the butterfly spread is the limited risk of trade. The maximum risk is established with the purchased premium plus costs of trading, and it is not a trade that needs adjusting unless the trader has sufficient reason to believe that the market has found a direction.

The spread can be applied with the anticipation of the market moving within a certain range between the present and expiration. If market fundamentals change or a technical trend develops that will take the market outside the range of the butterfly during the term of the trade, one or more options can be liquidated in order

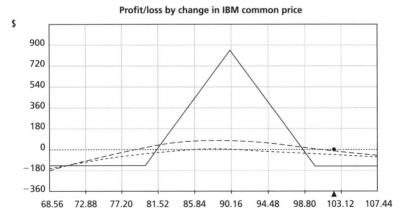

Figure 8.3   Long put butterfly—Powered by Option Vue 6

for the trader to take a direction on the market. If the short options are liquidated, then, just like the call spread, the profit or loss from the short option trade would be applied to the long premium of both purchased put options.

Butterfly spreads can be placed on both sides of the market to create a double butterfly which is one spread on each side of the market to capture a very wide range the with limited premium outlay and limited risk. If we take both examples of the IBM butterfly and combine the trades in a model, it will look like the chart shown in Figure 8.4.

The model in the figure shows the butterfly spread on both sides of the current market with limited risk across the trade. The difficulty with multiple strategies like this is that we have not yet accounted for the six to eight (options on futures are charged individually) commissions generated, and the risk-to-reward ratio has already dropped to less than 1:2. Whenever you are considering multiple option strategies such as the butterfly spread, always take into account the risk-to-reward ratio.

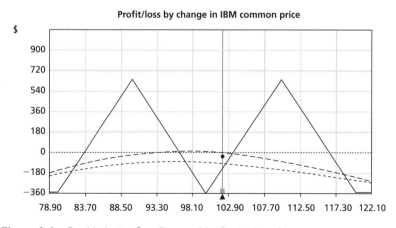

Figure 8.4 Double butterfly—Powered by Option Vue 6

Long Butterfly Strategy and Summary

When you are trading long butterfly spreads, always consider whether there is a reasonable probability that the underlying market will remain or move to the range of the butterfly at or near expiration. Butterfly spreads can be very effective in high volatility markets because you are selling an inflated premium which can be used to reduce the costs of the money option purchase over time, without having to take on the additional unlimited risk of a ratio spread.

The butterfly spread can allow you to take advantage of selling high implied volatility options in limited risk. It can provide a further advantage when the implied volatility of the at-the-money and near-the-money options is lower than the out-of-the money options. You should be looking for out-of-the-money options that may be inflated in anticipation of an upcoming market event, but that anticipation is not based on expectations of a large market move.

Situations in which the implied volatility of the options is significantly affected can potentially skew the value of the options during the term of the butterfly and cause negative equity on the spread for the intermediate time. Be aware that theses spreads have that potential margin risk in increasing volatility.

Butterfly spreads that have excellent implied volatility on inception may achieve zero premium outlay. We tracked a wheat spread at 60 cents per bushel and were able to apply even premium. The implied volatility held so strongly through the term of the spread that even though the wheat market had remained inside the window of the butterfly for most of the 90-day term, the spread gained no value until immediately before expiration. A spread of this nature would normally have a positive premium requirement at inception, and often, as time decreases, the volatility value will reduce leaving some profitability, especially if the underlying trades near the short premium. The spread worked out well, but the ability of high volatility markets to cling to value is sometimes remarkable and should not be discouraging.

Risk control on a butterfly is fairly straightforward, but here are some helpful hints on using butterfly spreads:

- It is a limited risk purchased premium spread. Plan on risking the entire premium on the spread.
- Apply butterfly spreads with as low a premium cost as possible. Try to keep your risk to reward above at least 1:3. A ratio of 1:4 risk to reward is preferred and is a sign of better than average volatility on the short option premium.
- Be aware that liquidating one or more options without liquidating the entire spread will expose the trade to risk that may not be limited.
- Be patient with these spreads; they can be very successful if they are left to do what they are designed to do at expiration.
- Make sure you are calculating your commission costs and premium into the spread breakeven prices.

At expiration if the trade is not liquidated prior to the expiration date, long butterfly spreads can have some interesting combinations of possibilities:

- If the original at-the-money option is the only in the money at expiration, the trade will be assigned the represented shares or futures contract, and the remaining options will expire leaving exposure of the outright shares or contract. If the option is a call option, you will be responsible for the purchase of the shares or the long futures position margin. If it is a put option, you will have the margin requirement for a short market position.

- If the at-the-money option and short options are in the money, then the long option and one short option (if it is a 2:1 butterfly) will be assigned their representative positions on the underlying asset, but they offset each other. The remaining short option, if it is a call option, would be assigned a short position, while the short put option would be assigned a long position on the underlying asset.
- If all four options in the examples are in the money, then all the options will be assigned their respective underlying positions, but they will offset each other as you would have two longs and two shorts.
- If all the options are out of the money at the time of expiration, then all would expire as worthless and the entire premium plus costs of trading would be lost.

Iron Butterfly Spreads

The iron butterfly is another variation on neutral delta, neutral market spreads. Truly the spread is nothing more than a protected short straddle. You can look at it as an at-the-money credit spread on both sides of the market. To create the iron butterfly, you are selling an at-the-money put and at-the-money call while buying an out-of-the-money put and an out-of-the-money call. The idea behind the iron butterfly is to capitalize on reductions in implied volatility with limited risk. If option implied volatility is high, then the short option premium may have the potential to be reduced against the long options during the term of the option spread.

To demonstrate the iron butterfly, let's look at the SPDR S&P 500 exchange-traded fund (SPY) option chain shown in Figure 8.5. In the figure we can see that the SPY is trading at 84.26 which makes the 85 call and put the at-the-money options. If we consider selling the May SPY 85 call option for 4.00 and the May SPY 85 put option for 4.70, we capture a total short premium of 8.70. Along with the short we would purchase out-of-the-money cover positions for each option by buying the May SPY 95 call option for .72 and the May SPY 75 put option for 1.46, thus giving us a total premium capture of 6.52.

The combined theta on the trade is the key to success with the iron butterfly. You should consider the iron butterfly for short-term expiration options to take advantage of the accelerated time value under the 60-day mark. In this case the combined theta of the shorts is greater than −10.0, while the combined theta being lost daily is around −7.0. The iron butterfly takes advantage of time value decay. It also takes advantage of decreases in vega during the term of the trade. If implied volatility collapses, the short option

Actuals	SPY Common			Legend								
	84.26	+0.83	Trade	Last	Chg							
Options	MAY <43>						JUN <78>					
110 calls	MktPr	MIV	Delta	Gamma	Theta	Vega	MktPr	MIV	Delta	Gamma	Theta	Vega
105 calls	0.12		1.40	0.28	-0.62	1.71	0.34	31.5%	5.03	0.77	-1.01	4.88
100 calls	0.22	30.9%	4.63	0.82	-1.22	4.00	0.84	33.3%	10.9	1.39	-1.82	8.35
95 calls	0.72	32.5%	11.9	1.81	-2.59	7.24	1.73	34.8%	20.1	2.06	-2.67	11.9
90 calls	1.94	35.2%	25.2	3.34	-4.23	10.3	3.16	36.4%	31.9	2.59	-3.39	14.5
85 calls>	4.00	37.6%	44.2	4.21	-5.09	11.5	5.25	38.3%	45.2	2.82	-3.81	15.4
80 calls	7.00	40.5%	63.6	3.91	-4.97	10.4	8.35	42.5%	58.5	2.73	-4.02	14.6
90 puts	7.85	37.0%	-74.8	3.34	-4.46	10.3	9.65	36.9%	-68.1	2.59	-3.41	14.5
85 puts>	4.70	37.4%	-55.8	4.21	-5.02	11.5	6.69	38.3%	-54.8	2.82	-3.77	15.4
80 puts	2.66	39.9%	-36.4	3.91	-4.85	10.4	4.40	39.9%	-41.5	2.73	-3.73	14.6
75 puts	1.46	43.4%	-21.7	2.69	-4.02	7.94	2.81	42.3%	-29.7	2.37	-3.37	12.5
70 puts	0.74	46.6%	-12.3	1.77	-2.88	5.36	1.72	44.8%	-20.0	1.87	-2.79	9.81
65 puts	0.38	50.6%	-6.65	1.06	-1.93	3.31	1.05	48.0%	-12.8	1.36	-2.18	7.10

Figure 8.5 SPY option chain — Powered by Option Vue 6

vega will outpace the long option loss and create the potential for profits prior to expiration.

Now let's look at the model for this trade in Figure 8.6. This model looks exactly like a long butterfly spread. You have an area of maximum profit on the at-the-money strike price on the sold option premium and a maximum risk to the outside legs of the spread when either underlying price exceeds the protective option on the outside of the spread.

This spread is designed for high implied volatility so as to maximize profit potential and reduce risk on the spread. You should be cautious of the cost of these trades. You are creating four trades which means four commissions in either equities or options on futures. The commissions, in addition to minimal gains over the course of several spreads, can result in a false sense of success. One trade at the maximum loss can offset several winning spreads. A significant spike in implied volatility will also cause the premium on the spread to be out of line until the time value is exhausted and the volatility declines. Some traders recommend buying additional call or put

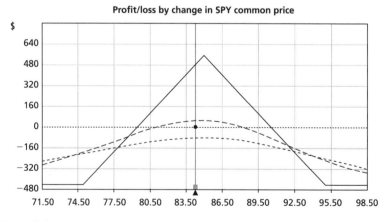

Figure 8.6 Iron butterfly SPY model—Powered by Option Vue 6

premiums on the outside of the trade to correct the delta in a major market move. This strategy may be successful if the market trends in the direction of the options quickly, but as with any short-term out-of-the-money option position purchase, the risk of decreasing volatility and accelerated time value decay is significant for these additional positions. Adding additional call premiums to the spread also has the potential for negating any profitability for the trade. The total reward of the iron butterfly can be fairly small, and adding an additional premium will increase risk and reduce reward if it is unsuccessful.

The iron butterfly differs from the long butterfly at expiration in that if the spread is placed at the money, some portion of the spread will be in the money if it is held to expiration. If both options on one side of the market are in the money, you will experience the maximum loss on the spread. The goal is to have the market between the protective strike prices at expiration. If the spread is held to expiration and the protective long option positions are not in the money, you will be assigned a long or short on the market depending on which side is in the money. You will need to be prepared for the cash and margin or outright margin of the assigned call or put options. Ideally, we would be looking to cash in on the time decay sometime shortly before expiration or right at expiration in order to avoid the exercise into the underlying.

The only time the exercise is preferred is if the value between the bid and offer on the options is disadvantageous to the spread. Sometimes with option positions, the volume can get thin and create a disparity between theoretical value and the current market price. It may be necessary to allow the option to be exercised and offset it immediately with the opposing underlying position.

The iron butterfly can also be reversed with the base of the trade being the long straddle rather than the short straddle. This would be the opposite position to the iron butterfly in that you are buying in a period of extremely low implied volatility and in a market that has a defined trading range.

The reversed iron butterfly is created by buying the at-the-money call option and the at-the-money put option while selling premium on the outside of each option. It is essentially a bull call and bear put spread at the money.

The reversed iron butterfly can be difficult in high-volatility situations, similar to the long straddle because, if volatility declines, the short options on the outside of the spread will not likely offset the volatility loss. The reversed iron butterfly would not be a spread held to expiration unless both options on one side of the trade are in the money or at least one side is strongly in the money in order to recapture the long premium spent. The long iron butterfly is a debit spread with a maximum loss of the premium paid for the spread plus the costs of trading

Like the iron butterfly, the reversed iron butterfly generates four commission charges for the option position, and these must be added to the premium for applying the trade.

Iron Condors

The *iron condor* is another member of the wingspread group of neutral delta or near neutral trading strategies. Understanding the condor is fairly easy; the condor is an out-of-the-money credit spread on both sides of the market. The condor is created by selling an out-of-the-money call option while buying a call option that is farther from the market and selling an out-of-the-money put option while buying a farther out-of-the-money put. Each of these options is in the same underlying asset and the same contract expiration.

A favorite market for iron condor trading takes us to the Chicago Mercantile Exchange and the big board S&P 500 futures contract (Symbol: SP). The CME S&P 500 futures contract is an index contract on the S&P 500 with a very large contract size of 250 times the index price. The contract is sized as a hedge instrument for large portfolios and is used by individual and commercial traders. If the S&P 500 index is trading at 1,000, then the contract represents $250,000 worth of S&P 500 index stocks per contract. The advantage to this contract for the iron condor is the substantial premium on the options. The disadvantage to this contract is that you trade this one with limited risk positions unless you have really deep pockets.

A chart for the big S&P 500 is shown in Figure 8.7. You can see from the chart that implied volatility remains fairly high in comparison to history and that there is somewhat of a trading range developing in the last couple of months before this capture. The ideal situation for neutral short trading spreads is high volatility with a reasonable probability of remaining within a trading range. The high-volatility activity in the market makes probability forecasts more difficult and less accurate with the wide trading ranges created.

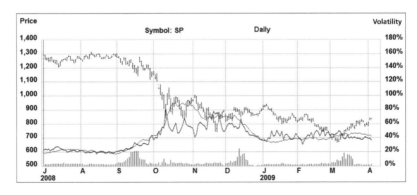

Figure 8.7 CME S&P 500 Futures (SP) chart—Powered by Option Vue 6

Futures	JUN <77>		SEP <168>		DEC <259>		MAR <350>		
	840.00	+4.50	833.00	+0.90	829.10	....	Last	Chg	Trade
Options	MAY <43>					JUN <77>			
870 calls	MktPr	MIV	Delta	Gamma	Theta	Vega	MktPr	MIV	Delta	Gamma	Theta	Vega
865 calls	30.60	36.0%	35.3	0.34	-119	284	45.70	36.8%	39.5	0.27	-91.7	383
860 calls	32.80	36.1%	36.9	0.34	-120	286	46.30	35.8%	40.7	0.27	-89.5	384
855 calls	35.10	36.4%	38.6	0.35	-122	287	50.40	37.1%	42.0	0.27	-93.0	384
850 calls	37.50	36.6%	40.3	0.36	-123	287	50.00	35.5%	43.3	0.27	-88.8	384
845 calls	39.90	36.8%	42.0	0.36	-124	287	53.30	36.2%	44.6	0.27	-90.5	384
840 calls>	42.50	37.0%	43.7	0.37	-124	287	55.80	36.3%	45.9	0.28	-90.6	383
845 puts	49.70	40.9%	-58.0	0.36	-137	287	65.50	40.9%	-55.4	0.27	-102	384
840 puts>	47.30	41.2%	-56.3	0.37	-138	287	63.00	41.0%	-54.1	0.28	-102	383
835 puts	44.30	40.8%	-54.6	0.37	-136	286	60.10	40.9%	-52.8	0.28	-101	382
830 puts	42.70	41.7%	-52.8	0.38	-138	284	57.80	41.1%	-51.5	0.28	-102	380
825 puts	40.50	41.9%	-51.1	0.38	-138	282	55.90	41.5%	-50.2	0.28	-102	378
820 puts	38.50	42.2%	-49.4	0.38	-138	279	53.70	41.6%	-48.9	0.28	-102	375
815 puts	36.50	42.4%	-47.6	0.38	-137	276	51.50	41.8%	-47.6	0.28	-101	372

Figure 8.8   CME S&P 500 Futures option chain—Powered by Option Vue 6

We can use the option chain in Figure 8.8 to construct our condor spread. The options listed are $250 per point, and we would typically be looking at an option spread that is much wider than what is displayed so as to allow the market significant trading room, but we can get down the basics of the spread. We consider selling the May options because of the accelerated time decay and decreased time for the market to break outside the trading range. Assume a sale of the May 855 call option at 35.10 and the purchase of the May 865 call at 30.60 while selling the May 825 put for 40.50 and buying the May 815 put for 36.50. On the call side we net a credit of 4.50, and on the put side we net a credit of 4.00 for a total credit of 8.50. Our maximum risk is the distance between the two strike prices on either side of the market minus the premium captured, so in this case our maximum risk is 1.50 × $250 or $375 plus costs of trading four option positions. The maximum profit in this example is 8.50 × $250 or $2,125. The risk-to-reward ratio on this condor is exceptional. Let's look at a model of the iron condor for profit and loss in Figure 8.9. The model shows the maximum risk on both sides of the spread if the price was out of the range of the purchased option strike prices.

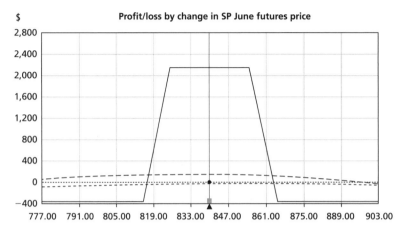

Figure 8.9   CME S&P 500 condor model—Powered by Option Vue 6

The flat spot at the top of the model represents the maximum profit from the position between the two short strike prices.

This example is hypothetical and based on the settlements for all the options on the day of the capture. Placing an iron condor spread with this advantageous a premium is not terribly likely, although it is possible in the right volatility conditions The real bid-and-offer process for executing this trade would have a natural spread between the bid and offer for each option which may make the spread premium capture less and the overall risk higher.

The iron condor can be placed as one order, or you can leg into the spread by creating each of the credit spreads separately. In a high-risk market like the S&P, you should not be trading naked on any side of the market unless you have the ability to carry the full risk of the S&P 500 futures contract. Be prepared for the full risk of the underlying asset if you are legging into a spread. The difficulty with legging is that markets move quickly and could remove any chance of profitability if the underlying changes price before the trade is covered.

Iron Condor Strategy and Summary

To successfully utilize the iron condor there are a few factors to keep in mind,

- With the iron condor we are looking for elevated implied volatility and a market with a reasonably defined trading range. Also we like to see probabilities of under 30 percent for hitting the outside strike prices, so make sure your condor is wide enough to account for the trading range.
- Condors have multiple commissions and fees that must be calculated into the breakeven. The effect of the commission on the breakeven will be greater in futures trading because each option generates a commission, and in equity trading the commissions will increase in trades that represent over 1,000 shares in most cases.
- Risk for a condor should be considered as the entire spread on one side of the trade plus costs of trading. You can certainly set any of the risk strategies we have discussed for the condor, from monetary stops to a percentage of the premium, but be prepared for slippage resulting from liquidating four options at the market on a stop.
- Make sure your risk-to-reward ratio doesn't exceed 3:1 on the iron condor. If your risk is higher than three times the premium captured, you are not creating enough premium or selling enough volatility. The trade demonstrated is the opposite of this, but it is not common for the reward potential to be substantially higher than the total risk in a short wingspread.

- Avoid the "fix it" trap. So many traders roll sides of the condor this way and that trying to "fix" the spread and keep it neutral. When you roll to fix the spread, you are liquidating one side of the position, likely at a loss, to adjust to a more distant strike price. Making an adjustment to the spread to widen the range can be done, but you must have adequate reason to believe that the market will return to the trading range and that you will be able to create enough premium to make up for the loss and the additional commissions and fees. Micromanaging spreads is one of the biggest mistakes that novice traders make. Advanced strategy trading in volatile markets means you will have to exercise discipline in risk management.

- Another common error for traders is when they reach a risk point on the condor on one side of the spread, they will remove only one side instead of the entire spread hoping to capture the remaining premium. Markets can cycle, and you may end up with the remaining credit spread in a losing position. Make certain that, if you remove only one side of the spread, you have adequate technical or fundamental justification for the market to continue away from the remaining short spread or that the spread is close enough to expiration to have little or no chance to reverse enough to endanger the other spread. Most often the largest losses on condor spreads result from being hit on both sides from market fluctuation

- Be patient with the spread; it is limited risk, and the reason for making sure you understand that you should be prepared to risk the full amount of the credit spread on one side is that markets cycle up and down. It will bounce around, and if you understand your maximum risk, you will be more apt to allow the spread to function in the trading range and lose time value.

- Trade condors in the short term—normally we say under 60 days, but if you can find a decent premium on a 30-day or less condor, it is all the better. The less time on the trade, the less time the market has to adjust against your positions, and the more advanced the time decay will be on the position.

At expiration the condor is like the butterfly spread. If either of the short options is in the money, you will be assigned the underlying long for the short put or short for the short call. If you do not exit the spread at expiration, you will have the responsibility of the underlying asset cash or margin. If both options on one side are in the money, you will have experienced the maximum loss, and the assigned underlying assets will offset each other.

Double Diagonal

The last spread we cover is an evolution of the condor spread called the *double diagonal*. This spread is simply a condor spread with diagonal cover trades on the outside, meaning that the purchased options on the outside are in a different contract month. You can also look at this spread as a near-term strangle against a deferred strangle.

The best double diagonal is one placed with the short option in the near-term month and the long options in a deferred month. This takes advantage of accelerated time value decay on the front short options and the reduced time decay on the long options.

An example of the double diagonal is in the S&P example selling the May 855 call option for 35.10 and buying the June 865 call option for 45.70 while selling the May 825 put for 36.50 and buying the June 815 put for 51.50. Assuming that the market stayed within the range of the trade, you would capture 71.60 against the purchase of 97.20 on the deferred options.

The double diagonal is an excellent method of building premium against the long spread when the market stays within the range of the short options. The ideal scenario is this: once the time value has reduced or been exhausted from the short options, you would roll the short strangle forward to the next contract month to create the iron condor with some extra cash already built into the spread. This is an excellent method for increasing premium returns using the same cover trade positions one or more times. In the example we would need to capture only about 26.00 additional points between the two new June short options to create the iron condor for a credit.

This also gives the flexibility of having a reduced cost long strangle if the market is not in a position to short additional premium on the June.

For risk control on the double diagonal, typically you have to have the same risk control setup as for the iron butterfly or iron condor. For the double diagonal, however, it is not uncommon for traders to allow the near-term spread to be exercised and create a synthetic option with the deferred option position. As with the iron condor, you want to avoid too many rolls to "fix" the spread delta because you will accept the loss and costs of the roll and may not recover the premium.

The double diagonal is a high-volatility friendly spread, but if implied volatility collapses during the trade, the short near-term options may not have the vega to make up for the losses on the long option positions.

If you are trading a double diagonal spread using options on futures, you need to account for any basis difference between the underlying contract for the near-term options versus the deferred contract. There can be substantial price difference between futures contract that may cause the near-term strangle to be misaligned with the deferred. The example we used with the S&P is a futures-based spread, but it works beautifully because the May S&P options are serial options based on the June futures. This avoids basis differences between underlying contracts.

A common mistake for novice traders is to look at the long double diagonal spread as "free trade" by buying the near-term options at a lower premium and selling out-of-the-money deferred options at an equal or higher premium. The difficulty with this spread is that the Greeks are not in your favor. The volatility effect on the deferred short option is likely to be greater than the near term and thus create significant volatility risk. The theta will be much greater on the short-term purchased options causing the purchased options to lose value much faster regardless of the movement of the underlying asset.

Chapter 9

INDICES AND EXCHANGE-TRADED FUNDS

Index-based securities make up one of the largest trading markets, with instruments based on a wide variety of various indices from the Dow Industrials and S&P 500 to energy and gold. In simple terms an *index* is an average of a basket of stocks, bonds, commodities, or other securities averaged and calculated to a usable price. There are several types of indices, but the major indices reported as standards of market behavior fall in to two basic types:

- *Price-weighted index.* A price-weighted index generates value from the totaling of the share price of each component of the index usually divided by a divisor of some sort to balance the index for dividends and stock splits. The Dow Jones Industrial Average (DJIA) is an example of a price-weighted index. The 30 components of the DJIA are added together and divided by a divisor which is published frequently for investors to keep track of. A price-weighted index means that price changes in higher-value securities will have a greater effect on the index than will lower-value securities.

- *Market-capitalization–weighted index.* A market-capitalization–weighted index generates weighting scale from the total capitalization of its components. Companies with larger market value gain a higher weighting in the index than do smaller lower-cap companies. The S&P 500 is an example of a market-capitalization or market-value index. Many of these type of indices have changed slightly to become floating indices in which only the outstanding shares in play in the market are included. Restricted shares would remain out of the calculation. Like the price-weighted index, the total value of the outstanding shares of the index components are divided by a divisor published regularly. The divisor is designed to create a more manageable point or dollar value to the index. Without the divisor system, the point value for the S&P 500 might be ten or eleven digits. Cap-weighted indices can also be referred to as modified cap-weighted indices when there are limitations placed on the percentage a particular company may represent. Many of today's indices are a hybrid of float and modified cap.

There are other weighting standards for variations on the major indices such as total shares, earnings, and book value. There are also unweighted indices where the index assumes the same dollar amount invested in each component regardless of size.

Indices are also divided by their coverage area in the market:

- *Broad-based indices.* A broad based index covers a large group of securities across many sectors in the market. The S&P 500 and Russell 2000 are examples of broad-based indices. Broad-based indices are also considered major indicators for the overall economy worldwide. The impact of changes in the economy show up well in an average of the 500 top companies.

- *Narrow-based indices.* A narrow-based index covers a small sector or specific industry such as the Nasdaq Biotech Index which covers biotechnology and pharmaceutical companies. Narrow-based indices are useful to investors with interests in specific industries. The indices help them gauge the temperature of the industry rather than the overall economy. Many industries do well even in tough economic conditions. The chart from McDonald's earlier in the book (Chapter 7, Figure 7.22) demonstrates that well. Narrow indices help investors seeking opportunities to move funds from one sector to another or control risk on certain portions of their assets.

The components and weighting structure of the indices are published regularly and are readily available on the Internet. The major broad-based indices are reported on regularly in television and radio reports as is the overall action of the market, but the reports can be deceiving. It is interesting reading to take a look at an index like the S&P 500 and how the components measure up to one another. It is not uncommon for the top 10 components of the S&P 500 to represent a significant portion of the total index. The same is true in other indices where the top few companies represent a sizable percentage. As an index investor, it is important for you to know the structure of the index and which companies will cause dramatic changes in the index and which will have minimal effect.

In managing your portfolio, you should keep track of the weight ratio of these components because, as you invest in either broad- or narrow-based indices, each component could enhance the effect on investments already in your portfolio, for the good or bad. If you are already outright long Microsoft, then you should be aware of how much Microsoft you will be adding to your portfolio by adding a position in an index. Conversely, as we get into hedging the portfolio, you will need to understand how much offsetting value you receive on a particular security with the index position.

On cap-weighted or modified cap-weighted indices, finding out what the percentage of the individual stock represents is fairly easy. Determine the total market capitalization of the individual component, divide it by the total market capitalization of the index, and the result is the percentage.

The same would be true for price-weighted indices. Take the individual share price and divide it by the total share price of all components to obtain a percentage of the index. You can ignore the divisor here because it is the same denominator for each component.

Index Investing

If you are not familiar with index investing, there are three major methods of investing in indices. Most people are familiar with at least one of these, but we cover all three:

- *Index funds.* You can be a part of the whole index world by investing in one of hundreds of index-based mutual funds. Mutual funds pool funds from large groups of investors to invest in the components of the various indices. The investments are structured and are maintained at the same ratio as the structure of the index. Mutual funds tend to have some sort of maintenance fee or management fee, although few have front-end commissions any more. These funds often outperform their managed counterparts because investors follow the index rather than managing and trading within the fund. Index mutual funds have their disadvantages in that the net asset value (NAV) is calculated at the end of the day, and all transaction orders for that day are completed based on the end of day NAV. Mutual funds may not be traded intraday or sold short, and they do not have options associated with them. Some index funds allow small, regular, individual investments into the funds; but in general index funds are primarily funded by institutional money. The advantage to index mutual funds for individual and business investors is the long-term nature of the funds. Index funds are designed to as closely as possible represent the performance of the underlying index. Commonly the fees are not terribly out of line in comparison to managed mutual funds which may be attempting to outperform the market and have much larger expenses.

- *Exchange-traded funds (ETFs)*. We get into ETF trading a little further in the chapter, but the exchange-traded fund is another method of index investing. ETFs, like index mutual funds, are often track index securities, but the ETF is traded like a stock and will generate a commission. ETF shares can be traded intraday and have options capability that index funds do not.

- *Futures markets*. The major indices have futures contracts that are traded on the Chicago Mercantile Exchange (CME), the Chicago Board of Trade (CBOT), and the Chicago Board Options Exchange (CBOE). If you are working with a large portfolio or a larger-scale investment into the indices, the futures market offers significant bang for your buck. The leverage in the major indices in the futures contracts multiplies the value of the index by the contract rate. Currently the active contracts include many of the major indices including DJIA, S&P 500, Nasdaq, and Russell along with a host of smaller index contracts. In recent years as index trading has increased significantly on equity exchanges thus spreading index trading funds across a wider area, products like e-mini index futures have exploded in volume on commodity exchanges. These contracts have always been a haven for adrenalin junkie speculators, but they have become valuable as well as of option premium and portfolio management tools.

Exchange-Traded Funds

Exchange-traded funds (ETFs) are becoming widely utilized by individual and sophisticated investors alike. These securities have similarities to mutual funds and track broad and narrow indices alike. ETFs represent a basket of securities or commodities, but they differ from mutual funds in that the ETF is managed by the basket of securities tied closely to the index, not the whims of a fund manager. In addition, these unit investment trust-based products trade intraday like individual stocks and can be bought, sold, and day-traded like any other open market security. The value of the ETF is established by trade and end-of-the-day net asset value settlement. EFTs also have options that trade on the ETF as the underlying security. The options trade intraday as well and are building a strong market following. These options, like all options, carry risk.

The benefit to the ETF comes in the form of diversification. Investing in today's market and the markets of tomorrow means dealing with elevated volatility and elevated risk. It has been said that diversification is the best answer to controlling and reducing market risk and that the ETF constitutes built-in diversification by investing in a basket of securities or commodities. Some estimates put true diversification at over 50 stocks in today's volatile market. It can be difficult for investors to manage a portfolio that is truly diversified, especially when mixing growth-oriented objectives with income-oriented stability.

The ETF offers the ability to invest in both growth and income in a diversified fashion. ETF offerings come in income varieties with debt securities as the basket as well as dividend-yielding common or preferred stocks. There is little end to the usefulness of this diversification tool. Once you add the ability to capture premium, enhance growth, and/or manage risk with options in an ETF, you have an investment strategy all in itself.

A potential downside to trading in the ETF market is the current lack of direct regulatory supervision of the flow of money and day to day holdings within the ETF. It is likely that this will be looked at by regulatory agencies in the future which may increase costs. Mutual funds may have the advantage in this area as the regulatory structure is more established.

Index Options

Index options have been around for many years. The largest market for index options was initially the Chicago Mercantile Exchange (CME) contracts with the S&P 500 index futures and options. As the market grew, new products emerged and have blossomed into the large offering of option trading choices today.

These options trade in the same fashion as the equity and commodity options. Let's take a look at an example of a popular index and the options trading on that index. In Figure 9.1 we show the chart for the popular Nasdaq 100 index power shares ETF. You can see the daily activity of the QQQQ power shares Nasdaq 100 ETF. This pattern is nearly identical to the Nasdaq 100 chart in Figure 9.2.

In comparing the two charts, you can see that the actual differences are negligible, except for the price. The Nasdaq is trading at 1,373 in Figure 9.2 and the ETF is trading at 33.69 share value.

If we were to consider trying to play further upside in the QQQQ, but we want to have some distance between our price and the current market, we could take advantage of one of our spread strategies on a broad market index.

Using the option model shown in Figure 9.3 we could consider using a sell-buy-sell strategy to capture premium on both sides of the current market and give ourselves plenty of time for the Nasdaq to continue the upside trend. In the figure we show the option chain for QQQQ. If we assume a hypothetical position of

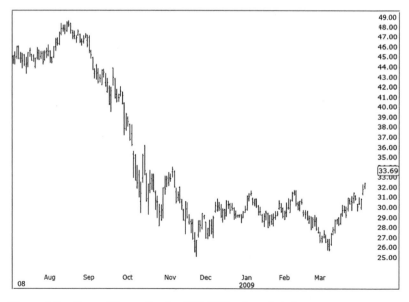

Figure 9.1   Power Shares Nasdaq 100 ETF—freestockcharts.com

Figure 9.2   Nasdaq 100 Index Chart—freestockcharts.com

Actuals	QQQQ Common			Legend									
		32.35	+0.59	Trade	Last	Chg							
Options			SEP <169>						DEC <260>				
39 calls	MktPr	MIV	Delta	Gamma	Theta	Vega	MktPr	MIV	Delta	Gamma	Theta	Vega	
38 calls	1.08	33.0%	29.4	5.16	-0.72	7.32	1.61	32.1%	36.9	4.70	-0.62	9.88	
37 calls	1.36	33.7%	34.3	5.37	-0.79	7.86	1.70	30.6%	41.2	4.71	-0.61	10.3	
36 calls	1.59	33.4%	39.4	5.48	-0.82	8.28	2.28	33.5%	45.6	4.67	-0.70	10.6	
35 calls	2.02	34.9%	44.6	5.47	-0.90	8.58	2.62	33.7%	49.9	4.56	-0.71	10.8	
34 calls	2.44	35.8%	49.8	5.37	-0.94	8.73	3.00	33.9%	54.2	4.40	-0.73	10.9	
33 calls	2.90	36.5%	55.0	5.17	-0.96	8.75	3.62	36.0%	58.5	4.19	-0.77	10.8	
33 puts	4.04	41.9%	-45.0	5.17	-1.07	8.75	4.50	38.3%	-41.6	4.19	-0.77	10.8	
32 puts>	3.24	39.1%	-40.0	4.89	-0.98	8.63	4.10	39.8%	-37.5	3.95	-0.79	10.7	
31 puts	2.97	42.0%	-35.2	4.55	-1.03	8.40	3.66	40.7%	-33.6	3.68	-0.79	10.4	
30 puts	2.41	41.0%	-30.7	4.16	-0.97	8.05	3.20	41.1%	-29.9	3.39	-0.78	10.0	
29 puts	2.07	42.1%	-26.6	3.75	-0.94	7.63	2.82	42.0%	-26.5	3.09	-0.76	9.62	
28 puts	1.77	43.3%	-22.8	3.33	-0.91	7.14	3.05	49.1%	-23.3	2.79	-0.86	9.14	
27 puts	1.53	44.8%	-19.4	2.79	-0.87	6.60	2.15	43.6%	-20.4	2.43	-0.71	8.62	

Figure 9.3   QQQQ option chain—Powered by Option Vue 6

buying five December QQQQ 33 call options at 3.62 while selling five of the December QQQQ 37 calls for 1.70 and selling five of the December QQQQ 27 puts for 2.15, our net option premium for this trade is a small credit of .25.

With the sell-buy-sell we create a window of profit opportunity with the bull call spread and reduce the cost of the trade with the short put position. If you look at the QQQQ chart, you will see that the location of the 27 put option corresponds closely with the 1,100 mark on the Nasdaq 100. With this spread the short put will give us the obligation to be long the QQQQ at 27.00 if the put is not liquidated on a risk control prior to that point.

Now let's look at the model for this trade and see how the profit and loss works out in Figure 9.4. You can see the unlimited risk of the spread as well as the profit potential. The sell-buy-sell trade has a fairly aggressive delta because of the short put premium and will gain value at a better pace then the outright bull call spread. This type of trade works well in index markets because of the typical growth rate of index pricing. In recent years, we have seen times when indices have extreme growth rates, but if you are placing your short options in the neighborhood of 10 to 20 percent, it is reasonable to assume that the index will remain in that range on an annual percentage rate basis.

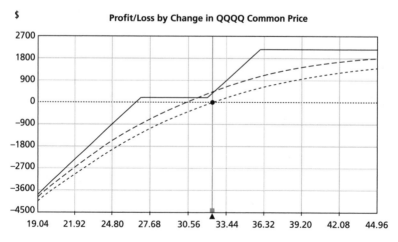

Figure 9.4 QQQQ sell-buy-sell model — Powered by Option Vue 6

There are different settlements for various index options:

- *Stock settled options.* A stock settled index option functions like traditional stock option in that the holder of the option would be assigned 100 shares of the underlying index stock for each option, long or short depending on the position. Margin rules would apply for options requiring a short market position in the underlying. The example QQQQ is a stock settled option index. Most, but not all, stock settled index options are also American style options so they function like traditional equity options and can be exercised into the underlying shares at any time.

- *Cash settled index options.* Some index options are cash settled rather than stock settled, meaning that if an option is exercised, the option position will be converted to cash. For example, if you were long an XYZ 50 call option and the underlying XYZ index was at 60 at expiration, rather than the 100 shares at 50, the call option buyer would receive $1,000 cash, the seller would be out $1,000 in cash (excluding the original premium). Most, but not all, cash settled index options are European style options in that they can be exercised only at expiration. It would make little sense to convert to cash prior to expiration in most cases because of the loss of time value premium.

- *Option on futures.* Index options with the underlying being futures contracts have varying expiration rules as well. Futures index contracts are cash settled for the most part, but the options are exercised into their respective underlying futures. Most of these contracts are American style in that they can be exercised at any time. Many of the index contracts themselves have only quarterly contracts; however, the options often have monthly expirations which create a serial option situation. Serial options on index contracts expire into the next contract month. For instance, an April or May S&P 500 option will be based on the June S&P 500 futures and, if it was to be exercised, would become a June futures contract. Cash settled futures contracts and their options often expire on the same day when it is not a serial option. The exchanges publish contract specifications online and by request. Many brokers have convenient calendars available with specifications for all futures contracts.

It is important to check with the individual prospectus or specifications of the index options you are looking at for expiration terms and expiration style. European style expiration options on indices are commonly used to prevent hedge traders from being exercised in the middle of a hedge strategy.

When you're trading in index options that may have some liquidity issues, you should be careful with European style options. When liquidity becomes an issue, the American style ability to exercise the option at any time is a significant exit door that does exist with European style options.

Another issue regarding expiration with index options is the time of day the option is settled. Options can be settled on an a.m. or p.m. basis. An a.m. expiration leaves the option trader open to some uncontrollable circumstance. And such an expiration means that the option expires at the close of the day, but the index price calculation for the settlement is not calculated until the opening of the shares in the index the next morning. The opening prices become the index settlement price for the option. This can leave a trader who was not in the money the previous evening in the money the next morning from a large change in share value overnight. It is common but not typically a significant change, but you should be aware of the risk with a.m. settlement options. A p.m. expiration option settles the index price for the option expiration on the closing prices of the day of expiration. Here again, you need to be well informed about the product you are trading as to how the option is settled.

Index and ETF Strategy

Now that we have a fairly decent understanding of index and ETF products, we can look at how we utilize these products in everyday trading. The options market on many index and ETF products is fairly active. The most active markets will be the ETF products that follow broad-based indices. In these products you will find active option trades where liquidity is of little concern.

We can apply a number of methods to index options for diversified investing. As a product that follows an index, you are receiving the benefit of diversification in a single investment action. If we consider utilizing ETF investments, as we would an individual stock, we have numerous strategies that apply. If you are trying to gain a long position in the market with a growth objective utilizing options, consider these strategies for index ETF options:

- *Selling put premiums.* With a short put strategy on broad-based indices, you are capturing premium on markets that statistically year after year have gains. When selling a put premium, your goal is to have the market at least remain steady. History would certainly be on your side with this strategy aside from the occasional recessionary trend. Risk control should be in place with any short option position.

- *Sell-buy-sell.* A position like the QQQQ we demonstrated earlier provides you with a long market opportunity with little or no out-of-pocket premium and minimal margin. Control risk just as you would for the short put.

- *Covered call spread.* The covered call employs a strategy similar to the one used for a short put, counting on statistical long-term gains in the market, with some risk offset with an out-of-the-money call premium.

- *Married put.* "Married put" is an equity term that does little to describe the position—buying or holding the outright shares, while purchasing a put option. (We discuss married puts more in portfolio management.) Be careful not to spend too much on your cover trades and eliminate what is likely to be single to low double-digit annual growth in broad-based indices.

- *Buying call and vertical spread options.* Buying outright call and vertical call spreads is always an acceptable and conservative approach to working with any market. In index options it is important to be disciplined in your implied volatility research and ensure that the implied is in a midrange to low area. With the modest annual returns of indices, a poorly timed or high-volatility option purchase can hamper annual returns. If you are buying in elevated volatility, find some offsetting premium with a bull call spread, ratio spread, and so on.

- *Back spreads.* In low-volatility periods a back spread may be highly effective, but be aware of total movement of the spread. Indices may not have the effective range that an individual stock or commodity may have because of the diversification. The back spread requires a fairly substantial price change to be effective, so it is important to consider the back spread as very long term and try to place the spread within the range of reasonable annual return for the index.

- *Double diagonals.* Double diagonals are a favorite among professional index option traders. The double diagonal capitalizes perfectly on the moderate range of the index versus singular components by selling a front premium to capture the accelerated time value decay while leaving the back month purchased options to gain value following the expiration of the short premium. This situation creates a long strangle in the index after the expiration of the front options with the choice to roll the short options forward into the short condor or maintain a directional position with one of the long options by allowing the shorts to expire. The spread is limited risk and an excellent choice for range-bound index markets. As always, have your risk control in place.

It can be more difficult in narrow indices, industry-specific ETF products to find heavy volume. If you are interested in trading in more narrowly based option products and you do not have the volume desired, be patient with your orders. Place priced orders and avoid market orders that will subject you to the price of the opposing position. Do not chase orders in thin markets. The same trading strategies apply to long market positions for narrow ETF positions, but we recommend sticking to American style options unless you are fully prepared to maintain the position through expiration.

The ability to use short an ETF gives another excellent dimension to the index and basket products. In the past short market positions were limited to futures contracts and the large margin and leverage associated with them. With ETF opportunities in the major indices and other products, traders have the ability to capitalize on diversified downward movement in the market. Along with short market positions, there are opportunities to capitalize on down moves with short call options, put options, or combination trades such as the short sell-buy-sell and covered puts. We discuss more about using index options on the short side of the market when we discuss portfolio management.

Summary

Index options offer exceptional flexibility when you are trading for diversification or outright investing without having to maintain a broad portfolio of individual securities. Index options can be beneficial in reducing overall trading costs and providing limited risk positions on both sides of the market. Remember to pay attention to the specifications for expiration style and type as well as implied volatility for your options positions.

Chapter 10

INTEREST-RATE PRODUCTS

Interest-rate derivatives are said to be the largest and most liquid market in the world. Options on these products are traded on multiple exchanges and of varying contract specifications. Interest-rate products often operate in opposition to the equity market as a safe haven for capital in rough market seas. Our focus for interest-rate markets is not to get into a detailed strategy discussion on commercial credit, swaps, and commercial hedging, but to discuss how options function on the market and to highlight some of the options used for defending a portfolio against changes in interest rates.

Interest-rate products in the United States are mostly traded on two major exchanges: the Chicago Board of Options Exchange (CBOE) and the Chicago Board of Trade (CBOT) which is now part of the CME Group. These two exchanges trade interest-rate products based on the same underlying assets, but in very different ways:

- *CBOE.* CBOE interest-rate products are based on the underlying assets of U.S. Treasury bills, 5-year U.S. Treasury notes, 10-year U.S. Treasury notes, and 30-year U.S. Treasury bonds. CBOE option products are derivative-based products trading on the current yield or yield to maturity of these underlying assets thus providing traders a means to utilize options for direct speculation or hedging of changes in interest rates based on changes in yield.

- *CBOT.* CBOT products are futures-based products trading on U.S. Treasury bills, 2-year U.S. Treasury notes, 5-year U.S. Treasury notes, 10-year U.S. Treasury notes, and 30-year U.S. Treasury bonds as well as eurodollars, swaps, Fed funds, and London Interbank Offered Rate (Libor). These products provide the investor with the ability to trade or hedge the redemption value of the securities both now and in the future. These products have significantly higher leverage than their CBOE cousins as the contract value represents from $100,000 to $1,000,000, depending on the contract. The contracts have an option in each month and quarterly underlying contracts.

These contracts are traded by individuals, businesses, and institutions for speculation and hedging, and they make one of the most active and liquid markets in the world.

Many of these contracts involve physical delivery, which means that investors in these products must monitor the notice dates for the contracts involved and be prepared to roll to different contract months or deliver or take delivery of the physical instruments themselves.

Bond Basics

Before we can begin with the specifics of trading interest-rate options, we need to make sure we have a basic background in the underlying instruments. Interest-rate products are based on some type of bond, cash deposit, or loan rate. We'll focus mostly on the bond aspect as related to U.S. Treasury securities as the primary instruments for interest-rate trading and hedging.

A bond is a term debt obligation to the issuer backed by the assets and/or revenue of the issuer. U.S. Treasuries are backed by the full faith and credit of the United States and the revenue stream from U.S. taxpayers. Through the years U.S. Treasuries have maintained one of the highest credit ratings in the world. However, recently there is a bit more risk associated with the skyrocketing U.S. national deficit, but the credit rating of U.S. Treasuries is not expected to move off AAA any time soon.

U.S. Treasuries come in several varieties:

- *U.S. Treasury bill.* The Treasury bill, or T-bill, is a zero coupon bond issued for terms of one month to one year. The T-bill is considered to be the safest U.S. Treasury security because of the short term. T-bills are sold at auction by the Treasury Department and are usually purchased by institutions or governments. Most individuals purchasing T-bills are doing so in the secondary market—that is, purchasing them from an institution—although recently the U.S. Treasury has made T-bills available directly to the public. Since these bonds have no coupon interest rate, they are sold at a discount at their face value. The appreciation between the discount price and the par value or face value of the bond between issue and maturity represents the return on investment or yield of the bond. T-bills are quoted in 1/32nds at their discount price, which is a percentage of their face value. A $10,000 bond quoted at 97–16 would be a $9,750.00 issue price. The remaining $250 would be the interest available to maturity.

- *U.S. Treasury notes.* Treasury notes are issued in terms of 2, 3, 5, 7, and10 years. T-notes, like T-bills, are sold at auction to institutions and governments and are an interest-bearing or coupon bond. These notes have a rate determined at auction which in turn determines the yield. Once auctioned, the notes can be held by the buyer or resold in the secondary market to individual investors and businesses. The selling price at auction and in the secondary market is a function of the par value or face value of the note plus the revenue stream from the bond over the term until maturity. T-notes are quoted in 1/32nds as a percentage of their face value as well. These notes are not necessarily issued or traded in the secondary market at a discount; they are often traded at a premium to the face value because of the value of the revenue stream from the coupon rate.

- *U.S. Treasury bonds.* U.S. Treasury bonds, also known as long bonds, are issued in 30-year terms. The T-bond is a coupon bond like the T-note with interest paid over the term of the bond. T-bonds are also publicly auctioned at issue and have an active secondary market. Treasury bonds also frequently trade at a premium to the par value of the bond because the revenue stream from the coupons is greater than the interest that can be achieved from other high credit-rated investments. Long bonds with higher interest-rate coupons that were auctioned during periods of higher interest rates will trade at a substantial premium to the par value during periods when current interest rates are low. As an example a 6 percent 30-year T-bond that has, say, 15 years left, may trade at 120 percent of par value when interest rates are lower. In contrast, as interest rates rise, the secondary market value of long bonds will fall.

- *Treasury inflation-protected securities (TIPS)*. TIPS are inflation-indexed bonds issued by the U.S. Treasury. The rate of return is adjusted to the consumer price index (CPI) as a measure of current inflation. The coupon rate is determined at auction like other Treasury securities, but have a yeild generally lower than T-Bonds or notes. The advantage to TIPS is that you are generating a real rate of return because the coupon rate is adjusted to account for inflation. This protects the bond holder against the negative effects of inflation over the term of the bond. TIPS are currently offered in 5-year, 10-year, and 20-year maturities. TIPS have an active secondary market as well, and in periods of low interest rates and/or expectations for increasing inflation, these bonds can be very popular.

Price versus Interest Rates

On the secondary market for bonds, as interest rates rise, bond prices fall and inversely as interest rates fall, bond prices rise. This is to the result of new issues being auctioned at the new interest rate.

Yield

Bond market returns are measured by the total return of the issue including the coupon rate over the term. This is referred to as *yield*. Bonds, especially Treasury issues, are quoted in the form of yield to maturity. When you see information regarding the bond market, you will often see the results of the day quoted in yield.

Calculating the current yield of an issue is easy; current yield is a simple function of price and rates:

$$\text{Current yield} = \frac{\text{annual interest in \$}}{\text{price paid for bond}} \times 100\%$$

As annual interest rates rise, bond values or the price of the bond falls. As interest rates rise, the current price of the security will be affected

Calculating yield to maturity is best done with financial software or a financial calculator for accuracy. The yield to maturity of a bond that is held to maturity must account for the gain or loss of value in comparison to the face value. When a bond is bought at a discount, yield to maturity will always be greater than the current yield because there will be a gain from the purchase price when the bond reaches maturity plus the coupon rate over the term the bond was held, thus raising the yield. When a bond is bought at a premium, the yield to maturity will always be less than the current yield because there will be a loss of value from the purchase price and the face value of the bond which decreases the gains from the coupon rate over the term the bond is held. Yield to maturity also assumes that the coupon rate of the bond is being reinvested over the term the bond is held. If you are withdrawing payments from the bonds, then the yield of the issue is going to be different.

The important thing to remember about yield relates to its sensitivity to interest-rate changes and what anticipated and actual interest-rate changes occur.

Yield Curve

The yield curve is the relationship between interest rates and the time to maturity of a bond or group of bonds. Treasury bonds, notes, and bills have varying interest rates and discount and premium levels for each type of issue and term. In a standard yield curve the lowest yielding instrument will be the shortest-term instrument, while the highest yielding instrument will be the longest-term bond, such as the 30-year T-bond. This makes sense in that the compounding of coupon interest will accrue on top of the par value over the course of the bond's life causing a higher yield, while the short-term T-bill has only it's discount rate for yield. Look at an example of a normal yield curve in Figure 10.1.

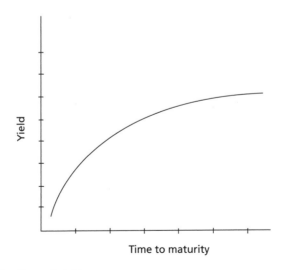

Figure 10.1 Normal yield curve

A normal yield is a sign of a stable interest-rate picture for the time being. If the curve begins to become misshapen, there may be anticipation or expectation building in the market for changes in interest rates.

As the threat of interest-rate changes increases or actual short-term interest rates such as the Fed rate begin to increase, there will be changes in the yield curve. Most financial news Web sites and services produce a daily yield curve, especially on Treasury issues. As short-term rates begin to rise, the curve will become more shallow, meaning that the yield is increasing on the short-term instruments in relation to the long-term secondary market instruments. This change indicates a potential need for action in your portfolio in any interest-rate–sensitive areas such as fixed income securities. Let's look at an example of a changing yield curve shown in Figure 10.2.

In the flat yield curve we can see that short-term rates are beginning to increase, which in the case of Treasuries would be T-bills or short-term T-notes. The yield is beginning to balance between

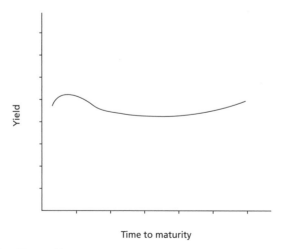

Time to maturity

Figure 10.2 Flat yield curve

short- and long-term rates meaning that there is a significant risk of inflation or that rates are being adjusted to meet inflation. This increase in short-term rates signifies significant risk to fixed income value unless the bonds are held to maturity. Extended issue yields remain slightly higher, but as time passes, bonds that were issued at lower yields will perform less well than short-term instruments.

This situation creates a future risk of an inverted yield curve similar to the one shown in Figure 10.3. When an inverted curve occurs, the long bonds are significantly underperforming the short-term issues because of recent increases in short-term rates. The long bond values have plummeted because, as new issues are auctioned, they are receiving a higher rate of return. Previously issued bonds with a lower coupon rate will have a higher value because their overall rate of return in the secondary market will be less than that of new issues.

Portions of the portfolio that might be in fixed income or interest-rate–sensitive areas need to be monitored and protected from changes in interest rates unless the bond holder has no intention

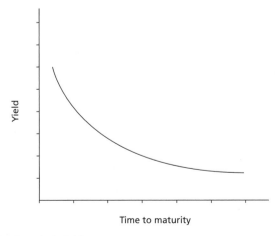

Figure 10.3 Inverted yield curve

of marketing the securities prior to maturity. This is an unusual case, and investors should be advised of the risk to the value of the bonds from changes in interest rates.

Interest-Rate Futures

Interest-rate futures exist to provide a means to hedge risk against interest rate changes as well as to predict the future value of secondary market issues. Investors often ask what the futures contract is based on. The prices do not match the current auction prices from the Treasury at all or the bonds in their portfolio. This is a true problem with the futures market, because the futures contracts are based on what is called cheapest to deliver (CTD). Since the futures market remains a physical delivery market, the investors who have written short call options or may be short the underlying futures have the obligation to deliver the bonds themselves. If they own the bonds in their portfolio, they will deliver the lowest-cost instrument. If they need to purchase the securities in order to deliver, they will find and purchase the lowest-cost bonds and deliver those. Cheapest to deliver for 30-year bonds and T-notes is usually around halfway through the cycle to maturity. CTD issues can be found on most major financial news sites in the quote section or on your financial quote system.

The major concern to the portfolio is the underlying value of the securities. The risk of increasing interest rates is real loss of liquidation value. This value can be protected through a combination of futures contracts. In the case of rising interest rates, futures can be utilized to be short the instruments that will be most effected by the raise in rates and to defend the value of the security. The downside to a straight out short is that it may not match the makeup of your fixed income portfolio because it may not be the CTD securities. You may have longer- or shorter-term maturities that are incompatible. You can either accept the differences as a sort of basis to the futures contract or utilize a ratio of issues with different terms to match your maturity cycle. If your maturity is seven years, then you may want a 5-year T-note contract and a 10-year T-note contract to get you somewhere around 7.5 years in maturity.

When you're using derivatives, just remember the leverage you are pulling with each contract. Table 10.1 shows a sample of the contract specifications for many interest-rate products.

You might notice from the last part of the table that the U.S. Treasury instruments are $100,000 per contract, except the two-year note which is $200,000. Use caution with the leverage these markets represent, especially when working a ratio delta of maturities. The two-year note is double the size of the remainder of the contracts.

Interest-Rate Options

Before we get into a discussion about using options on interest-rate products, especially for hedging positions against changing interest rates, it should be clear that the Treasury futures markets are by no means a hedging method for the small investor with a $10,000 fixed income portfolio. If you are worried about the changes in the discount rate on under $100,000 in T-notes, or T-bonds, your best bet is to hold to maturity, liquidate the position for a money market or a nice dividend yielding preferred stock, or consider rolling any long-term instruments into shorter-term bonds where the effect of rate change will not be as dramatic.

Table 10.1 Interest Rates

Instrument	Exchange	Description	Expiration Months	Trading Hours	Contract Value
10-year Taiwanese government bond futures	TAIFEX	10-year government bonds having face value of NT$5,000,000 and 3% coupon rate	H, M, U, Z	8:45-13:45 M-F, 8:45-24:00 Last trade date	NT$250
30-day commercial paper futures	TAIFEX	30-day financing commercial paper with face value of NT$100,000,000	All 12 months	8:45-12:00 banking days	0.005 = NT$411
10-year Australian government bond	SFE	A$100,000	H, M, U, Z	8:32-16:30; 17:12-7:30 (d)	.005%/annum ~ A$40.00
3-year Australian government bond	SFE	A$100,000	H, M, U, Z	8:30-16:30; 17:10-7:30 (d)	.005%/annum ~ A$14.00
90-day bank bill	NZFOE	NZ$1,000,000	H, M, U, Z	17:40-7:00; 8:30-16:30	.01%/annum
90-day bank bill	SFE	A$1,000,000	H, M, U, Z	8:28-16:30; 17:08-7:30 (d)	.01%/annum ~ A$24.00
Canadian bankers' acceptance	ME	C$1,000,000	All 12 months	6:00-7:45; 8:00-15:00; curb until 16:00	.005 = C$12.50 nearest 3 months; .01 = C$25.00 all other months
10-year Canadian government bond	ME	C$100,000	H, M, U, Z	6:00-8:05; 8:20-15:00; curb until 16:00	.01 = C$10.00
2-year Canadian government bond	ME	C$200,000	H, M, U, Z	6:00-8:05; 8:20-15:00; curb until 16:00	.0005 = C$10.00
3-month Euribor	EUREX	€1,000,000	H, M, U, Z	8:00-19:00	.005 = €12.50

Contract	Exchange	Contract Size	Delivery Months	Trading Hours	Tick Value
3-month Euribor	LIFFE	€1,000,000	All 12 months	LIFFE CONNECT 1:00-21:00	.005 = €12.50
Euro BOBL	EUREX	€100,000	H, M, U, Z	8:00-22:00	.01 = €10.00
Euro bund	EUREX	€100,000	H, M, U, Z	8:00-22:00	.01 = €10.00
Euro buxl	EUREX	€100,000	H, M, U, Z	8:00-22:00	.02 = €20.00
Euro schatz	EUREX	€100,000	H, M, U, Z	8:00-22:00	.005 = €5.00
2 year euro swapnotes	LIFFE	€100,000	H, M, U, Z	LIFFE CONNECT 7:00-18:00	.005 = €5.00
5/10-yr euro swapnotes	LIFFE	€100,000	H, M, U, Z	LIFFE CONNECT 7:00-18:00	.01 = €10.00
Eurodollar	CME-G	$1,000,000	All 12 months	7:20-14:00; Globex 17:00-16:00	½ tick = $12.50
Eurodollar	LIFFE	€1,000,000	All 12 months	LIFFE CONNECT 7:00-21:00	.005 = US$12.50
Eurodollar	SGX	US$1,000,000	All 12 months	Electronic 7:45-19:00; MOS 21:20-4:00	.005 = US$12.50 (a)
Eurodollar, mini-sized	CME-G	$500,000	H, M, U, Z	electronic 18:00-16:00	.005 = $6.25
3-month Euroswiss	LIFFE	SF1,000,000	H, M, U, Z	LIFFE CONNECT 7:30-18:00	.01 = SF25.00
Euroyen	CME-G	¥100,000,000	H, M, U, Z	7:20-14:00; Globex 17:00-16:00; MOS 21:20-4:00	.005 = ¥1,250.00
3-month Euroyen	TFX	¥100,000,000	All 12 months	8:45-11:30; 12:30-15:30; 15:30-20:00	.005 = ¥1,250.00

(Continued)

Instrument	Exchange	Description	Expiration Months	Trading Hours	Contract Value
Euroyen (LIBOR)	SGX	¥100,000,000	H, M, U, Z	Electronic 7:40-19:05; 20:00-22:55	.005 = ¥1,250.00
Euroyen (TIBOR)	SGX	¥100,000,000	H, M, U, Z	Electronic 7:40-19:05; 20:00-22:55	.005 = ¥1,250.00
30-day Fed funds	CME-G	$5,000,000	All 12 months	7:20-14:00; electronic 17:30-16:00	$10.42
3-month HIBOR	HKEx	HK$5,000,000	All 12 months	8:30-12:00; 13:30-17:00	.01% = HK$125.00
ID × U.S. dollar spread	BM&F	US$pt. value × unit price	Consult exchange	GTS 9:00-16:00	0.00%
30-day interbank cash	SFE	A$3,000,000	All 12 months	8:34-16:30; 17:14-7:30 (d)	.01% = A$24.66
5/10-year Japanese government bonds	TSE	¥100,000,000	H, M, U, Z	9:00-11:00, 12:30-15:00, 15:30-18:00; elec. 8:20-15:20, 15:30-18:20	.01 point = ¥10,000
Japanese government bonds, mini	SGX	¥10,000,000	H, M, U, Z	Electronic 7:45-17:15; 18:30-22:55	¥.01 = ¥100
Japanese government bond	LIFFE	¥100,000,000	H, M, U, Z	LIFFE CONNECT 7:00-16:00	.01 = ¥10,000.00
3-year Korean T-bond	KOFEX	KRW 100,000,000	H, M, U, Z	9:00-15:00	.01 = KRW 10,000
1-month LIBOR	CME-G	$3,000,000	All 12 months	7:20-14:00; Globex® 17:00-16:00	.0025 = $6.25

Instrument	Exchange	Contract size	Months	Trading hours	Tick value
Long gilt	LIFFE	£100,000	H, M, U, Z	LIFFE CONNECT 8:00-18:00	.01 = £10.00
30-day overnight repo rate	ME	C$5,000,000	All 12 months	6:00-7:45; 8:00-15:00; curb until 16:00	.005 = C$20.55
Short sterling	LIFFE	£500,000	All 12 months	LIFFE CONNECT 7:30-18:00	.01 = £12.50
Singapore dollar	SGX	S$1,000,000	All 12 months	Electronic 8:45-17:00	.005 = S$12.50
10-year swaps	CME-G	$100,000	H, M, U, Z	7:20-14:00; electronic 17:30-16:00	$1/2$ of 1/32 = $15.625
5-year swaps	CME-G	100,000	H, M, U, Z	7:20-14:00; electronic 17:30-16:00	$1/2$ of 1/32 = $15.625
10-year swaps	CME-G	100,000	H, M, U, Z	7:20-14:00; Globex 17:00-16:00	.0025 = $25.00
2-year swaps	CME-G	500,000	H, M, U, Z	Globex® 17:00-16:00	.0025 = $25.00
5-year swaps	CME-G	200,000	H, M, U, Z	7:20-14:00; Globex 17:00-16:00	.0025 = $25.00
30-year U.S. T-bonds	CME-G	$100,000	H, M, U, Z	7:20-14:00; electronic 17:30-16:00	1/32 = $31.25
10-year U.S. T-notes	CME-G	$100,000	H, M, U, Z	7:20-14:00; electronic 17:30-16:00	$1/2$ of 1/32 = $15.625
2-year U.S. T-notes	CME-G	$200,000	H, M, U, Z	7:20-14:00; electronic 17:30-16:00	$1/2$ of 1/32 = $15.625
5-year U.S. T-notes	CME-G	$100,000	H, M, U, Z	7:20-14:00; electronic 18:00-16:00	$1/2$ of 1/32 = $15.625

Using these markets for hedging should be for a legitimate hedge on $100,000 or more per contract in held securities. If you are trading interest rate products with protecting a portfolio as a goal, make sure you are in balance in futures versus the underlying asset. If not, you are speculating, and the risk to the portfolio from these markets is significant.

There is nothing wrong with speculating in futures markets. In fact there is a great deal of money to be made in speculative derivative trading, but there is just as much to be lost, so be sure to have your trading objective clear and you and/or your clients are aware of the risks involved.

With that said, in interest-rate markets we come up against another set of terminology. For example, buying protection to the long side of the market is a cap; buying for the downside is a floor. We are going to keep it simple. Understand that if you are buying a limited risk cap, you are buying a call option. The same is true with the floor—a put option.

Before you can properly utilize options for interest-rate risk control, you should have an idea of the interest-rate risk you are exposed to. After reading the financial papers regarding hedging interest rates and making your fourth trip to the bottle of aspirin, you might discover that there are several ways of calculating the sensitivity of a bond position to interest rates, none of which the common investor with anything better to do is going to make heads or tails of. To bridge this gap as best we can, let's look at the simplest method. DV01 (dollar value on a 1-basis-point change) is a commonly used method for determining the price change of a bond from changes in interest rates. Software is of course your best solution, but if you really want to do the math, here is the formula for DV01:

$$DV01 = -\frac{DP}{10,000 \times DY}$$

- Delta P = change in price on the bond
- Delta Y = change in yield

The simplest method for calculating a DV01 is to average the absolute price changes of a particular treasury security for a 1-basis-point (bp) increase and decrease in yield to maturity.

In a simple example we use the 30 year bond trading at 122–08 or $122,250.00 which is a 6 percent coupon bond with 15 years remaining until maturity. This is roughly the CTD bond at this time with the price based on the current U.S. Treasury bond futures contract. A change in price of $100 will equate to 1 bp up or down in yield. To get the absolute DV01, you would need to do 1bp up and 1bp down and divide the total by 2 to have a true DV01.

Let's assume, for example purposes, that this bond represents the fixed income risk to interest rates in your portfolio. In reality you would need to find the DV01 for each income asset and find the appropriate maturity issue or ratio of cheapest to deliver (CTD) treasury issues to account for the maturity differential between your assets and the CTD futures. As yield rises 1 bp, the risk to the price of the asset is $100. If you had $1 million in these securities each basis point would be $1,000 loss of value. So a standard interest-rate hike in short-term rates of 25 basis points that is carried through into the long maturity market could affect the portfolio value by $25,000. Long-term interest rates rising by 2.00 points could cost this bond holder $200,000. When current Fed rates are at 25 basis points to zero and long-term mortgage rates are in the 4 percent range, the risk of a 2.00 point hike is substantial.

Certainly the potential to sell the underlying futures contract and lock in the current yield is tempting, but there can be a substantial margin risk for each futures contract. We have covered a great number of option strategies, so now we can look at applying these option strategies to interest-rate problems, which in the years to come is likely to be an issue to combat inflation developed from low to zero interest-rate conditions. As the yield curve begins to distort when the Fed raises the discount rate to combat inflation, short-term instruments may have value risk. We know we can utilize several strategies to control the yield risk on medium- and long-term maturities where the yield risk is most substantial:

- *Selling an out-of-the-money or at-the-money call premium.* Selling out-of-the-money calls brings in cash flow against a held long position. Essentially you are creating a covered call of sorts in that you are long the physical bond and shorting. As an example, the December 122 call option is trading for 4–21 or $4,328 per contract. Selling this call option provides coverage for nearly a half point move in yield in nine months. Not out of line and still leaves profit ability up to 126–21.

- *Buying put premium.* Buying puts in U.S. T-bond options is an excellent floor for the value of this instrument. The disadvantage to buying put options is the cost. If we look at buying the at-the-money put option for December 2009, the quote is 6–15 or $6,234 for the 122 put option — $6,2340 on $1 million in value. This being the at-the-money put, we would gain at a 50 percent delta, but we have the significant risk of time value decay and volatility decreases.

- *Risk reversal.* The risk reversal is a perfect trade for this situation; it is exactly we can cover the interest-rate risk while also reducing the cost. Going back to the December options, the 122 put was 6–15. If we look to sell some premium to cover the cost of this position, we could certainly consider limiting the upside to the bond value by selling the 125 call options and bringing in half of the premium cost of the 122 put option. The 125 call is quoted at 3–06 or $3,093. Now the net cost would be $31,410 on $1 million. We can always reduce the hedge position by purchasing an out-of-the-money put and creating a window in the market. The 120 put option in this example is trading at 5–15, a full $1,000 less per contract.

- *Sell, buy, sell.* Given the limited potential for rate hikes in 1 year, one might decide that risking that yield can increase only so much on the 30-year bond in the term of the option trade. The sell-buy-sell further reduces the cost of the at-the-money option. Consider buying as before the 122 put option, while again selling the 125 call option and adding the sale of the 112 put option for 2–24 or $2,375. Now we have reduced our cost further by selling the out-of-the-money put. We have limited downside, but if the risk of premium is greater than the assumed risk of the market falling through 112 in 9 months, then the sell-buy-sell may be very effective. So our cost on the risk reversal of $3,141 per contract is now reduced to $766 per contract or $7,660 on $1 million. The YTM at 112 on this same bond would be 4.86 percent at 112.00. So we have covered 86 basis points of risk with $7,660 on $1million.

- *Short-term covering long exposure.* Another feasible strategy for covering long maturity exposure is to consider buying puts or selling calls or short market spreads on shorter maturities with the logic that the yield curve will flatten and the shorter maturity will have a more dramatic effect by increasing interest rates before longer maturities. In recent years, long-term rates have responded in step or shortly following increases in the Fed discount rate and T-bill discounts. This strategy may be effective if the logic regarding the yield curve holds, but it is also likely that long-term rates will respond quickly and cause any hedge effect to be useless or minimal at best.

- *ETF options.* Last but not least is to utilize option positions in Treasury index-based exchange-traded funds. The same hedge philosophy applies with selling calls, buying puts, or utilizing one of our spread strategies for short market positioning. Determine or you may be able to look up the DV01 for Treasury index funds and compare the DV01 to your portfolio. If you can find a comparable sensitivity to rates or find a ratio of income index funds to match your portfolio, the index provides a diversified method of carrying interest-rate risk without direct involvement in Treasury futures. This may be considered a more conservative approach with less risk and potentially less margin risk. The disadvantage is the contract size in that the U.S. Treasury bond contract represents $100,000 per contract, while the index fund will likely not have as significant a per-basis-point value to the portfolio. Conversely, if your exposure is based significantly in fixed income ETFs or mutual funds and you have an exposure greater than the

$100,000 per contract, the Treasury futures and options offer a single commission per $100,000 for buying put options or at least a much smaller number of commissions than the ETF options because of the contract leverage.

Summary

This chapter is based on Treasury issues. Corporate bonds respond in similar fashion only with the reactivity being reduced by the speed at which new corporate issues are sold with increased coupon rates or deeper discounts on zero coupon issues. The hedge philosophy is the same for corporate, municipal, foreign government, and U.S. Treasury issues. The interest-rate contract specs we lay out show a significant number of contracts available for rate hedging from Eurodollars and LIBOR to foreign securities and U.S. issues. The option strategies we demonstrate offer many creative solutions for controlling interest-rate risk in your fixed income portfolio. Institutions favor credit swaps for hedging in many cases, but with the potential for regulation and basing OTC swaps on the exchanges for credit and credit default to help control the risk to the counter party, the OTC market may end up doing much the same in the future as the regulated side with the current futures.

Chapter 11

OPTION PRICING

Option prices are developed based on the same system as their underlying asset counterparts. The prices are actual trades between two parties to establish the quote you see on your computer screen. Determining the price at which an option should be bid or offered is a process of calculating the value of the option in relationship to the underlying asset.

Several option models have been developed over the years to establish the theoretical value of options in relation to the trade of the underlying and are a continuous source of academic debate regarding the pros and cons of each system. We won't get into a mathematical discussion of each system, but being familiar with the systems and potential market participants that may be following each system is important to your trading success.

There is a wealth of information on how option pricing models function and how the data is developed, but as an investor or portfolio manager your purpose is to put the information to work for you. In the age of trading software, we have easy access to the academic effort on option pricing. We want to focus on what do with the information to develop successful trading strategies.

It is important to understand the importance of the pricing models, the theoretical value of an option, and how implied volatility affects you as the trader. As an example, the latest and greatest cute little furry talking toy in September has a retail price of $20. A holiday fad could cause any one of the cute little furry talking toys to go for hundreds if not thousands of dollars and create throngs of toy crazed shoppers. History tells us that sitting on the shelf right next to the latest and greatest talking toy is a similar toy with a different name that no one will want and that there will be thousands of these on the shelves in warehouses waiting for the after-holiday sales to dump them at a discount.

If you were to buy or sell a call option on a group of those toys with a December expiration, how would you price the option? Only one of a few possible toys would be the winner, so how would you price a $20 call option, even if you did know which toy was going to go crazy?

This is where option models come into play. We can plug in the current underlying toy value of $20 and then extrapolate what will happen to each option strike price created for the toys from $20 to infinity. We can look at the holiday history of hot little fur balls and derive a probability assessment of the size of the change in price for this year's toy. Your option model can then tell you that if the little fur ball was to rally to $100 per toy, a particular option would be worth x number of dollars in this much time.

You can perform as many theoretical probabilities as you wish using your model, but at this point we must separate reality from theoretical value. The investor who extends an offer to write the December fur ball $20 call option creates the market for the option. This price is up to the writer of the option, not the option model. The assumptions for this investor's pricing may be one of a thousand different probabilities calculated in the model. There is no way to know the price until an investor places an offer. As an option seller you can choose to sell for less, the same, or more; or as the buyer you can buy or not buy. There is no physical price for the option until the buyer and seller find a price together to trade the $20 fur ball call option. Until an option writer agrees to take the risk at that price, there is no market for the option.

The difference between the practical function and the academic research of option pricing is liquidity, variables in pricing models, and the subjective risk assessment of the seller. If an option trades at a particular price, that price is the option's tradable value, regardless of theoretical or fair value indicated by the option model.

If you are the one bidder on an option in a thin market, you may have to pay the seller's subjective price or not trade your option. This is common in out-of-the-money deferred options in both equity and commodity markets. When that trade hits the pricing model, the volatility may be completely out of line, and it may appear to be an overvalued option, but in reality that is the option's value, overvalued or undervalued. That price will remain until the next seller and buyer come together on a price for the same option.

Experienced active option traders often have a different view of option pricing from those in research departments and classrooms. An active option trader will view the option market as a fluid pricing model in itself. The vast capability of arbitrage traders to research and quickly identify variance in option pricing between the underlying asset and their respective options creates a system of active value for the retail market. Unless an option market is thinly traded or the contracts are deferred, an active option market will have fair value versus the underlying given the volatility most of the time.

If options have elevated implied volatility in high volume, the value is justified by the demand of high-volume traders such as hedge funds and arbitrage traders. High implied volatility in high volume creates more legitimacy to the theoretical option value. In thin markets implied volatility can have a different skew because of the odd option trade at higher-than-expected implied volatility.

Thin markets also offer opportunity for the brave sellers who may choose to sell in uncharted territory. When offering options that do not yet have trade established or where little trade has been established, you will be relying on your option model to provide a best-guess theoretical value for the option in question. These are usually speculative opportunities and not necessarily part of any portfolio hedge strategy since they cannot be counted on to fill in a timely fashion.

On a broad basis if we look at active options as fairly valued most of the time because of the ability of large traders to take quick advantage of arbitrage opportunities between the underlying asset and the related options. We mostly have to be concerned with why the implied volatility of an option is high and what forces would cause the volatility to remain high, go higher, or go lower.

The forces that drive markets are also what drive options, both technical and fundamental. Options can have independent forces resulting from a particular high-volume trader or group of high-volume traders targeting a specific strike price or group of strike prices. In our bond example in the last chapter, we discussed selling call options on the December U.S. T-bond 122 call option as a potential hedge for interest-rate changes. Our example was on $1 million or 10 options. What if a trader was doing 1,000 of those call options to cover $100 million in value? One hundred million dollars in Treasury bonds is something just over a drop in the bucket. What kind of effect would be applied to a single option strike price if 1,000 or 10,000 call options were offered at a certain price?

If the trader needed to get the trades done and was willing to allow some price discretion, somebody might notice and begin pulling bids to see how low the offers would go before arbitrage traders would pick them up. Is there a chance that the option may trade at a discounted implied volatility? Absolutely, especially in markets with less volume. Conversely, if someone was buying the hedge, the option might trade at a premium or higher implied volatility.

When we talk about implied volatility, one of the items we are looking at is the skew of the implied across the available strike prices. At times you will find that out-of-the-money options have a higher implied volatility compared to the at-the-money or in-the-money options. This is known as the volatility smile (see Figure 11.1).

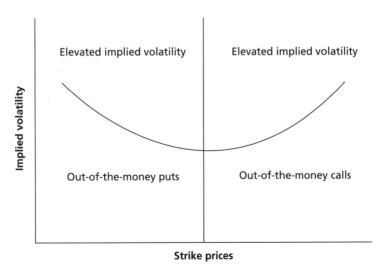

Figure 11.1   Option volatility smile

The volatility smile you see shows that typically out-of-the-money options have higher implied volatility. This also often includes the in-the-money-calls on the left side and the in-the-money-put options on the right side. The cause of the volatility smile is option demand. In markets where the volatility is increased and the market believes there is a potentially volatile trading range or break out potential for the underlying asset price, the implied volatility will be elevated. It is simply demand driven.

The inverse of the volatility smile is the volatility frown shown in Figure 11.2; although the volatility frown is a less commonly used term. This phenomenon happens frequently with stable equity assets. You will notice that the representation is a shallow curve rather than a deep curve like the smile. Typically when a stock or commodity is in a period of quiet fundamentals, stable, and in a narrow trading range, investor demand moves away from the out-of-the-money options to at-the-money positions. This is not the smartest play in the world given that you are buying higher implied volatility at

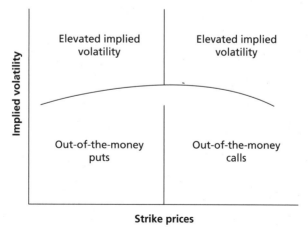

Figure 11.2 Volatility frown

the money, but it is a reality nonetheless. Again, this is driven by supply and demand. If you have an abundant supply of option writers away from the market or a weak group of buyers, the implied is likely to retreat. If the market appears to have little or no potential for growth or disaster, you will see a similar situation.

What we can learn from the volatility smile is to spot when we have distortions that we may be able to capitalize on. Selling call and put premiums on the outside edges of a steep volatility smile is likely to be a good opportunity to capture the volatility. Someone is or has been willing to buy these options at high volatility for the smile to exist so you must be certain of your fundamental and technical analysis.

You can extrapolate from the smile what strategies might be most effective in each situation. You have to reverse your thinking and consider trading implied volatility and not the market fundamental itself. If volatility is low in the-at-the-money options and elevated on both ends, we might consider a short out-of-the-money condor, short strangle, long straddle, long at-the-money call or put, bull call or bear put spreads, and ratio spreads covered calls and puts. All of these take advantage of out-of-the money implied volatility.

For elevated implied volatility in the center like the frown, we have another set of trading strategies: a short iron butterfly, short straddle, long strangle, back spreads, long out-of-the-money calls or puts, and long condors. These trades take advantage of your being able to purchase low out-of-the-money implied volatility in relation to the at-the-money positions.

Pricing your option trades based on volatility as much as on the price and on market fundamentals will do a number of things for your trading:

- It may help increase your success rate on option positions. Avoiding volatility risk and time value mistakes with short-term high-volatility options will improve your percentage of winning option trades. Everyone has losing option trades; it is the nature of the beast, but identifying volatility is the key to success.

- Paying close attention to the positioning of high-volatility options will key you into the movement of money in a particular underlying asset. If you begin to see the volatility curve dip down on the put side of the equation and increase on the call option side, there is a likelihood that large-scale investors are buying protection on short positions in out-of-the-money calls or there is speculative interest in the long side of the market.

- Evaluating option implied volatility will help you with your technical charting. If an option has a particularly large open interest, there may be an attempt brewing to pin the market to a particular strike price. Look at that strike price on your underlying chart and draw a line to it. Where does that take the market? Up, down, sideways? Better than drawing a trend line to the strike price, look at your most recent bell curve. Where does the curve hit the strike price? That strike price may end up as a feature of the bell curve. Are there any major support or resistance points around the strike price? gaps, or other technical features that would explain the open interest?

- Another key to success in using any option strategy is to analyze the option movement and implied volatility in the week or two leading up to your placement of the option spread. If implied volatility has been increasing steadily on the options, even over the underlying asset, this is a warning sign for using option purchase strategies. The increased implied may be a sign that other traders are already pricing the particular move into the market with individual option strategies or cover trades on underlying positions. What this means to you is that the implied volatility represents the potential of the market already built into the trade.

Option Models

Option models are a necessary evil and rather than heading for that bottle of aspirin over a bunch of calculus, let's look at the pros and cons of a couple of the popular systems. At the least it's important to understand the history and rationale of these formulas as well as their benefits and shortcomings. Let's look at the most popular formulas used to calculate theoretical option value and implied volatility and then we'll look at what is relevant and what is not relevant about these models.

The most prevalent formula for option pricing is the Black-Scholes option pricing model. The Black-Scholes formula was created in 1973 by Fisher Black and Myron Scholes. The model essentially changed financial markets by providing a means to estimate the future value of derivative positions given a certain set of variables. The Black-Scholes model makes certain assumptions that are important to understand because they represent some of the limitations of the model:

- *No dividends during the life of the option.* This is a serious limitation to the model. Stock dividends are common, and to adjust the model you must discount the underlying for the dividend paid to account for the variance. This unfortunately is a manual adjustment although some attempts have been made to modify the formula for the adjustment.

- *No American exercise.* European exercise terms mean that the option can be exercised only on the expiration date. American exercise allows the option to be exercised at any time during the life of the option. This is really significant only for deep in-the-money options or options near expiration, because investors in general are not going to exercise and waste the remaining time value in the option.

- *Markets are efficient.* The efficient market assumption says that it is not possible to consistently predict the direction of the market or individual investment. The model assumes a continuous random motion to the market.

- *No commissions are included.* We all have to pay commissions of one amount or another to execute trades. The model does not include commissions in the calculation of profit and loss or value.

- *Interest rates remain constant and known.* The Black-Scholes model uses the risk-free rate. Periods of heavy changes in interest rates can skew the model because it assumes a rate based on the T-bill with 30 days left which may be a bit different from the actual cost of capital during the period of the option.

- *Returns are log normally distributed.* This assumption suggests returns on the underlying stock.

With these assumptions in mind, the Black-Sholes model is the standard option model for most online and software applications. Most option analysis software has two or three choices for pricing formulas built in for the various needs of the user, but in general you will find that the default for the application is Black-Sholes.

Some of the disadvantages of the Black-Sholes model are corrected in the binomial pricing model or the Cox, Ross, Rubenstein model. Cox, Ross, and Rubinstein introduced the binomial model for pricing U.S. stock options in 1979. This model is a tree model with nodes or branches and, when viewed graphically, the stock price and option price steps through each interval period from origin to expiration. At each step, the stock price will either move up or down, with a probability defined by the volatility of the stock.

Each step or node in the tree represents a period in which the stock price can branch up or down. From each of these two points the stock price can either branch up or down at another point, creating another probability. The branches continue, making a larger structure through expiration.

Like the Black-Scholes model, the binomial model assumes a risk-free interest rate, but in contrast to Black-Scholes, this model can account for dividend yield.

Because of the tree structure of the binomial model, options can be evaluated as exercised prior to expiration. The model assumes that once time value has completely disappeared, the option would be exercised or expired.

The Cox, Ross, Rubenstein model corrects two issues with the Black-Scholes model, American option expiration and the model is able to account for dividend yield in the formula. The binomial model is said to be more accurate, but also takes significantly longer to calculate by hand.

Analysts frequently discuss the advantages and disadvantages of each formula, and there have been numerous adjustments to the Black-Scholes formula in an effort to account for the disadvantages. Black-Scholes is much faster, which is why traders rely on it exclusively, even with the disadvantages.

Keep-It-Simple Option Pricing Model

Before we leave option pricing, there is a wonderfully simple option calculator available to every trader. This option calculator is capable of telling you what your option will be worth at various times, at different strike prices and values. All you need for this simple little calculator is your eyeballs.

If we put up any option quote page, we have our calculator. Let's look at the example in Figure 11.3. In this option chain, we have two months represented in options. The June NYMEX crude contract and the July NYMEX crude contract. Let's look at this vertically for a moment, sticking strictly with the June contract. The market is at 54.57 and the 55 call option is trading at 4.50. If the

Futures	JUN <47>		JUL <81>		AUG <110>		SEP <140>		
	54.57	+0.25	56.37	+0.51	57.44	+0.49	Last	Chg	Trade
Options	JUN <42>					JUL <76>			
61 calls	Last	MIV	Delta	Gamma	Theta	Vega	Last	MIV	Delta	Gamma	Theta	Vega
60 calls	2.35	61.8%	33.5	2.94	-51.4	69.9	4.55	59.0%	48.4	2.70	-39.7	102
59 calls	2.94	62.4%	36.5	3.64	-53.3	71.5	4.89	59.3%	51.0	2.68	-40.1	102
58 calls	3.25	62.8%	40.0	3.82	-54.6	72.7	5.29	59.6%	53.6	2.65	-40.3	102
57 calls	3.60	62.9%	43.7	3.94	-55.3	73.5	5.60	59.5%	56.2	2.60	-40.1	102
56 calls	4.04	63.4%	47.5	4.01	-56.0	73.8	6.19	60.1%	58.7	2.55	-40.2	101
55 calls	4.50	63.8%	51.5	4.04	-56.2	73.6	6.49	60.4%	61.3	2.48	-39.8	99.9
54 puts	4.45	64.5%	-44.5	4.01	-56.3	72.9	5.30	61.3%	-36.1	2.41	-39.7	98.2
53 puts	4.39	65.3%	-40.4	3.94	-56.0	71.7	4.84	61.6%	-33.7	2.33	-39.0	96.1
52 puts>	3.73	65.8%	-36.4	3.81	-55.1	69.8	4.40	61.9%	-31.2	2.24	-38.2	93.6
51 puts	3.41	66.5%	-32.4	3.63	-53.9	67.5	4.00	62.2%	-28.8	2.14	-37.3	90.7
50 puts	2.90	66.8%	-28.8	3.02	-52.1	64.7	3.54	62.7%	-26.5	2.02	-36.2	87.5
49 puts	2.39	67.3%	-25.7	2.69	-50.0	61.4	3.28	63.2%	-24.3	1.90	-35.1	83.9
48 puts	2.05	67.9%	-22.8	2.49	-47.8	57.8	2.96	63.7%	-22.2	1.79	-33.7	80.1

Figure 11.3 NYMEX Crude Oil (CL) option chain—Powered by Option Vue 6

crude oil futures were to fall to 51.57, losing 3.00 per contract over the next three days, from this what would you suspect the value of the 55 call option to be? Look at the 58 call option at 3.25. This option would be the same distance from the current market as the 55 call would be if the market fell by 3.00. Knock off a few cents for time value, and presto. Instant theoretical value!

If we were short the July 52 put option at 4.40 and over 30 days the market had gone against the position by 2.00, how much would we be losing on the 54 put? Slide over to the June options and look at the 52 put there. The futures contracts are already 1.80 basis to each other, so we can account for most of the 2.00 loss right there. The traded premium of the June 52 put is 3.73, so theoretically the time value has offset the 1.80 loss in value, and we still might be making money on the trade. If we want to be more accurate, we can take 20 percent of the difference between the premium of the 52 put and the 53 put and add it to the 52 put premium, and we ought to be pretty close at about 3.85. The actual option calculator says 3.90. That's a pretty good estimation. You can do this on the fly, in your head. Serial options or contracts that have options in every month certainly help because it leaves less room for estimation. Options that are only quarterly are more difficult and require a bit more math, but nonetheless are very possible.

This does not just work for commodity options, let's look at Figure 11.4 showing Microsoft options. With stock options you do not have to be concerned with the basis between underlying contracts which is a perk over commodity options. The theta on MSFT is very small; the options actually hold value very well which is reflected in the basis between options. Going horizontal, if we purchase the MSFT 18 call options in October for 2.30 and we held the option for 91 days, the likely value would be that of the

Actuals	MSFT Common			Legend									
	MSFT		18.33	+1.27	Symbol	Trade	Last	Chg					
Options	JUL <116>						OCT <207>						
22.0 calls	Last	MIV	Delta	Gamma	Theta	Vega	Last	MIV	Delta	Gamma	Theta	Vega	
21.0 calls	0.76	41.5%	32.7	7.97	-0.65	3.70	1.32	42.9%	40.1	6.13	-0.55	5.26	
20.0 calls	1.10	43.4%	40.5	8.39	-0.75	3.97	1.71	44.7%	46.0	6.18	-0.59	5.40	
19.0 calls	1.44	43.3%	48.7	8.43	-0.77	4.09	2.01	43.9%	52.0	6.08	-0.58	5.42	
18.0 calls>	1.94	45.1%	57.1	8.09	-0.79	4.03	2.30	41.6%	58.0	5.85	-0.55	5.32	
17.5 calls	..s..						..s..						
17.0 calls	2.47	45.7%	65.1	7.40	-0.75	3.79	2.65	39.0%	63.9	5.49	-0.49	5.09	
16.0 calls	2.95	42.1%	72.5	6.45	-0.60	3.42	3.50	45.2%	69.7	5.02	-0.52	4.76	
20.0 puts	3.15	50.0%	-59.6	8.39	-0.86	3.97	4.47	61.0%	-54.0	6.18	-0.79	5.40	
19.0 puts	2.81	57.6%	-51.3	8.43	-1.01	4.09	3.85	61.5%	-48.0	6.08	-0.79	5.42	
18.0 puts>	1.83	47.7%	-43.0	8.09	-0.82	4.03	2.75	52.2%	-42.0	5.85	-0.66	5.32	
17.5 puts	..s..						..s..						
17.0 puts	1.55	53.4%	-34.9	7.40	-0.87	3.79	2.50	57.9%	-36.1	5.49	-0.70	5.09	
16.0 puts	1.05	51.2%	-27.5	6.45	-0.76	3.42	1.69	51.4%	-30.4	5.02	-0.58	4.76	
15.0 puts	0.85	56.0%	-21.0	5.38	-0.73	2.96	1.74	62.1%	-25.0	4.46	-0.66	4.32	

Figure 11.4   MSFT option chain—Powered by Option Vue 6

July 18.00 call at 1.94 if the market was still around 18. If the underlying was at 20.00, we could look at the 16.00 call option and guess at theoretical price of around 2.95.

Option models are more accurate, and you can specify dates, prices, volatility, and so on, but this is a simple on-the-fly method to use to calculate your option value.

Chapter 12

MARKET THEORY
AND PORTFOLIO
MANAGEMENT

The hurdles to success and profitability are growing rapidly in today's volatile market. In this chapter we look at market theory and risk strategies you can use to improve your portfolio management techniques and tactics through advanced option strategy.

Market Theory

In 20 years in the financial world my experience has led me to believe certain things about investors and markets. As a financial professional there are days I walk out of the office on top of the world—I am a genius. At about 8:30 a.m. the next morning the market has changed my opinion, and I am now the stupidest person ever to walk the earth. These are the markets; it is not easy. If it was easy, everyone would be driving a Ferrari.

There are the cynics among us who believe that the market is completely manipulated; others believe it is completely random.

The academic group is on an endless search for the silver bullet chart pattern or indicator, and the fundamentalists can tell you everything you didn't ever want to know about IBM. In order to understand how each of these groups affect the market, we need to understand more about the underlying theories.

First, let's talk about the random walk hypothesis because this theory is fascinating and controversial. Random walk market theory suggests that if you give the drunkest person you know a little shove, he or she will stumble down the street in a totally random stepping pattern. If you do it a a number of times, you will eventually have a pattern to chart, a randomly created pattern, but a pattern nonetheless. Random walk says that there is no predictability to the steps and that each walk will create an ever-expanding set of possibilities.

Being the mean friend that you are, you decide that your buddy's close encounter with the light pole in his drunken walk is hilarious, and you bring him back and do it again. This makes you a technical analyst. You bet cash with your friends that he hits the light pole; you have just become a technical trader.

The same theory extends to the market in that the random steps create a sort of histogram that eventually creates patterns of where random steps have occurred previously. Technicians will find predictability in these steps, but in reality this predictability is an illusion. Before the technical trading world starts sending me hate mail, let me qualify by saying that illusions have a reality of their own. When David Copperfield made the Statue of Liberty disappear in 1983, our senses said it was gone. It's not possible that it was gone, but it was not there. An illusion can be reality whether it is real or not. Things look different from different points of view.

Technical analysis is no different. The patterns formed by the movement of the market have been published as a particular signal of one sort or another, which in turn draws a particular investor who is following the pattern. A head-and-shoulders formation is a commonly followed formation, which means that there is money behind the theory. The more money, the more accurate the theory is. It is entirely self-fulfilling. A key reversal is another strong market technical signal that draws significant capital, therefore it works. So why don't all these patterns work all the time? Hundreds of thousands of pounds of paper and ink have been dedicated to the technical explanation for the movement of the market, but this is where the Brownian motion theory enters the picture. If you are not familiar with Brownian motion it is essentially a scientific theory of why a particle of dust will move in a random pattern floating on top of the water, even when the water is still. The dust interacts with the active molecules in the water. The molecules are constantly in motion because the atoms are constantly in motion. As the molecules bump into the dust, they propel the dust in one direction or another. There are sextillion little bumps pushing a behemoth particle of dust into motion. Here the market has similarities as well with millions of investors making trillions of dollars in little bumps pushing prices around. Some bumps are bigger than others, such as hedge funds and index funds bumping a particular company by buying heavily, but nonetheless they all represent the driving force behind the market.

The chart patterns are only as accurate as the moving molecules of money heading in a particular direction. This is not to disparage technical trading, but it is important to understand, when we start talking about systemic risk, that the illusion of technical trading is revealed when the broad market fails for economic reasons. When the Dow can lose years' worth of growth and value in a day or a week, the supportive technical capital becomes faithless and sidelined. Support does not hold because the response to the threat of loss activates the flight instinct in us, and we tend to run away.

Technical trading has a place in the market and is an excellent draw for speculative capital and liquidity. In today's marketplace managed index funds and hedge funds are chock full of technical analysts, which means that the majority of the markets' capital power is focused on technical aspects to some degree. Under normal market conditions certain technical indicators can be relied on because of the number and wealth of investors using those indicators. It is important to study the popular indicators and to try and get an idea of what kind of investors are using them. We don't put a significant number of indicators on our charts in this book because indicators are often "trendy" and change frequently, and these indicators are not necessarily relevant to our option discussion.

Some analysts base their trading decisions on several if not dozens of indicators. If these analysts represent significant capital, their methodology may be hard to discover, so when you manage risk with competing capital large or small, you must understand the main characteristics of the technical trade and follow your own guidelines.

On the flip side of this you have fundamentalists who base their trading on hard evidence. Fundamentals are things like balance sheets, price to earnings ratios, company news, weather, and so forth. Fundamentalists believe firmly in the validity of their research and probably have a more substantial argument on the reality of their systems than technical traders.

Past performance is not an indicator of future results. This disclaimer can apply to just about every product in the investment industry, and it is especially the case with technical and fundamental trading. Can you realistically say that, since the weather pattern in 1973 was the same as the pattern this year so far, the effect on the corn market pricing is going to be the same? You may have an argument for the weather effect on the crop minus 36 years in technology to offset weather risk, but outside of that similarity, the conclusions are going to be purely speculative. The same can be said for the history of any corporation. Given all the information available today on the Internet, the fundamentalist is armed to the teeth with real-time facts and figures about performance, earnings, news, and the CEO's shoe size.

The advantage to fundamentals is that they are based on fact and provide a foundation for a particular security when the chart is quiet. Fundamentals account for true growth in the market. Next year everyone is going to want a raise, which means that companies will have to charge more so they can pay their employees more, and in turn the employees will spend more on the higher-priced items giving the gross domestic product (GDP) its annual growth rate. We all want more money, so therefore the economy grows, well most of the time anyway.

"The markets are manipulated" is a common statement by a lot of investors, large and small, and every one of them is correct. In recent years, the amount of concentrated capital in the market is striking. Index funds and hedge funds have more money at their disposal than most people even know exists. This manipulation is all perfectly legitimate in most cases, aside from a giant Ponzi scheme or two, it is just massive quantities of concentrated cash, like the molecules pushing the dust around.

Just because the markets are manipulated to one degree or another does not mean that they are impossible to trade. It is simply a fact that should be assumed and add to the realization that risk control is essential in the new market. Options as we have discussed are an excellent means of coping with this risk.

Managed performance versus indexed performance has been a hot topic lately. In many cases the indexed portfolios have outperformed the managed portfolio, and now it seems that every manager's goal is to beat the index. It is a tough call on this, but in general over the long haul common sense would dictate that the best advice is to diversify. Use some of both. There will be times when managed funds far exceed the indices when the market struggles to recover from economic slowdowns. Not all managers are equal, and certainly the more aggressive the manager, the more risk and the more potential for reward. Index products such as index ETFs are excellent tools and should be utilized thoroughly, but having a manager to assess risk in choppy times will likely be beneficial. We have all been a bit spoiled, and there are a number of young traders who don't remember much of an S&P 500 at 300 chopping around for two years to recover from the 1987 crash, much less further back. We have been spoiled by the volatility in the market and are relying on years of index growth that is not likely to not occur in negative or flat GDP. The S&P lost nearly 40 percent, and at an average 10 percent annual rate of return in the S&P, will it take four years to recover? Probably not, but there is a decent chance that the managed portfolio will surpass the indexed portfolio.

Portfolio Management

The first priority in portfolio management is to identify areas of risk and to look for solutions to current and future risk. We can divide portfolio risk into three categories:

- *Systemic risk.* Systemic risk can be viewed as the risk of the major markets and the economy. Investors, especially small investors, are often caught off guard by systemic risk and changes in the overall economy. Many investors identify risk to the individual investment without measuring the collective risk of the entire portfolio. This oversight can become significant when the entire market suffers a downturn. The burst bubbles in 2000 and 2008 are perfect examples of systemic risk that many investors and professional managers were very unprepared for.

- *Sector or industry risk.* This is the risk represented by a group of companies in a particular industry or an index related to a particular industry. Sectors can be large, such as the technology sector, or related to a small industry. Sector risk is commonly understood by a broad range of investors. They often have a sectored view of risk because a lot of analysis done on sector risk in the media. Small investors are often more familiar with sector risk because of the structure of mutual funds. The early mutual funds were objective-based with general terms such as total return, growth, income, or some combination of these. As funds have grown, they have followed a pattern of tracking indices and sectors to provide customers with more diversity and a greater selection of funds. In recent years the ETF has increased the view of sector diversity with so many ETFs following sector indices or industry groups.

- *Individual component risk and diversification.* Risk in a portfolio is made up of the risk to the individual components of the portfolio. If one component of the portfolio suffers a large loss, it affects the profitability of the entire portfolio. Individual risk also applies to the areas that might be higher risk capital and that are somewhat beyond the portfolio objectives such as taking a shot at a particular high-risk investment.

Risk Management Strategies

The number one convention of risk management is diversification. The purpose of diversification is to spread the risk across a range of components so that if one component suffers a loss, the balance of the components in a well-diversified portfolio will absorb and make up for the loss.

The problem with diversification as a sole risk management strategy is the lack of protection from systemic risk. No matter how diversified the portfolio, when the bulk of equities on the planet go down, the portfolio will go down. This is not unusual, nor does it mean that something is wrong with diversification. It is just a fact. As we discussed earlier, investors are often taken aback by the effect of negative economics on their portfolio. This is because so much emphasis has been placed on diversification that investors are unprepared to manage systemic portfolio risk. This often includes large portfolio managers as they struggle to maintain the balance between aggressive returns and managing risk.

There is no silver bullet for risk management; it is a problem with a many-faceted solution. Let's look at the types of risk and identify the shortcomings of risk management strategies.

When managing systemic risk, you have several tools available. Certainly diversification is the primary tool, but the downside to diversification is a loss of individual component or sector performance. If you are diversified into 30 different stocks such as the Dow Industrials stocks, a strong performance in one stock may be offset by a negative performance in another, or at least growth will be checked by any poorly performing components.

The S&P 500, QQQ, and Russell 2000 are well diversified on their own. These broad indices generate year-on-year returns and also make excellent hedging instruments for systemic risk. If you are a long investor in ETF or futures products in broad indices, option trading strategies for defense against negative economic conditions need to be looked at. The difficulty with broad indices is the hedge cost versus the return. Leaving out 2008 for the time being, we can fairly state that the S&P 500 has had an average annual return of around 10 percent. There were years with 20 percent plus gains and a few with 20 percent or more lost. In 2008 the S&P lost 38.6 percent, the third largest drop since inception.

Let's take the S&P 500 and look at three different strategies for systemic risk control that also could be utilized in narrow-based applications. With an average annual return of 10 percent, we can use that 10 percent as our focus point for an option premium in a covered call style. Let's say hypothetically the SPY ETF is trading at around 92.00. Ten percent in either direction is just under 10 points. We assume that the SPY 102 call option for September is trading at around 2.20 with 140 days left. If we sell this call option, we bring in just over 2 percent of the value of 100 shares of SPY over 140 days. Selling this call option caps the gain for the SPY shares during the period to 12 percent. If the market rises beyond the 102 during the period of the option's life, you can be satisfied with the 12 percent or remove the option at expiration and allow the shares to continue. Selling this call option also reduces the risk to the shares by 2 percent. It is not a significant benefit, but in contrast to outright holding it is a minor improvement. If you were able to execute this trade twice over the course of the year, you have the potential to increase the profitability of the 10 percent average annual return by 4 percent.

If we take this a step further and bring the option premium closer to the market, we pick up a significantly larger premium. The 94 call in this scenario is trading for 5.50. In selling this call, we bring in roughly 6 percent of the total value of the spread and leave just over 2 percent gain potential for the market. We have reduced the potential gain for the market over the course of the option's life to 8 percent, but we have added 6 percent to our risk protection. So over the course of 140 days if the SPY is above 94, we will have an 8 percent gain and the ability to remove the option according to your objective or at expiration. We can also allow the short option to offset the SPY with an 8 percent gain in 140 days. Managing this position twice in the course of the year can add up to enhanced gains over the average annual return of the S&P.

The broad-based ETF is an excellent tool for managing systemic portfolio risk. If we look at using a short market position in a broad-based index against an individual component or sector-based port-folio, we can accomplish a reduction in overall risk without limiting the strength of individual returns. Narrow portfolios have higher risk because of the reduced diversity and theoretically higher returns. By utilizing a risk strategy on a broad index versus your sec-tor investment, you decrease the systemic risk to the portfolio along with leaving a larger portion of the upside open for profitability on the sector-based indices.

The outright short call options or the risk reversal are the best positions to use to offset risk across the broad indices. When you are outright selling a call, you are not able to set a floor, but you are bringing cash against the potential downside risk in the portfo-lio. The risk reversal of buying a put and selling a call option allows you to place a floor on the broader market while the sector or indi-vidual investments remain intact. You must use care when buying put options on broad indices. With the average 10 percent return for the S&P 500, it is very easy to spend 10 percent of the index in put premium over the course of the year, which leaves you with nothing. The short call is very critical to ensuring that you are not burning up profits on premium.

Managing risk on sector components or sector indices can be handled in much the same fashion—selling calls and buying puts. This may sound like a broken record, but it is a strategy that works. Consider if you were able to capture a 5 percent index premium selling an at-the-money call premium every quarter. When we discuss spreads, we talk at length about the covered call, but apply the idea to portfolio management. Capturing 5, 10, or 15% annually in call premium against held positions in broad indices or individual components adds a great deal to the bottom line in the long run.

Offset your put premium costs with short call premium as much as possible, unless you are able to buy puts in a flat or negative volatility curve. If you are able to place a floor under the market with a low implied volatility put, there is usually a reason why the put options are cheap. A small number of people think that this particular security is going down soon. This does not mean that you should not buy the put option; it just means that you will get it at a better price and that you should be cautious on the short call premium.

In our option strategy and spread discussion we talk about managing risk on individual components, so we won't be redundant here. The risk to individual component management, especially with options, is micromanagement. Diversification will take care of a portion of individual risk when the portfolio is viewed as a whole. High-risk components are the best candidates for individual management, but you should avoid micromanaging. Even the best portfolio managers fall victim to micromanaging from time to time, which is one of the reasons why the indexed funds outperform managed funds at times. Micromanagement of a portfolio is costly—trading commissions, missed opportunities from being out of a market, and missed objectives from overtrading. What is most critical is identifying and isolating your high-risk products and separating them in your mind from the diversified portfolio. When your objective is to place your portfolio risk somewhere centered on the efficient frontier, you have high- and low-risk components to that objective. If the high-risk components have a risk reversal, sell-buy-sell, or short option premium built around the position, you can raise the efficiency of your risk.

Of the many spread strategies we discuss, the best tools for management of risk are the simple option spreads selling premium or using short delta to offset risk.

You can be an excellent portfolio manager by following some simple rules about markets and using options:

- Options are a fantastic independent investment and addition to any portfolio. Options create opportunity to manage risk or capitalize on movement with decreased risk. The keys discussed throughout this book are that you watch your volatility and use some other people's money to pay for your positions by selling premium.

- Don't overanalyze. We all overanalyze everything in financial markets. We find unnecessary reasons for growth where growth is natural. Setbacks in growth and periods of negativity are also natural. It has happened several times before and will happen again.

- Use your option strategies wisely. The worst thing to watch is a trader who will spend 90 percent of his option investment adjusting and protecting an option trade until there is no way to win.

- If you're wrong the market, be wrong and learn from it. Risk controls should be hard objectives even if you cannot place a hard order. Second-guessing their initial assessment of the risk of a situation is the first mistake managers make.

- Keep it simple. Too many people make things just too difficult and make mountains out of mole hills. The more complex your risk strategy, the more difficult it is to manage and likely the more expensive it is. Buy and hold is not a bad strategy; it has proven to be successful, but you will be old and gray by the time you get to enjoy it. There is money to be made in the market, short and long term—truckloads of it. To be successful keep your investment and risk strategies simple and easy to read, analyze. Understand where the risk is going at all times. Nothing is worse than to look back at a group of strategies and think, where did the money all go? Track what you can manage.

- Diversify. Diversify. Diversify. Have your ETF products, add some managed funds, toss in a few short strangles and condors, and pick up that ridiculously cheap I-don't-care-if-it-goes-to-zero stock, sell some bond calls, and buy some risk-free rate instruments. Whatever the combination you put together, spread it out. Cover your systemic risk in the broad indices and spread out the wealth to many areas, industries, and securities and futures products.

We have covered a great deal of the influence of fund traders on the broad market throughout the book. A final thought to take from the discussion of risk regarding the funds is that they, in many cases, are a significant representation of the broader market sentiment. Because funds represent chunks of capital from large and small investors, they are in themselves a market barometer.

The "bubbles" of the 1999 and 2008 demonstrate that funds like the rest of market investors funds must perform to draw capital. It is difficult to say if and when the funds will have the same capital influence on the market they have had in the past, but it stands to reason that what has happened before will likely happen again.

As a skilled investor in the new market the challenge will be to manage the systemic risk generated by swelling market capital in funds or any other new investment vehicle created for the future.

Some final advice:

Years of experience in option trading has demonstrated for me that the most successful methods involve a balancing act between short and long option premium. Overall most option traders would agree that carrying a balance of option premium weighted to short or written options has a higher percentage of success. This is also offset by those who have experienced a significant market run against a short option in which they lost significant capital. In order to find the balance and avoid many of the pitfalls there are some commons sense rules to short option trading:

- *Track your short option value.* This means that you should be constantly aware of the total amount of short option premium written and what the reasonable risk is to that premium on a total account basis.
- *Scrutinize your delta.* We discussed delta at length on a individual trade basis, but what is your account delta on a total market basis. Are you net long, short, neutral and by how many shares or contracts overall? If the broad market fails, what is your total exposure? By having a watch on your total exposure you can better manage systemic risk.

- *Diversify neutral delta.* When working with short or written options, think in the same terms you do with investing in general, diversify. When selling options consider not only neutral delta strategies such as the strangle, straddle, condor and butterfly spreads, but doing these spreads in multiple markets with opposing objectives. This method helps to ensure the exposure is less significant in sector or regional risk situations and may also help with systemic risk. With this in mind, do not trade more than you can keep track of at any given time.

- *Bring home the premium.* As an option seller or writer it is easy to become over-confident after a series of option expirations in your favor. Set yourself a limit to the premium captured versus risk capital. Some have had success at writing 50% or more of their determined amount to risk for any given period or expiration cycle. In other words, if you have $5000 to risk, writing $2500 in premium is a expiration cycle. If that cycle is short, the dollars and cents can become very exciting as can the risk, but it is important to set boundaries immediately as to your total risk in short premium or short option value.

Summary

Advanced option trading is an essential skill for the successful advisor, investor, or trader now and in the future. Honing your option knowledge and techniques will add significant resources to your market tool bag. After many years of working with individual and professional traders and investors the biggest lesson I have learned is that there is never an end to the learning. I hope you enjoyed Advanced Option Trading and please visit my website at www.kkraus.com.

INDEX

ABOUT THE AUTHOR

Kevin Kraus is currently president of Ember Financial, a Texas-based investment advisor, and author of *How to Start Trading Options* (McGraw-Hill Professional Publishing). Kevin has also been featured on weekly radio talk shows and is the author of *CSM Trade Outlook*. Kevin coauthored two-top selling instructional video series on option trading as well as the Option Tutor Course, a Web-based options training program. For more information, visit his Web site at www.kkraus.com.